Qualitative Methods in Inter

Research Methods Series

General Editors: **Bernhard Kittel**, Professor of Social Science Methodology, Department of Social Sciences, **Carl von Ossietzky** Universität Oldenburg, Germany and **Benoît Rihoux**, Professor of Political Science, Université catholique de Louvain (UCL), Belgium

In association with the European Consortium for Political Research (ECPR), Palgrave Macmillan is delighted to announce the launch of a new book series dedicated to producing cutting-edge titles in Research Methods. While political science currently tends to import methods developed in neighbouring disciplines, the series contributes to developing a methodological apparatus focusing on those methods which are appropriate in dealing with the specific research problems of the discipline.

The series provides students and scholars with state-of-the-art scholarship on methodology, methods and techniques. It comprises innovative and intellectually rigorous monographs and edited collections which bridge schools of thought and cross the boundaries of conventional approaches. The series covers both empirical-analytical and interpretive approaches, micro and macro studies, and quantitative and qualitative methods.

Titles include:

Alexander Bogner, Beate Littig and Wolfgang Menz (*editors*)
INTERVIEWING EXPERTS

Audie Klotz and Deepa Prakash (*editors*)
QUALITATIVE METHODS IN INTERNATIONAL RELATIONS
A Pluralist Guide

Lane Kenworthy and Alexander Hicks (*editors*)
METHOD AND SUBSTANCE IN MACROCOMPARATIVE ANALYSIS

Research Methods Series
Series Standing Order ISBN 978–0230–20679–3–hardcover
Series Standing Order ISBN 978–0230–20680–9–paperback
(*outside North America only*)

You can receive future titles in this series as they are published by placing a standing order. Please contact your bookseller or, in case of difficulty, write to us at the address below with your name and address, the title of the series and one of the ISBNs quoted above.

Customer Services Department, Macmillan Distribution Ltd, Houndmills, Basingstoke, Hampshire RG21 6XS, England

Qualitative Methods in International Relations

A Pluralist Guide

Edited by

Audie Klotz and Deepa Prakash

Department of Political Science, The Maxwell School of Citizenship and Public Affairs, Syracuse University, USA

First published 2008
Published in paperback 2009 by
PALGRAVE MACMILLAN

Palgrave Macmillan in the UK is an imprint of Macmillan Publishers Limited, registered in England, company number 785998, of Houndmills, Basingstoke, Hampshire RG21 6XS.

Palgrave Macmillan in the US is a division of St Martin's Press LLC, 175 Fifth Avenue, New York, NY 10010.

Palgrave Macmillan is the global academic imprint of the above companies and has companies and representatives throughout the world.

Palgrave® and Macmillan® are registered trademarks in the United States, the United Kingdom, Europe and other countries.

ISBN-13: 978–0–230–54239–6 hardback
ISBN-13: 978–0–230–24175–6 paperback

This book is printed on paper suitable for recycling and made from fully managed and sustained forest sources. Logging, pulping and manufacturing processes are expected to conform to the environmental regulations of the country of origin.

A catalogue record for this book is available from the British Library.

A catalog record for this book is available from the Library of Congress.

Printed and bound in Great Britain by
CPI Antony Rowe, Chippenham and Eastbourne

Contents

List of Tables

List of Figures

Acknowledgments

Three groups of people deserve our heartfelt thanks for their influence on this project. Without them, there would be no book.

The initial idea derived from discussions between Audie Klotz and Cecelia Lynch related to their co-authored *Strategies for Research in Constructivist International Relations*. That book focused on the toolbox. Since it could not include everything, here we concentrate on the tools. While Cecelia did not contribute a chapter of her own, she greatly influenced our emphasis on pluralism. Delivering the tools, of course, would not have been possible without the contributors, all of whom responded enthusiastically to our invitation to write about their use of methods. They probably never imagined how demanding their editors would be! We appreciate their willingness to rethink and rewrite, sometimes more than once.

A number of people at the Maxwell School of Syracuse University influenced the particular form of the project. At Peg Hermann's suggestion, and with her invaluable financial support through the Moynihan Institute of Global Affairs, most of the contributors presented their first drafts to a live student audience. The Moynihan staff provided logistical assistance for those visits. Peg also generously hosted a seaside dinner in San Diego during the 2006 annual meeting of the International Studies Association, the only opportunity for most of the authors to talk in person. Gavan Duffy originally created PSC 694, Qualitative Political Analysis, and he graciously let us commandeer it for 2 years. Azamat Sakiev provided research assistance at the earliest stage, and both his and Deepa Prakash's work were funded by the Political Science Department.

Most books are written by professors, who supposedly know best how to teach their subject matter. In contrast, learners played a central role in this project. We especially thank all student commentators in the Fall 2005 cohort, who provided detailed suggestions and prodded our visiting experts in insightful ways. Revised versions had to pass muster with a second group of students in Fall 2006, although they did not have the fun of grilling the authors in person. In addition, students in both years experimented with these guidelines in their individual homework assignments, often in very creative ways. The editors tried to channel all of this feedback, but any credit for making the chapters accessible goes to these students. We are grateful for their willingness to contribute to work in progress and to embrace learning as a process.

A.K. and D.P.
Syracuse, NY

Notes on Contributors

Brooke Ackerly, Associate Professor at Vanderbilt University, is co-editor of *Feminist Methods in International Relations*, among other work bridging feminist political theory and international relations.

Samuel Barkin, Associate Professor at the University of Florida, has published on a wide range of topics in international relations, including international political economy, institutions, environmental politics, and theory.

Jeffrey T. Checkel is Professor and Simons Chair in International Law and Human Security in the School for International Studies, Simon Fraser University, and Adjunct Research Professor in the Centre for the Study of Civil War, International Peace Research Institute, Oslo.

Gavan Duffy is Associate Professor at Syracuse University, where he investigates political conflict and conducts formal and computational linguistic analyses of strategic political interactions.

Kevin C. Dunn, Associate Professor at Hobart and William Smith Colleges, works at the intersection of international relations and African politics. He is author of *Imagining the Congo* and co-editor of *African Guerrillas, Identity and Global Politics*, and *Africa's Challenge to International Relations Theory*.

Hugh Gusterson, Professor of Cultural Studies at George Mason University, offers an anthropological perspective on science and technology issues in international affairs, including two books on nuclear scientists, *Nuclear Rights* and *People of the Bomb*. He also co-edited *Cultures of Insecurity* and *Why America's Top Pundits are Wrong*.

Margaret G. Hermann is Gerald B. and Daphna Cramer Professor of Global Affairs and Director of the Daniel Patrick Moynihan Institute of Global Affairs at the Maxwell School of Syracuse University. She is a widely published expert on comparative foreign policy, political leadership, and political psychology.

Matthew J. Hoffmann is Associate Professor at the University of Toronto. His research interests include global environmental governance, social constructivism, complexity theory, and agent-based modeling. His book *Ozone Depletion and Climate Change* explored social norm dynamics in environmental politics with both computational simulations and process tracing case studies.

Audie Klotz, Associate Professor at Syracuse University, is the co-author of *Strategies for Research in Constructivist International Relations*, among other publications. Her current research on state identity compares immigration policies in South Africa, Canada, and Australia.

Anna Leander, Associate Professor in the Department of Intercultural Communication and Management at the Copenhagen Business School, works on issues of private authority in international relations, focusing on the use of force.

Iver B. Neumann is Professor of Russian Studies at Oslo University and Research Professor at the Norwegian Institute of International Affairs. He has used discourse analysis in studies of diplomacy and popular culture, including his co-edited book, *Harry Potter in International Relations*.

Jerrold M. Post, Professor in the Elliott School of International Affairs at George Washington University and Director of its Political Psychology program, has developed personality profiling as a framework for both scholarly and applied analysis of political leaders.

Deepa Prakash is a PhD candidate in Political Science at Syracuse University. Her research interests are in critical security studies, the discourse on 'terrorism,' and the identities of non-state actors, with a focus on South Asia.

1
Introduction

Audie Klotz

Debates across the social sciences rely on philosophical markers, notably the contemporary polarization between the so-called 'positivists' and 'post-modernists.' These labels are contested. Few 'positivists' rely on a narrow definition of falsification, and many 'post-modernists' reject extreme relativism. But the division is also grounded in some legitimate ontological and epistemological differences. For instance, positivists resist including language as a form of observable behavior, and those who reject by assumption the salience of culture or language need not debate how best to study meanings. Post-modernists, in turn, generally see concerns over rigorous analysis as a hallmark of a putatively flawed scientific approach to human action. One unfortunate result of this pervasive divide is a limited appreciation of the insights offered by scholars working within alternative frameworks. It leaves little common ground for analyzing the role of rhetoric in foreign policy choice, for instance.

Despite their abstract nature, the main terrain of these disputes is the realm of empirical research, including the delineation of legitimate research questions, allocation of funding for projects, and employment in the profession. For example, the conflation of ideas with ideology in the traditional 'Realist' characterization of 'Idealism,' still dominant in the field of International Relations (IR), privileges materialist explanations. The epistemological question of interpretation gets sidelined, because ideas are assumed not to matter as much as military capabilities. As a result, IR privileges a certain form of diplomatic history that lacks serious consideration of discourse analysis. And that can make it harder for scholars employing post-modern inspired approaches to get published in mainstream journals or get jobs at research universities (particularly in the United States).

Much has been written about this situation (see Hall 1999 on the philosophical issues and Steinmetz 2005 on the disciplinary ones). It has even spawned a 'perestroika' movement in Political Science aimed at opening up that discipline (Monroe 2005). But we still lack true intellectual engagement. Discussion remains an abstract positioning at the level of ontology or epistemology. Yet researchers need practical answers at the level of methodology: How *should* scholars interpret meanings? In IR, recent literature provides plenty of useful illustrations (such as the diverse contributions in Katzenstein 1996 and Weldes *et al.* 1999) but little about the practical trade-offs between techniques for analyzing language. What is at stake in selecting from discourse, speech acts, and semiotics – or even content analysis? When might it be justifiable to combine tools drawn from different analytical traditions – can discourse analysis or semiotics inform the construction of a dictionary for context-sensitive computerized coding, for instance?

We think that refocusing on methodological questions can break down the insularity of scholarly communities, because the justification for practical choices in empirical research exposes underlying ontological and epistemological assumptions (Klotz and Lynch 2007). We concentrate on IR (broadly defined) to provide a degree of empirical overlap. This helps to reveal how researchers wrestle with similar sorts of decisions that require the translation of abstract assumptions into concrete practices. Why do researchers define key concepts differently? How much 'data' is enough? What makes one interpretation better than another? We may still disagree on procedures and standards, but dialogue over methodology forces us to state the goals of our research, clearly define our core concepts, and set out our theoretical assumptions. Then, if warranted, researchers can expand their tools, or at least be able to understand a broader range of relevant literatures.

Many advocates of pluralism already seek to bridge the qualitative–quantitative split through the use of mixed methods. Statistical analysis can certainly be combined with case studies to capture causality in terms of conditions and mechanisms. Yet the presumption remains that positivism and post-modernism are incompatible. For instance, Sprinz and Wolinsky-Nahmias actively promote pluralism, including formal models, but (mis-) characterize post-modernism as lacking methodology (2004: 5). Consequently, we have no guidelines for determining when post-modern analytical techniques are *similar, complementary,* or *incompatible* with prevailing positivist approaches. For instance, both rational choice and literary criticism offer theoretical templates for historical narrative, but these remain *very* distinct literatures. Pluralism, as currently practiced, falls short.

Our starting point is 'qualitative' methods, because of the absence of sufficient guidelines for applying these tools. In contrast, courses in a wide array of statistical techniques are readily available. This gap creates a misperception that historiography and ethnography, for example, do not need to be taught to students and that experienced scholars intuitively know how to use interviews or textual analysis. Researchers of all generations continue to share tales of frustration about learning the trade through trial and error.

An increase in qualitative methods books and courses across the social sciences recognizes this need for practical lessons (for a sampling, see the syllabi posted on the website of the Consortium for Qualitative Research Methods hosted at Arizona State University, that many publishers are expanding their offerings in this area is readily evident in their current catalogues). Those written by political scientists remain oriented toward testing theories and making causal arguments (King *et al.* 1994; Brady and Collier 2004; George and Bennett 2005; Goertz 2006; Trachtenberg 2006; Gerring 2007). Most ignore post-modernism or reject it explicitly; a few offer asides about limited compatibility. Two notable exceptions lean the other way, in defense of critical theory and interpretation: the compendium by Ackerly *et al.* (2006) of feminist approaches in IR and the commentaries compiled by Yanow and Schwartz-Shea (2006).

We adopt a broader view, taking seriously the goals of *both* post-modernist and positivist researchers. This book starts from the assumption that 'qualitative' methods are somehow linked to meaning. But we leave open the boundaries of what should be labeled qualitative, as well as the possibilities for combining qualitative with quantitative and formal approaches. The chapters in this book present a cross-sample of perspectives, ranging from interpretation inspired by Foucault to mechanism-seeking process tracing all the way to agent-based modeling. While the authors work within the field of IR (or international studies, as some might prefer), they bring the insights of other fields, opening up an interdisciplinary conversation.

The contributors offer detailed guidance on how to apply specific tools of analysis and how to circumvent some inherent limitations. All are accomplished scholars who share, with extraordinary candor, their successes and failures. Since fostering use of a broader range of analytical tools requires breaking down the barriers constructed by epistemological polarization, we also asked them to consider whether it would be appropriate (and if so, when) to combine their primary tools with other qualitative, quantitative, and/or formal techniques.

Part I segues from ontology and epistemology to methodology via research design. Any project is grounded in particular literatures, and the theories contained in those literatures provide a specific vocabulary to characterize the empirical world. Theories, by their nature, simplify and privilege certain aspects of that world. Yet few works on methodology help aspiring researchers get from those ontological assumptions, manifest in theories and concepts, to methodological choices. Illustrating with applications of Pierre Bourdieu's field analysis, Anna Leander, in Chapter 2, offers four steps for translating key concepts into empirical work: asking questions, exploring the relationship between key concepts, figuring out how to apply those concepts, and reflecting on the ways in which those concepts, in turn, can create social realities.

Extending Leander's comments on reflexivity, Brooke Ackerly, in Chapter 3, points out that some concepts, notably gender, embed scholars in their own social environments, presenting researchers with a series of potential dilemmas in the design of their studies. Tensions start with the formulation of key questions and range from very practical issues of sampling to the ethical implications of publishing. For those striving to sensitize themselves to inequalities, in both theoretical formulations and research practices, she offers 'curb cutting' as a pedagogical tool that trains people to view the world through different interpretive lenses.

Leander's and Ackerly's shared emphasis on context and interpretation are, for many, the hallmarks of 'qualitative' case-based research. But in Chapter 4, Audie Klotz uses their insights to challenge the common treatment of case studies as a 'method.' Case selection, she argues, is part of research design, and a variety of methods can be used to analyze them. Researchers should, therefore, clarify their questions, their concepts, and their logic of comparison before tackling the two tasks specific to case selection: defining a 'case' *of* something and mapping out the universe of *possible* cases (including non-cases). She then assesses three strategies: single cases, paired comparisons, and the elusive category of 'More-than-Two but Not-a-Lot.'

Especially for the Classic Qualitative Tools covered in Part II, we selected authors who would draw on examples from IR because researchers in our field lack teaching materials that address the particularities we face. Discourse analysis by a literary theorist, for instance, may operate at an aesthetic level that does not capture politics or policy concerns. In contrast, Iver Neumann, in Chapter 5, suggests ways to turn censorship into an analytical advantage, among other insights. He translates the meta-theory of discourse into four methodological steps. The first is a precondition: a degree of cultural competence. From there, he guides readers through the delimitation of texts and subsequent mapping of the representations that comprise discourse. The final step is to untangle the layering of dominant and subordinate discourses.

Diplomatic history's narrative approach has long dominated qualitative analysis in IR (even after the 'history' versus 'science' debates of the 1960s) and is amply represented in the burgeoning methods literature (Elman and Elman 2001; Trachtenberg 2006). Alternatively, offering a post-modern perspective in Chapter 6, Kevin Dunn shifts down from Neumann's macro-historical level to explore agency in the creation of representations and contestation over them. After clearly situating his work ontologically and epistemologically, including its differences from causal analysis, he offers concrete advice on tracking down archival materials destroyed by arsonists and coping with the overwhelming amount of textual, visual, official, popular, and other materials appropriate for his genealogical approach to history.

Unlike historiography, ethnography appears infrequently as a tool of analysis in IR, perhaps because advice from an anthropologist working in a rural village is of limited use to someone seeking to do participant observation in a government department. But anthropology as a field is shifting away from the local in isolation, and as Hugh Gusterson demonstrates in Chapter 7, participant observation and interviewing can indeed help to answer questions about international security. Security clearance may be a distinctive barrier, but access to any field site presents challenges. Starting, like Neumann and Dunn, from a theoretical perspective informed by Foucault, Gusterson presents ethnography as a tool for mapping meanings, but he carries this out at the micro-level of individuals within their communities.

Given the penchant for qualitative analysis in IR to focus on individuals as key actors in historical narratives, Jeffrey Checkel's use of process tracing, in Chapter 8, presents an extension of a traditional approach, rather than an alternative one. By linking process tracing to the study of causal mechanisms generally, and by illustrating with independent and dependent variables beyond the foreign policy arena narrowly defined, he opens up possibilities for its application at diverse levels of analysis and across fields of study. Checkel also discusses some practical considerations of using elite interviews, official documents, and secondary sources to distinguish various dynamics of decision-making and collective identity formation as micro-level mechanisms of socialization.

Part III continues this focus on individuals and micro-level analysis, albeit in radically different ways. Each in its own way challenges what typically would be considered a qualitative method yet still captures some element of its hallmarks: meaning, interpretation, and context. Therefore, we call these Boundary Crossing Techniques, because they force researchers to reconsider what, if any, characteristics should define qualitative research.

In Chapter 9, Jerrold Post brings psychology and psychiatry to the task of figuring out what makes leaders 'tick.' His technique of Political Personality Profiling is a variant of the single case study, one which draws on personal history and comparison via personality type. No special training is required, he points out, only a sensitivity to psychologically minded types of observations that enable the researcher to identify the characteristics and patterns that clinicians use for diagnosis. More generally, his approach offers one answer to questions about how deeply analysts can delve into the minds of their research subjects.

Margaret Hermann, in Chapter 10, asks many of the same research questions about political leadership as does Post (and as many analysts of foreign policy do), but she uses Content Analysis as her tool for analyzing individuals at a distance. She delineates eight generic steps that any researcher should think through in order to analyze large quantities of textual (and visual) materials. Along the way, she challenges some of the myths that many interpretive scholars have about this approach; current software programs, for example, do allow for context-sensitive coding.

Gavan Duffy remains skeptical about getting into the minds of these leaders, even at a distance, and offers an alternative approach in Chapter 11 that concentrates on communications between individuals (such as foreign policy makers). Influenced by Anglo-American speech act theory, he applies formal logic to texts in order to create replicable interpretations. Pragmatic Analysis contrasts with the post-modern inspired approaches of Neumann, Dunn, and Gusterson, as Duffy holds out the future possibility of using computers to provide systematic analyses of discourse.

Taking formalization one step further, Matthew Hoffmann makes a case, in Chapter 12, for adding agent-based models to the interpreter's toolkit. He argues that this particular form of computer simulation can capture key dynamics of mutual constitution. Yet he insists that all models are heuristics, and, therefore, remain the basis for interpretation rather than objective analysis.

Part IV steps back from particular tools to Implications for pluralism in research and teaching. In Chapter 13, Samuel Barkin returns to the broad debates alluded to in this introduction. He remains skeptical of the term 'qualitative' and cautions against any naïve embrace of pluralism. More optimistically, Deepa Prakash in Chapter 14 highlights teaching tools that work especially well. She draws on her own experiences and those of her peers as they experimented with the guidelines offered in the manuscript versions of this book, as well as her perusal of assignments described in other syllabi. Together, these two chapters give scholars plenty of ideas for teaching and learning without falling into the trap of reifying the category of qualitative methods.

This book provides both an introduction to unfamiliar techniques and a guide for better application of familiar tools. Those designing a course might want to assign the chapters in order, while someone looking primarily to use a particular approach can safely skip to that section. Others may wish to concentrate on particular themes, clustering the chapters that focus on textual analysis, for instance, or perhaps those concerned with individuals as agents. Cross-references within each chapter provide suggestions for identifying such threads. Readers trying to figure out how to combine various techniques would benefit from reading the Research Design and Implications sections before delving into the toolbox. While controversies in contemporary IR and Political Science instigated the creation of this book, we hope that these chapters – in whatever order they are read – will prove useful to researchers seeking to practice pluralism across the social sciences.

Part I: Research Design

2
Thinking Tools

Anna Leander

In 1984, I moved to Paris to begin my undergraduate education at the *Institut d'Etudes Politiques de Paris* (Sciences Po). Sciences Po offered a series of seminars ostensibly to help foreigners (including me at that time) pass the entrance exam. What I remember from these is a chain smoking 'M. Thomas' doing his utmost to convey the message that Sciences Po was an elite institution, that entering it was like entering a 'gulag' and that only the best would 'survive' (his expressions). I also recall finding M. Thomas and his universe rather bizarre. A few years later, this was no longer true. I looked at French education in a new way just as Iver Neumann (in this book) looked at women differently after working with fur-coats. But more significantly, I had become intensely aware of the (often inarticulate) hierarchies and power relations of *practices*.

A year and a half after my first encounter with M. Thomas and the practiced hierarchy of French higher education, I came across the work of sociologist Pierre Bourdieu and more precisely his book *Distinction* (1984). (All references here refer to his work in translation but I recommend the originals in French, which tend to be considerably longer and more elaborate.) By that time, I was thoroughly puzzled by the idiosyncrasies of the hierarchies surrounding me as well as by the fact that those on the receiving end of these (students, including myself) kept accepting them. *Distinction* provided some clues, since it is an analysis of social hierarchy in France. But more significantly for a discussion of method, it contained a *vocabulary* for asking questions about power. These were embedded in a Social Theory of the grand kind: an updating of such classics as Marx, Durkheim, Weber, or Levi Strauss informed by philosophers such as Pascal, Kant, and Heidegger (such as Bourdieu 1996a, 2000a). No wonder I was impressed.

11

This chapter conveys some basic ideas regarding the 'thinking tools' this vocabulary provided that will be useful for applying any theoretical framework to empirical research. Bourdieu has attracted attention from all branches of the social sciences and the humanities, including international relations, resulting also in a momentous secondary literature. Clearly this is not an obscure method that seduced me because of my experience at Sciences Po. The chapter you are about to read cannot possibly 'cover' it or introduce an uncontested version of it. My presentation is selective, geared primarily towards the social science side and towards providing some practical advice based on my own experience in using it. Those who find Bourdieu's particular tools potentially useful will also have a basis to find out more from his own work.

I will do this by discussing how the thinking tools relate to the key issues all researchers face when selecting and applying appropriate 'methods.' I begin with the kinds of questions that Bourdieu's thinking tools are useful for raising and answering, namely questions about symbolic power and violence. I then discuss the conceptualization of the thinking tools in general terms, and proceed to highlight three crucial decisions to be made when 'operationalizing' these to answer a specific research question. The chapter concludes with a discussion of how to distinguish good research from bad (validity), with an emphasis on the centrality of reflexivity.

Research questions: ask about symbolic power/violence in practices

The method a study uses cannot be dissociated from its research questions. Methods serve a purpose. One does not drill holes with a hammer or fix nails with a drill. Similarly, when working in the social sciences it is important to acknowledge that methods can do different things. The method one chooses is related to what questions one is answering. Inversely, as anyone embarking on a research project (and any supervisor) knows, formulating a good research question is key to a successful research project. Methods textbooks explain that 'good' research questions are anchored in existing literatures and theoretical approaches. There is a two-way relationship between research questions, theoretical approaches and the methods tied to them.

Consequently, the first thing to consider about a method is whether or not it is useful for formulating and answering the kind of research question one wants to ask. The 'thinking tools' introduced here interested me precisely because they gave me a vocabulary for considering the questions I found important about my Science Po experience, namely questions about symbolic power and violence in social practices. I have continued to find these significant in my work in international political economy and international relations, ranging from the politics of foreign direct investments in Turkey to security in Africa and in the West (see, for example, Leander 2001, 2002).

Asking questions about symbolic power amounts to looking at how 'symbols' (broadly defined) are an integral part of power relations (Bourdieu 1992). This seemed of essence in the 'gulag' that M. Thomas was introducing, but it kept striking me as an essential aspect of all power relations, including in the very hard material things. To stick with Sciences Po, there was clearly a strict hierarchy; there were dominated and dominating people. This hierarchy had some material manifestations (material rewards for success, written rules, sanctions, institutionalized humiliations) but the common understanding of education and of one's own role in the system seemed so much more important. It seemed to shape the material manifestations of power relations as much as (if not more than) the other way around. Asking questions about the working of symbolic power hence seemed an obvious priority. The thinking tools were helpful in that they directed my questioning towards three central aspects of these power relations.

The first of these was the extent to which 'symbolic violence' was an integral part of symbolic power. The power relations at Sciences Po could not have worked if the 'losers' of these relations had not themselves gone along and followed rules, which so obviously placed them at a disadvantage. As in so many other situations, the victims were their own perpetrators. Women perpetuate gender inequality, military establishments accept benchmarking practices favoring private security companies, development planners contribute to a displacement of the focus of development thinking towards security issues. Symbolic power relations rest on 'symbolic violence' where victims perpetrate their own powerlessness. Power therefore works all the more effectively as there is a degree of what Bourdieu would call 'misrecognition' or *illusio*, an idea with parallels in Gramscian and Foucauldian thought. For similar reasons, power is all the more effective when it rests on understandings which appear disinterested or unrelated to hierarchy, for example, based in science, culture, or art (Bourdieu 1993, 1996b). In my own work, technocratic competence, efficiency, humanitarian work, and local empowerment have been central for obfuscating power relations and symbolic violence. To 'discover' this, asking questions about symbolic violence has been crucial.

The second aspect of symbolic power relations that the thinking tools help focus attention on is the centrality of practices (what people do) rather than overarching discourses and representations (captured by what they say and write). At Sciences Po, rules were upheld more by what was *not* said and written anywhere than by what was. Power rested on the innumerable practices people engaged in without thinking much about it, just because it was the right thing to do, and they all somehow knew it. When you arrive as a foreigner, you notice simply because you do not know and (consequently) keep doing the wrong things. You would really like people to articulate the unwritten rules for you but if you ask, it turns out they cannot. For them, the rules are so obvious and natural that they do not seem to be rules but part of the natural world. Texts and discourses (and Sciences Po's written regulations) will of course reflect some of this, and you can capture this part by reading and acquiring a 'cultural competence' of the kind Neumann mentions (in this book). But the step from discourses to practice is a long one (see Dunn's discussion of the 'long conversation' in this book).

This brings attention to a third aspect of symbolic power highlighted by the thinking tools, namely its link to the material world (things like money, jobs, institutional positions, weapons, passports, or diplomas). Meaning and its practical implications change depending on the context. *What* you say matters less than *where* you speak from. The mystery of the minister is that her words can produce the material realities they purport to represent. But they do so *only* because of her position in social hierarchies. Similarly, the power of contemporary private security companies reflects not only the favorable bias towards them in risk and new public management discourses but also their links to policy makers, their evolving institutional role and their capacity to promote these economically. In addition, to some extent, what you say depends on where you speak from. As a student in Sciences Po, I did not count on having the same effect on our reality as our professors or as the minister of education. In fact, it did not even occur to me to try to have much influence at all. What I say (or not) is linked to my social position. This focus on material power and social hierarchies as an integral part of meaning production contrasts starkly with the 'internalist' focus of those discourse analysts who concentrate mainly or only on language. It has consequently been a key bone of contention between Bourdieusians and (some) post-structuralists (see contributions in Shusterman 1999).

To recapitulate, methodologies are linked to conceptualizations of the social world and so are the questions they are useful for answering. The approach introduced here is particularly helpful for asking questions about symbolic power and violence in social practices. This may not sound terribly original. Discourse analysis, process tracing, and gender studies methods – just to mention some methods discussed in this book – claim to raise and answer similar research questions. However, as just underlined, I find Bourdieu's approach particularly helpful because of the specific focus it gives to these questions. It keeps questions about power in the center of the analysis. It directs attention to the centrality of the dominated in power relations. It is helpful for capturing the extent to which practices reflect and reproduce a mixture of economic, cultural, and symbolic power. With this specific focus comes a set of methodological tools. Consequently, the next steps are to get a hold of these in the general toolbox (conceptualization) and then decide how you would like to use the tools for your own purposes (operationalization).

Conceptualization: grab your thinking tools

A general conceptualization of the social world is an integral part of any methodology. It defines what to think about and what to look at (hence thinking tool). Methods rest on these assumptions about how the social world works. With vision come basic tools. Some authors in the social sciences become 'classics' because they challenge existing assumptions and make readers see the world differently. Luhmann, Braudel, and Foucault have made people think about how the social world works in novel ways. One cannot use Foucauldian discourse analysis or a Braudelean historical materialist analysis to answer questions about Luhmanian autopoietic systems. When Neumann (in this book) advises you to begin by carving out a 'discourse,' he has already equipped you with the basic thinking tool for analyzing the social world: not the carver but the discourse. Bourdieu-inspired methods rely on three such basic thinking tools: Fields, *Habitus*, and Practices (some would add *doxa* and capital). Indeed, earlier versions of this paper talked about the FIHP (Field, *Habitus*, Practices) method.

The first of these thinking tools is the field, the centrality of which leads some scholars to label the method 'field analysis.' In order to make sense of the social world, it is useful to think of it as divided into relatively autonomous sub-systems following their own logic. These subsystems are called fields but the general idea is rather widespread and reminiscent of Luhmann's relatively autonomous social systems. Sciences Po might be thought of as a field, relatively autonomous from the field of social sciences internationally, from the French economy, and so on. A field is defined by the fact that those who are in it share an understanding (often unarticulated) of the rules of the game or the 'stakes at stake' in that given area of social activity. In that sense, the field is essential for understanding power relations. It defines what counts as advantages, or (social, economic, or cultural) 'capital' in that field. People's (or institutions') relative *position* in the social hierarchy in turn is defined by how much capital they accumulate. In diplomacy, humanitarian aid, banking, or Islamism, different forms of capital confer advantages. While central bankers may hold dominant positions in the field of banking, they may be subordinate in the humanitarian field.

Fields are only *relatively* autonomous. They exist in the context of other fields. This means that capital can be imported from one field to another. For example, Halliburton could import the economic and political capital it had accumulated in the field of US construction when it began competing for security contracts in Iraq. Of course, there is no guarantee that capital in one field has the same value in another field. Halliburton's political contacts to the Pentagon and the State Department were certainly more directly valuable than were its contacts to local administrators in Houston, Texas, when it moved into security contracting. There is an 'exchange rate' for capital. One might think of the struggle over its value in terms of the general struggle for power in society, and it is in this sense that Bourdieu uses 'the field of power.'

That fields are only relatively autonomous also means that the logic of a field is continuously shaped by the logic of other fields. Some fields are particularly important because they influence a great number of subfields; one might think of these as 'meta-fields.' Education, with its role in defining legitimate knowledge, is one example. The State, with its claim to a 'monopoly on legitimate symbolic violence,' is another. The shift in a meta-field sends ripples across a number of other fields. For example, the revalorization of neo-classical economics, including econometric modeling and degrees from the United States or Britain, triggered changes in most other fields, such as public administration, where these assets become valued and new public management thinking central. In turn, this shifts the positions and capital of actors in a range of subfields. In security, for example, private firms found themselves considerably advantaged. The meta-field of education has been crucial in reshaping the subfields of public administration and of security. These linkages between fields, and in particular the existence of meta-fields, are useful for understanding the broader (re-) production of power and domination in society.

Fields are not only static entities where actors occupy immutable positions according to their 'objectively' measurable capital endowments.

Fields are also dynamic terrains of struggle. People may seek to improve their own position by increasing their capital, they may strive to alter the field increasing the value of the capital they have or they may try to shift the boundaries of the field to alter both the value and the amount of capital they have. It is surprising that this struggle is not more intense and explicit. To explain this and to give substance to struggles that do take place, the second central thinking tool of the approach, the *habitus*, becomes pivotal.

The idea of the *habitus* is that while people have resources (capital) granting them a position from which to act, they also have taken-for-granted understandings, or 'dispositions,' that guide how they act. These are largely habitual and unreflected in nature, hence the term *habitus*. But they are essential for power relations. The *habitus* shapes strategies for accumulating capital and for reshaping fields or the failure to have such a strategy. But more than this, dispositions – such as eating habits, cultural interests, manners of speech, dress codes, and lifestyles – give shape to the body and body language. These become incorporated and embodied capital. Ataturk's dress codes (prohibition of the Fez and the veil, detailed dress codes directed at state officials) and the contemporary struggle over them are good illustrations of efforts to shift the value of incorporated capital and more profoundly of the dispositions going with them. Ataturk wanted a modern and Westernized Turkey. Present day Turkish Islamists wish a Muslim and independent one.

The *habitus*, like capital, is produced in specific fields. It reflects the values and discourses of a field, which in turn are shaped and reproduced by the people in that field. It provides the link between general structures and discourses – to which the Bourdieuian *doxa* is a rough equivalence – and the variety of practices they result in. Hence, the *doxa* is useful for the analysis of broad overarching understandings (such as Bourdieu's analyses of the state) or for the analysis of relatively undifferentiated societies (such as Bourdieu's analysis of Kabyl society in *The Logic of Practice* [1990]). However, to understand why a person or groups of people reflect general discourses in varied ways and why people follow the kind of 'strategies' they do, the *habitus* is a better tool.

The *habitus* is indeed an agent or group level thinking tool. As such it is subject to variation and change. A person is part of multiple fields in the course of their life. A person entering a new field (me entering Sciences Po, International Alert activists entering diplomatic circles) is bound to miss many unwritten rules and consequently appear clumsy and ill-adjusted. Over time, these rules become incorporated into the *habitus* of the person, whose behavior becomes less awkward. Alternatively, the logic of the field might evolve so that the behavior is no longer at odds with its logic. Often both processes occur. Activists of major non-governmental organizations, such as International Alert, have learned the rules of international diplomacy and to some extent these rules are reflected in their *habitus*. At the same time, they have been major drivers of change in international politics. For example, their mere presence, which is at odds with traditional diplomatic state-based politics, has resulted in far-reaching changes in what actors can claim to be part of the field (extended to a range of non-state actors), what resources are valued (adding democratic resources, media power, and human rights credentials to military and economic might), and what understanding about international politics is taken for granted (such as in resolutions passed by the UN).

This takes us to the third thinking tool, practice. The basic idea with practices is that what people do rather than what they say is of essence. In part, this is so because a large share of their behavior is not consciously reflected but habitual and shaped by the position they act from. Practices capture the 'structuring' effects that shape action. (For a Foucauldian perspective on this issue, see Dunn and Gusterson in this book.) It is a way of capturing the reasons and situated rationality of action by repla-cing it in context. It is a guard against the very common tendency to impute a rationality to people (usually the rationality of the researcher) and then be forced to explain behavior that does not follow this ration-ality as stupid, irrational, or deviant, a tendency Bourdieu referred to as the 'genetic fallacy.'

More centrally, practices capture what people do in context, and this *relational* aspect of practices is of essence. We may be able to under-stand the action of International Alert in calling attention to small arms trade in the UN context by looking at its capital and the *habitus* of key members. However, we can only grasp the *habitus* and the capital if we think in relational terms. Moreover, if we want to understand the consequences of their actions for power relations in international politics, we need to place this action in relational context. We need to look at the practices of International Alert, how these are shaped, and, in turn, how they affect the practices of other actors in the field. Since practices are thought of as relational, they capture the overall pattern of interactions in a field and are differentiated from individual strategies of action.

This leads to a last essential point about practices: they are 'gener-ative.' Practices create meanings, entities, and power relations. When International Alert enters international politics, practices are shifted.

It is not simply that power relations change because (given) people gain and lose in terms of some (predetermined) resources. Rather the resources and the people that count in international politics themselves are reshaped. A generative process is in motion. Similarly, contemporary political practices resting on opinion polls and media-mediated political action 'generate' politics as the aggregation of atomized individual interests on topics over which individuals have little to say and often few thoughts (see contributions in Wacquant 2005).

In practices, one can observe the relations of (symbolic) power and violence. It is hence not surprising that many consider 'practices' pivotal to the approach. They would argue that any Bourdieu-inspired study should depart from practices and build up an understanding of field and *habitus* from these. More generally, they would side with those who consider Bourdieu's work as key to the 'practice turn' in the social sciences. However, as pointed out above, the *habitus* and field have similar status for other scholars. My own position is that the three thinking tools are related to each other and work together. Perhaps this is because I first read *Distinction*, where the analysis is framed as [(*habitus*) (capital) + field = practice]. But more likely it is because I have worked with all three thinking tools and find them all important.

To sum up, the toolbox of this approach contains three basic concepts for thinking about the social world: field, *habitus*, and practices. Using these thinking tools together is the basis for explaining and understanding symbolic power and violence. Many scholars consider one tool to occupy a more central and logically primary position. My own understanding is that they work together, that one can begin by using any tool. Moreover, most studies make more use of one tool than the others. Certainly Bourdieu's own work did; note the difference between *Distinction, Outline of a Theory of Practice* (1995) and *The Weight of the World* (1999). The decision of which tool to use and how much to take the two other tools out of the toolbox are decisions about how to employ the general thinking tools in one's own context. As this indicates, the third step, after asking questions and conceptualizing, is to operationalize.

Operationalization: decide on boundaries, level and scope

The thinking tools have been used to look at symbolic power and violence in practices ranging from those related to artistic production, the state, international law, elites in Brazil, the family, the suburbs of Paris, the media, European politics, and public administration (and elsewhere). As this diversity signals, there can be no firm guidelines for what exactly to look at, what evidence to gather or in what kind of quantities (nor can I possibly list here all the fascinating secondary literature applying Bourdieu). Annual income, bonuses, thinking in terms of financial economics, interest in extreme sports and participation in professional meetings may be essential for understanding the field, *habitus*, and practices of investment banking but have little relevance for understanding those in the field of artistic production.

It is impossible to 'operationalize' field, *habitus*, and practices before the research. Fleshing them out in order to analyze symbolic power and violence is what the research is about; 'operationalization' is a key aspect of research. This said, if it is to work well, there are three central decisions to be made about the study: (i) where to draw the boundaries of the field; (ii) at which level to work with the *habitus*; and (iii) how to limit the scope of the study (possibly through a selective use of the thinking tools).

Drawing boundaries around the study to delimit the field and the practices at the center of the research is necessary: we obviously need to know what symbolic power/violence we are interested in. Yet, the stakes are high. The delimitation of the field both includes and excludes. The drawing of lines therefore shapes the analysis and its results profoundly. Consider two studies analyzing changes in international security after the Cold War. In one, the boundaries of the field are narrowly drawn around diplomatic practices (Pouliot 2003). In the other, the boundary is drawn to include the gamut of security professionals, including police, military, and commercial networks (Bigo 2005). The subsequent analyses differ in content, coverage, and style. And they reach opposite conclusions about the nature of change in international security. Pouliot argues that security greatly increased after the Cold War, as the bloc confrontation has been replaced by a security community. Bigo concludes that insecurity has greatly increased, as a consequence of the evolving practices of security professionals.

It is therefore important to be conscientious about the decision to draw boundaries. Mistakenly drawing lines may distract attention from essential practices and power relations, and hence obscure precisely the things the analysis purports to clarify. It is particularly important to watch out for two common pitfalls. The first is to draw the boundaries of the field so that the symbolic power/violence relations one aims at analyzing fall outside it. Although there is an international diplomatic practice and field, it may be a serious mistake to assume that symbolic power/violence in the definition of international security can be analyzed in terms of it. The pivotal role of security professionals and their routine practices, for example, is entirely left out.

The second pitfall is to assume that links between a field and other fields deprive the field studied of its own logic. All fields exist in context. This does not make it impossible or meaningless to study them. The crux is to draw the line between the field and practices that are central and those shaping them from elsewhere. The practices of private security companies can be studied in terms of a field in its own right, even if this field is obviously tied to a number of other fields, notably fields of national security which shape the field of private security professionals and which these in turn influence. However, for the sake of a study it is of essence to set the boundaries of which relations of symbolic power/violence one wants to focus on.

This leads to a second crucial decision that has to be made: what level to work on, or more specifically, how to operationalize the *habitus*. At one extreme, one might work from the individual. Hence to capture symbolic power and violence in the Caucasus, Derlugian (2005) has constructed his research around the biography of Musa Shanib to clarify and explain the (sharply diverging) political trajectories of Checheno-Ingushetia, Kabardino-Balkaria, and Abkahzia. At the other extreme, one might imagine working at the level of the entire practice and field studied, as Ashley (1989) did in IR, where he argued that the shared (Realist) assumption, or *doxa*, that community in international anarchy is impossible resulted in a diplomatic practice blocking the possibility of 'global governance.' Both extremes have serious drawbacks.

Using the *habitus* at an overly general level makes the social world seem uncomfortably 'automatic and closed,' as Lahire (1999) rightly points out. It overemphasizes the structuring effects that weigh on actions. The variation in the *habitus* of different groups and people due to their social positions and past experiences is simply eliminated by fiat, as is the role of emotions in social relations, such as love, family, friendship, or enmity. If the *habitus* is merged with the *doxa*, it can no longer provide the link between general discourses, structures, and agency. Its role as a separate thinking tool disappears. Working with the *habitus* on the individual level is no more persuasive. Here the *habitus* becomes a collation of individual experiences and pasts, in which it is difficult to distinguish what is of more general utility for understanding the symbolic power and violence of social practices. The *habitus* runs the risk of being watered down to an individual history with limited analytical clout.

Consequently, I find the best strategy to be one of trying to work with the *habitus* at a level between these two extremes. More concretely, the *habitus* works best when differentiated according to key groups in a study, as in Bourdieu's analyses of the educational field in France (for example, *Homo Academicus* [2000b] or *The State Nobility* [1998]). This is also how it enters my analysis of the field of private security, where groups of individuals share a common general understanding of the stakes at stake but differ fundamentally in how this is articulated in their readings of the social world. This 'middle of the road strategy' can usefully be complemented by analysis at the individual level to retain the sense of depth in the study. Like the *Economist* uses boxes to detail an example, one can use examples to flesh out a point. I have often relied on extensive quotes from interviews with security contractors, job announcements, and advertisements by firms to make arguments about the *habitus* of contractor groups more tangible.

The third and final decision to be made is when to stop or how to limit the scope of the study. This is a central question for analysts using any method, and certainly in studies drawing on Bourdieu, it is an essential one. The empirically grounded theoretical set up easily produces overly ambitious studies. Evidence – including statistical data, biographical information, photographs, art, literature, classical texts, diplomatic archives, public speeches, newspaper clippings, and interviews (depending on the question) – tends to pile up but could always be completed with even more. This requires subjecting 'evidence' to a thorough analysis. Finally, writing and structuring the analysis is inspiring, but word limits, stylistic requirements, and the like quickly become a nuisance. This is one reason for Bourdieu's foundation of the journal *Actes de la recherches en sciences sociales*, where there were NO word limits and one could publish non-conventional material including pictures, art, and news clippings. It is probably also the reason *Distinction* is 660 pages and *The Weight of the World* is 1460 pages.

Most of us do not have the privilege of publishing books or writing dissertations of that length. Nor do many journals accept articles on the conditions of *Actes de la Recherche*. But even if we did, it is really hard work as Bourdieu often sneered at those who shun empirical studies. Hence my strong and articulate preference for good 'thick descriptions' (Geertz 1973) based on the analysis of a range of evidence is tempered by my self-preserving instincts and pragmatic approach to the needs of those completing their dissertations. I am persuaded that deciding on scope, as early as possible, is of essence.

I have tried both of the two most common ways of limiting the scope of my studies, and they both work fine. The first is to reduce the empirical focus of the analysis: focus on small groups of agents and practices. Restricting the scope of an empirical analysis does not have to be done at the expense of its theoretical ambitions. For example, in *The Social Structures of the Economy* (2005), Bourdieu uses an empirical analysis of the housing market in France to make a general theoretical point about the significance of social structures for the operation of an economy. The second way to limit scope is to work selectively with the 'thinking tools': instead of trying to provide an analysis based on field, *habitus*, and practices, rely on one of these, leaving the others in the background. This strategy is also used by Bourdieu in short lectures and essays, such as those in *Practical Reason* (2002), to concentrate on an argument. But perhaps the most important is to put strict deadlines and time limits. (Or as Gusterson notes, in this book, the grant money runs out.) That is a very unscientific but effective way of limiting scope, making sure that a project does not swell and become more ambitious than there is room for it to be.

The thinking tools introduced in this chapter are malleable. They can be used to raise questions and analyze power in almost any context. Yet, when using them in any specific context they have to be fixed. The field, *habitus*, and practices (*doxa* and capital) need to be given concrete and tangible meaning. This operationalization within a particular focus is a central part of the research process – no general blueprint can guide it.

Validity: work reflexively

As with all other methods, a Bourdieu-inspired approach needs to answer the basic question of how it distinguishes good research from bad. Since researchers using the thinking tools are left relatively free to apply these contextually, they will necessarily make different choices. How can one judge which account is better if two accounts, such as the studies of (in)security discussed above, reach different conclusions on the same question? But more centrally for most people, how can one assert the quality and validity of one's own work? The answer seen from the perspective of the thinking tools is simple: 'work reflexively.' Reflexivity hence becomes an integral part of the 'method,' which is consequently sometimes referred to as 'reflexive' sociology (Bourdieu 1985). I outline here three distinct understandings of what working 'reflexively' means for research practice and end with a note of how it is reflected in research writing. (See Ackerly, in this book, for a complementary elaboration on these issues.)

At the most simple, working reflexively may mean reflecting on the quality and validity of the study in a methods textbook's sense. Evidence for a thinking tools study is similar to evidence used in any empirical work. It relies, variously, on statistical information, life span data, interviews, texts, photographic evidence, or pictures. Consequently, the usual standards apply. Issues such as the accuracy, adequacy, representativeness, and relevance of the information are essential for evaluating whether the 'evidence' of a study supports its conclusions. For example, if people are assigned positions in a field on the basis of information that can be shown to be false or irrelevant, that assignment is mistaken. If a scholar argues that an actor's position in the field of international security is greatly enhanced by the cultural capital linked to the mastery of Copenhagen School concepts and the educational capital that comes with a diploma from the Political Science Department of the University of Copenhagen, he or she is simply wrong. Similarly, a generalization about the *habitus* of private contractors based on the movie *Blood Diamonds* can be taken to task for generalizing on too thin a basis. Finally, the approach is set up to produce accounts about real-world symbolic violence and power and social practices. If these can be shown to follow very different patterns from those suggested in an account, it is wrong. These conventional checks on the validity of a study deserve being taken seriously (see the other chapters in this book for answers to these issues reflecting the authors' diverse thinking tools).

However, reflexivity at this level is insufficient. As all studies that take the role of meaning in social contexts seriously, studies made with the thinking tools approach have to answer some tricky questions regarding the status of the observer in relation to the observed. Specifically for this approach, it would be inconsistent to claim that the field of the social scientists was a field – the only one – where people did not have a *habitus*, did not struggle over positions, and were not engaged in practices producing symbolic power/violence. Since the approach makes no such claim, it needs a way of dealing with the tainting that the dynamics of the scientific field must give to its 'scientific' accounts of the social world (Bourdieu 2004).

This is where the second understanding of reflexivity comes in: working reflexively also means using 'epistemological prudence.' The basic idea is that researchers should 'objectify the objectifying subject,' that is, use the thinking tools to analyze themselves. This caution about the way knowledge is produced has direct implications for research. It is the only road to limit the bias entailed in looking at the world from one's own perspective, such as me looking at the world of private contractors as a female French/Swedish Copenhagen Business School employee. It is also important in interacting with the people researched. The impact of my physical appearance, reactions, gestures, social status, and use of language tends to have an immediate impact on what interviewees say and leave out from their accounts. I cannot abolish this, just as I cannot, through reflexivity, eliminate my own bias in order to look at the world from nowhere. I can, however, do my best to limit its impact and also be aware of it when I analyze the results. This is 'epistemological prudence' in research practice.

Third, the researcher exists in a broader context, in a social world where privileged knowledge, such as that produced in universities, is of essence. Scientific practices 'loop,' to use Hacking's (1999) term, back into society and reshape its 'reality.' Categories and representations create their own social reality. Educational institutions are meta-fields that shape knowledge in other fields not only by producing categories but also by sanctioning careers. When scientific practices have looping effects, we need to be reflexive about what kind of 'reality' these research loops constitute. Epistemological prudence is a beginning. It can be used as a guard against the collective hypocrisy and self-delusion of assuming or pretending (rather than showing) that research agendas sanctioned by a scientific field are those most socially important. This is an obvious concern in the current context of the commercialization and internationalization of universities.

However, limiting the role of reflexivity to one of prudence is arguably both naive and irresponsible. Instead of 'prudence,' one needs reflexivity in a third sense: as a 'realpolitik of reason.' Purportedly neutral and objective scientific knowledge all too often presents unrealistic and unreasonable accounts of a world devoid of symbolic power and violence. However, precisely because knowledge is so central to the social world, these accounts play an essential role in perpetuating power by obscuring it. This delegitimizes work that effectively deals with issues of symbolic power. In this context, reflexivity (at least in Bourdieu's view) should be used to promote a realpolitik bolstering serious scientific work (with emancipatory potential) while denaturalizing, historizing, and unmasking (to use some clichéd expressions) the fantasy world of much of what counts as 'science.'

The first two kinds of reflexivity are relatively straightforward and palpable. They sit well with classical understandings of reflexivity, even if the notion of epistemological prudence gives it a twist. The realpolitik take on reflexivity is more complicated. It runs against the idea of value neutral science with which most contemporary university education is imbued. It smacks of politicization. It has become (mistakenly I would argue) associated with Bourdieu's left-wing politics and hence understandably irritates people who do not share these. Ultimately, the question is one of alternatives. The alternative seems to ignore the looping effects of the sciences, unreflexively accepting their role. Any responsible thinking person (not only left-wingers) would presumably find this unsatisfactory.

By now, you are hopefully wondering how these three versions of reflexivity can possibly be stuffed into a research project. The short answer is that they cannot. If I write an article about intervention in Darfur, I cannot also include a full reflexive analysis of my own position in the academic field and the link of my study to the political context I am analyzing. There will most probably not even be much explicit reflexivity about the evidence used. There simply is not enough space; the reflexive grounding of the argument will most probably have to remain unarticulated. But then, that is the fate of most methodological and theoretical considerations that underpin a study of any kind. This does not diminish their importance any more than it does the utility of working reflexively, but it makes following the reflexivity of others more difficult. It also limits the time one sets aside to think reflexively. One may wish for a magical self-reflecting quill à la Neumann (in this book) to do the job, especially since most of us cannot spare the time to write the equivalent of Bourdieu's *Homo Academicus* to come to grips with their position in their own academic field or of his *Distinction* to come to grips with their position in society. However, I still contend that, even if the result remains unarticulated, working reflexively is sound advice.

Conclusion: thinking tools, dispositions, and irreverence

When I first read *Distinction*, I did not for a second imagine that I would one day be trying to distil some essential points about its 'method' into maximum 25 manuscript pages. The idea would have seemed absurd to me. For one, I did not picture myself as an academic. But more centrally, I did not think of it as a 'methods' book. I found the book interesting and helpful for strictly personal reasons but drew no link between it and my studies. As many students, I thought it essential to have neat and clear-cut concepts and methodological tools that simplify the world. The dense vocabulary, the shifting definitions, and the constant back and forth between theory and empirical observation in Bourdieu's book definitely did not fit this understanding of a useful method.

It was not until quite a few years later (well into my PhD) that my frustration with the Procrustean beds of neat and clear concepts and methods that effectively stymied interesting research pushed me to draw on Bourdieu. By that time, I had come to appreciate the relatively open and malleable thinking tools. These did not work as the strict universal categories that I had once thought indispensable. They were integral to something more useful, namely a disposition for thinking about power and symbolic violence in context.

This chapter has communicated my bid for the substance of that 'sociological disposition' and more specifically my understanding of its methodological translation. I have insisted that I think it disposes analysts to raise questions about symbolic power/violence and, more generally, social hierarchies. I have suggested that thinking of the social world in terms of fields, *habitus*, and practices is integral to it. I have drawn on the work done by myself and others to point to some key decisions to be taken in the course of operationalizing these general thinking tools. And I have argued that it logically suggests the importance of working reflexively.

This distilling exercise is absolutely irreverent. I have imposed a strictly personal order, priority, and logic on a complex and multifaceted conceptual framework, which can of course be understood and used differently. Moreover, to satisfy editors and readers, I have eliminated much of the conceptual apparatus and ('all that French') vocabulary that expresses it in the process of simplifying. But then, Bourdieu was a great advocate of the irreverent use of theories – of 'writing with a theorist against that theorist' – so I may just be following the tradition I claim to write about. The bottom line is that if this makes what I have called the thinking tools more accessible, it will have been worth it.

Acknowledgment

Readers of the very different earlier versions of this chapter have made helpful comments: Stefano Guzzini, Jef Huysmans, Hans Krause Hansen, Karen Lund Petersen, Dan Nexon, Ted Hopf, Rens van Munster, Trine Villumsen, and especially Audie Klotz, her students, and my co-contributors to this book.

3

Feminist Methodological Reflection

Brooke Ackerly

Feminist inquiry is not reserved for women or even for those who identify themselves as feminists. It invites every scholar to revisit his or her epistemology and core conceptualizations throughout the research process. Feminist theory and methods provoke self-reflection, empower the researcher to explore new questions revealed by such reflection, and guide the research process in ways that are attentive to the power of knowledge. To assume that only feminists or women could do feminist inquiry would be to ignore the scholarship that feminist inquiry requires. If we assume that some people understand power through their struggles with power and not through their scholarly study of power, we belittle the scholarship of those who struggle.

Feminists share critical sympathies with post-structural, post-colonial, and critical scholars and with social movements, particularly women's movements, local and global. Among these, *feminists* do feminist inquiry particularly well because (and when) they are attentive to: (1) power in all of its visible and invisible forms, (2) boundaries and their potentials for exclusion, marginalization, and incomplete or superficial inclusion, (3) relationships of power and obligation (between people in different parts of the global economy, between men and women, parents and children, researchers and research subject, reader and audience), and (4) the role for self-reflexive humility in maintaining attentiveness to these concerns.

Distinguishing feminist methodologies from other methodologies is less important than asking how critical reflection can improve the conceptualization, epistemological assumptions, and research design choices required for any research project. Feminist methodology encourages all scholars to acknowledge that there are hierarchies in our own scholarship and to acknowledge that our own inquiry is partial and ongoing. Without such consciousness, we are not only bad feminists, we are also bad scholars. In this sense, feminist methodology is not just applicable to questions about women (as Leander's contribution to this book illustrates). In addition to providing a huge range of particular tools for inquiry, the feminist contribution to methodology can be summarized as a tool for reflection that is guided by humility.

Whether a particular project calls for qualitative or quantitative methods, feminist inquiry entails reflection directed at all stages of the scholarly process. In coming up with a research question, we may ask whose interests are served by it. In conceptualizing our study, we may ask how language has historically conditioned the conceptualization of a problem. In operationalizing our variables and in collecting our data, we might use gender analysis. For example, an interview is a feminist interview when we reflect on the power dynamics between researcher and research subject in global context. (Gusterson's experiences with spouses, retold in this book, illustrates that men can do feminist interviews.) Publication is *feminist* when we attend to how our findings will be used and their effects on our research subjects.

Feminist theory has made feminist empirical work particularly challenging. Its commitments to exploring absence, silence, difference, and oppression have generated aspirations to do research that, if fully practiced, would leave many scholars forever in the field, always listening for new voices, always (respectfully) hearing cacophony, always suspicious of certain harmonies or recurring themes (Lazreq 2002; Dever 2004). Empiricists have to wrestle with this irony without allowing it to prevent them from doing their research. To allow such reflection to inhibit rather than inspire our research would be to perpetuate the invisibility of gendered absences, silences, differences, and oppressions, and the injustices that they conceal (Gluck and Patai 1991; Pettman 1992; Wolf 1992; Enloe 1993, 2000; Sylvester 1994; Wolf 1996; Stacey 1999; Staeheli and Nagar 2002).

In this chapter, I illustrate these concerns through my own work on human rights. I briefly introduce the critical ambitions inspired by feminist theory and then highlight the kinds of methodological challenges I faced when trying to be attentive to silence, marginalization, and absence. I reflect upon the relative merits of the options I considered and choices I made at important moments in the research process. In the third part, I offer a pedagogical and methodological tool, 'curb-cutting,' for inspiring one's own reflection.

Feminist inquiry in brief

Feminist inquiry is about revealing unquestioned differences and inequalities that conceal the exercise of power, including the power to conceal those differences and inequalities, and being attentive to the power exercised when researching these. All aspects of the research process are contestable. Attentiveness to the exercise of power extends not only to a field of study but also to its manifestation through academic inquiry.

Academic feminism has ethical responsibilities that reflect an ontological understanding of scholarship as *for* social change. Feminist theory educates feminist empiricists about the ethical importance of epistemological reflection at every stage of the research process. And feminist theory informs the methodological choices of any feminist researcher. Finally, most feminist research is self-consciously deliberate in its pedagogical purpose. The choices that feminists make about where and how to share and teach our scholarship are themselves methodological.

In empirical research, feminism encourages attentiveness to the challenges of seeing marginalization when the social, political, and economic authorities of a society render hierarchies either invisible or socially characterized as natural (Enloe 2004). It has been influenced by and has influenced many critical theoretical perspectives including post-structuralist, post-colonial, and critical theories (Fraser 1997; Narayan 1997; Ling 2002; Risman 2004) as well as movements for social justice (Collins [1990] 1991; Young 1990, 2001). At its best, feminist inquiry is attentive to the power of epistemological authority to mask political, economic, and social oppression as natural and accepted (Pateman 1988; Brown 1995; Ackerly 2000, 2008; Hirschmann 2003).

Such attentiveness to silence and inequality might well inhibit an empiricist from gathering or analyzing data by trapping her in a self-reflective mode. It might render a qualitative empiricist particularly incapacitated, afraid of exercising power over her research subject at every turn (D'Costa 2006; Jacoby 2006; compare Stern 2006). Juxtapose this potential incapacity with the emancipatory potential of feminisms (Agathangelou 2004). There is nothing emancipatory about fear – even the fear that one's own ideas may be corrupted by systems of power that one has internalized (Suu Kyi 1991; Ackerly forthcoming 2008). As Martha Nussbaum argues, 'In fear, one sees oneself or what one loves as seriously threatened' (Nussbaum 2001: 28). Threats may lead to emancipatory action, but threat itself is not emancipatory.

Moreover, while the feminist researcher may well have good theoretical and ethical reasons for leaving activism to activists (Bell and Butler 1999), there are no good ethical reasons for the feminist researcher knowingly to perpetuate the silence of the marginalized when she has the education and resources to reveal these (Smith 1999; Ackerly 2007b). And there are good ethical reasons for disrupting silence and marginalization. Yet, we know from critical reflection that feminists have also perpetuated some forms of marginalization, despite our best efforts. (Dunn, in this book, explores similar themes in the context of race and inequality.)

How then might the feminist empiricist proceed? Each choice she makes as a researcher should be evaluated as an exercise of power, just as it is understood to be an exercise of discernment. When the feminist empiricist attends to dilemmas that emerge during her research process, she may resolve them in the moment in order for the research to proceed. But they remain unresolved in the sense that at other stages in the research process, she may reflect back on earlier choices to note the epistemology that is privileged by those choices or the ways in which prior conceptualization has limited her ability to engage fully with the import of a particular dilemma. In the next section, I illustrate how I dealt with such dilemmas.

Methodological dilemmas in practice

From 1998 to 2001, I was a participant observer in online working groups of women's human rights activists (Ackerly 2001) and hosted with the Center for International Studies (CIS) at the University of Southern California a conference for scholars, activists, and donors. From these two projects emerged a puzzle: how could activists and other feminists who disagreed about so much understand their work for women's human rights as part of a shared project? Was this understanding an artifact of the resources (the online working groups funded by UNIFEM and the conference funded by CIS) that facilitated their dialogue? Was this the 'articulation' of a theoretical insight about human rights more generally? Or both?

Building on that work, I began a project exploring the notion of 'universal' human rights from a feminist perspective – a perspective attentive to absence, silence, difference, oppression, and marginalization that makes claims to universality both politically and theoretically suspect (Peterson 1990; Fraser 1999). Some of my methodological dilemmas affected the entire project, others only certain aspects of it.

Some could be attended to but never resolved; others could be provisionally resolved. I offer these not as representative of the dilemmas feminist qualitative methodologists face, but rather as opportunities for sharing how one feminist uses feminist methodology to think through them. As feminist researcher, I attended to:

- power in all of its visible and invisible forms,
- boundaries and the potentials for exclusion, marginalization, and inclusion to be incomplete or superficial,
- relationships of power and obligation (between people in different parts of the global economy, between men and women, parents and children, researchers and research subject, reader and audience), and
- the role for self-reflexive humility in maintaining attentiveness to these three concerns.

Jacqui True and I refer to these four as the 'feminist research ethic,' a shared tool of feminist empiricists. (We review the feminist work from which we derive this schema in Ackerly and True, forthcoming.)

For expository purposes, I discuss these dilemmas in an order that roughly reflects the chronology of a research plan. However, because of the way that the feminist research ethic guides our thinking about a given research dilemma, the feminist research process often requires deviating from the research plan and even retracing steps of the process. For example, dilemmas in sampling could make us rethink our question (see D'Costa 2006 for a particularly informative model of this). Each dilemma should provoke many questions and further reflection on related dilemmas. In order to share my work, I reconstruct key moments of methodological reflection, not to mask the non-linearity of the actual research process, but to enable others to comprehend the import of what are in retrospect decisive dilemmas in research.

My principle *question dilemma* was, should I ask the question, 'Are there universal human rights?' Is it a worthy theoretical enterprise for a feminist (who is attentive to the power of difference and the invisibilities of various exercises of power) to try to reason about *universal* human rights when most accounts of universals mask the particulars of privileged experience (MacKinnon 2006; compare D'Costa 2006)? In my preliminary work on the topic (in both the working group and the workshop), I came to know women human rights defenders. Many were working a third shift (after work and family care) to promote women's human rights in their communities, many others were working at risk to themselves, and they seemed to understand themselves as collaborating even while disagreeing. From the relative comfort of academe, I reasoned that I could start from the assumption that they were onto something. Therefore, the question was a means to interrogate power not to reify or conceal its exercise.

Having decided to ask the question of universal human rights, the *research design dilemma* was how to go about answering it. Feminist reflection about research design is similar to that of other fields at many levels. Feminists review the literature and consider the merits of various options relative to our research question. Like other researchers, we face decisions about locations, domain, sampling, data collection, data analysis, and publication.

However, some of the feminist considerations may seem unusual. For example, I considered broadening the use of the Internet as a source of insight, but I worried that continuing to focus on the online working groups would not yield an adequately diverse sample. Participants represented only a slice (and to a certain extent, disproportionately elite slice) of the women's human rights movement. In addition, the groups were becoming increasingly self-referential. Fewer new participants were contributing than when the groups were first launched. Generally, they were more privileged within this context: the relatively better resourced, those networked with the global North, those with local political networks, those with funding networks, those who were relatively more powerful within their organization (compare Ackerly 2007a). My question was not well addressed from the perspective of the privileged within their organizations and the privileged within the women's movement globally.

The ethical dimensions of research design may not always be anticipated by the researcher, but some can be. For example, I could have continued with the method of participant observation at meetings that I hosted. However, this approach raised ethical questions for the researcher–research subject relationship, some of which were related to the limited resources of women's movements globally (Clark *et al.* 2006; Ackerly 2007b). The meeting at CIS cost approximately $20,000. Replicating that meeting would likely cost the same (or more, as there were many expenses associated with that meeting that were not incorporated into the budget of the workshop). Should some of the few resources for women's human rights activism in the world be diverted to my project? It was not clear to me that the under-funded work of women's human rights activists was best supported by their participating in meetings organized by me. However valuable they were to my work and to those who were able to come, it was not obvious to me that this was the *best* use of funds.

I decided that I would do best to learn from activists in the women's movement transnationally and locally. Therefore, I looked specifically for activists marginalized in mainstream movements (for example, movements for street vendors) and for women marginalized within the transnational feminism movement (for example, women who were not part of the 30,000 women at the 1995 UN Conference on Women in Beijing).

Research design considerations include practical and ethical dilemmas around selecting research subjects, *the domain* of subjects from which we sample. Identifying my research subjects was an act of epistemological power that would have a definitive impact on my findings. What would be the best way to identify (to see and to locate) women in order to learn from them? What would be the domain of women activists? How would I sample among them in order to select activists to interview?

I had neither hope nor aspiration for a representative sample of the world's women or even of women's human rights activists. The movement is so huge, geographically diverse, and disbursed, and always shifting membership – all of the activists of the movement (the domain) would always remain unknown to me. To try to get a representative sample of an unknowable domain was a spurious endeavor. Moreover, my question could not be explored by a representative sample. Instead, I needed my inquiry to reveal different and competing ideas. Therefore, I needed to sample marginalized thinkers and those willing to voice disagreement.

Most systems that I thought of involved identifying visible organizations through Internet searches and my growing personal networks. These approaches would yield those who had made themselves visible to myself or others. For example, I might have studied recipients of small grants thereby relying on a third party to identify the organizations. Each of these approaches to identifying research subjects would have privileged the relatively powerful, even though some of those subjects might have identified themselves as relatively marginalized within global women's activism.

The international discussions leading up to the World Social Forum (WSF) and the Mumbai Resistance (which was a more anti-capitalist meeting that met across the street from the WSF conference) in 2004 indicated that these meetings might present an opportunity for me to witness people who felt marginalized in a range of contexts. By coming to the WSF, they would be exhibiting the willingness and ability to make the effort to overcome that marginalization by planning to network. At WSF, I would be able to hear their thoughts about the possibility of networking when they were most aware of their similarities and differences with other groups because they were confronting them daily during WSF. I would also be able to be a participant observer of movement organizations' efforts to be more or less inclusive of other movements and organizations. Because of all of these opportunities to hear difference and thoughtful reflection on difference, I decided to interview participants in WSF and Mumbai Resistance.

Again, there was cause for reflection on privilege. Would not these be the elites of the transnational movement as well? Possibly. However, women were using WSF as a space to influence global progressive movements. Mumbai WSF was an opportunity for women to see if alliances with other progressive movements were possible (World Social Forum Panel 2004a,b,c). Further, though some participants in WSF 2004 stayed in comfortable hotels, the cost of participation (including travel and lodging) was feasible for many (a total of 960 rupees or less than 18 Euros). This meant that the meeting drew a large number of grassroots activists from India. WSF was a place where I could observe activists expressing their ideas and their agency. (I went to Porto Alegre the next year and sent graduate students to Kenya for WSF 2007.)

To be confident that my sample did not create a bias toward a shared universal view of human rights, I needed a *sampling mechanism* that would result in the study being informed by people who disagreed with one another or who were willing to voice disagreement with certain parts of the movement. A research assistant and I planned out which panels we would observe, seeking to identify a range of feminists. At those panels, we sought to identify women (and men) who could offer perspectives we had not heard before or who had asked a question that went unanswered in the panel discussion. Only four interviewees were selected because the person was known or referred to me. But this snowball sampling did not get any bigger than that because I wanted the anti-snowball sample: a sample of the people who were at some degree of critical distance from the snowball of transnational feminist activism. I needed to seek those whose opinions might differ from the main arguments heard by well-networked feminists. I was listening for cacophony.

What kind of *data* should I collect in order to be able to record these people's insights and bring them home for further reflection? I considered asking for life histories and other forms of open-ended interviews that would give the interview subject the greatest opportunity to control the content she provided (compare Stern 2006; also see Gusterson's use of life histories in this book). However, these were activists who came to WSF to network, not to be research subjects. They were willing to take a break and reflect over a cup of tea or water, but they were not up for a long intermission in their own activist agenda in order to inform my academic agenda. With the ethical consideration of *their time* most central to my methodological choice, I decided on participant observation and an interview format, which treated the subject as the expert she was on the demands and possibilities for universal human rights from her perspective. I invited her to comment on some of the dominant threads of transnational feminism, to identify opportunities for networking and collaboration, and to offer accounts of obstacles.

Even while collecting the data, but most critically once home, I reflected on the ways in which *analyzing data* is an ethical practice: an exercise of power, of delimiting boundaries, of appreciating relationships, and an opportunity for self-reflection on all of these. If the interview subject was the author of her ideas, could I ethically do anything other than report them (Gluck and Patai 1991; Wolf 1992)? How was I to use her insights?

I decided not to take each interview as its own individualistic isolated 'text' but rather treat it as part of an ongoing dialogue with others, my other interview subjects, the others that the subject had had conversations with at WSF, the panels that she had participated in, even the interlocutors that she imagined. This was appropriate because participants were at WSF to dialogue with others. When they sat down with me, they were continuing a pattern that they were engaged in throughout their time at WSF – exchanging ideas with others. This dialogue was enriched when I went to WSF 2005 in Porto Alegre and to a meeting of feminists that preceded it. My understanding of WSF as a space for women's human rights activists changed as a result of these additional meetings, but the importance of reflecting on the differences among women's human rights activists was affirmed.

The dialogue was further enriched by sharing my insights. Though my interview subjects did not dialogue with each other, in my book I put their ideas in dialogue with one another. In a brief letter circulated to the interviewees, I shared a short account of the theory and the draft manuscript of the larger project. I solicited and received few comments from the participants. This stage of the inquiry was made particularly difficult by my choice of marginalized activist. Many of my interview subjects were difficult to find again. Their experiential reasons for not communicating with me could not be known to me, unless they communicated them to me. One wrote from Afghanistan,

> Thanks for your nice concern and yes!! You can publish my interview anywhere you want as you asked me in your last email.
>
> As you know we are living in a society where religious extremis are capturing all the social and political Sector, and my activities are very democratic so while launching some of my projects and programs for women empowerment I am receiving different threats, and I have to be careful about my live because they are very good in shooting people like us....
>
> (unedited personal communication, 25 February 2004)

In essence, she asked me to use her insights, whether or not I could find her. (Note that I have illustrated a common and yet unanticipated impact of analysis. It revealed the importance of dialogue and collaboration *for the analysis* of the data and therefore the need to have a second stage of data collection at WSF 2005 and another kind of data collected in the form of correspondence with interviewees.)

For most academics, *publishing* a piece of research is not a methodological decision; it is a professional decision about audience. In contrast, for the feminist it often is a methodological decision. In my case, what would be the value to the activists informing my inquiry of the theoretical treatise I was expecting to produce for an audience in my field, political theory? Taking their theoretical insights in order to produce what was for them a useless piece of scholarship, inaccessible in their familiar language, was an act of privilege inconsistent with the theoretical intent of the project. The epistemology and methodology of my project was supposed to break down the theory/practice dichotomy, yet the book produced for that project (and appropriate for my professional ambitions) could be inaccessible to the informants.

I dealt with this paradox of privilege in two ways. First, the book itself contains an argument unusual in political theory, a suggestion *to activists* about how they might change their work in light of the theoretical insights generated during *my* reflection on *their* insights. Second, *Universal Human Rights in a World of Difference* is not the final end of this scholarship. As I finish the book, I am beginning a research–scholar network whose central question is, what does it mean to do research *for* social justice (as opposed to *about* social justice)? We are developing a research practice in the area of global feminism to do academic research that serves organizations or communities engaged in women's human rights activism broadly (and problematically) defined. This scholarship has led me into ethical relationships with scholars and activists such that in addition to my academic interests, my ethical commitments require that I continue related scholarship *and* facilitate the opportunities for others to do research that strengthens women's activism around the world (Ackerly 2007b).

The academic–activist relationship developed during this scholarship has also created a pedagogical obligation (again, an *obligation* on my part, not just an interest, though that too) to bring into the curriculum of my elite university in the US theoretical reflection and empirical data that shine light on the marginal spaces of global politics where so many of the world's women work so hard against oppression, unacknowledged, unrecognized, and 'invisibly.' This scholarship is intended to reveal that 'their' marginalization, oppression, invisibility, and absences are evidence of 'our' privilege and 'our' exercise of epistemological power. How do we teach ourselves and our students to do this work?

Curb cutting as a pedagogical tool

Because gender hierarchy so often gets institutionalized in ways that render it invisible, researchers need to comprehend marginalization through experience, not solely through sociological study. Of course, we cannot directly experience *others'* marginalization. So we need to teach ourselves to be attuned to the possibility that there may be experiences that are invisible to us. I describe this to my students as 'curb cut feminism.' This same pedagogical tool can be a stimulating tool for scholars' (not just women's) methodological reflection. In this section, I show how researchers can stimulate reflections on their own research process similar to those I described in the preceding section.

In my own classrooms at an elite North American university, where all facilities are technically accessible, I use the metaphor of curb cuts to reveal the challenge of making privilege visible. Curb cuts are the cuts in a sidewalk that turn a step into a slope and enable a wheelchair to cross a street or driveway. They are accommodations that make spaces designed to privilege access for certain people accessible to all. 'Curb cut feminists' cut ramps into the curbs of injustice – such as structural inequalities and the politics of misrecognition – and then we all, including immigrant minority women with dependent parents and grandchildren and trafficked camel jockeys, can live in a world that is more just, and promote justice for some in ways that enhance justice for others. 'Curb cut feminism' also describes a theoretical perspective with a methodological commitment to be attentive to privilege and hierarchy not only as a subject of study but also as a *way of studying*. The metaphor may be best suited to North American university campuses where curb cuts, automatic doors, and blue disability symbols are part of daily life, but the aspiration to a form of emancipatory scholarship that works against *all* forms of oppression is important to many strands of feminist inquiry.

To illuminate the ways in which privilege gets treated as 'normal,' I ask my students to do basic daily activities – get coffee, pick up their mail, park for class – in a wheelchair. The purpose is not to simulate the perspective from a wheelchair (that cannot be done), but rather to make visible their own privilege that they did not see before. Through this activity, they gain a range of insights about (limits to) mobility created by the design of their institution and its accommodation systems. They notice steep hills, bumpy sidewalks, accessible side entrances and steps at the main entrances. One lesson that students quickly learn is that *accommodations* by no means mitigate the *privilege* of certain forms of mobility.

The exercise stimulates our desire and ability to notice additional forms of our own privilege, which we do not often notice. Further, by it I hope to cultivate the ability to reason in ways that make some of the experiences and challenges of those *unprivileged* by the basic spatial, political, economic, and social designs of our societies *visible*. Because I use the metaphor of curb cuts, one might misunderstand me to be priv-ileging some forms of disability over others or privileging disability over other forms of marginalization. The point is not to identify *a* perspective to privilege, but to deploy a device that destabilizes the perspective from which we 'know.' Aware of the presence or absence of curb cuts, only one door being accessible, and of library books on inaccessible shelves, we are more attentive to the *privilege* of the norm. Attentive to certain mobility privilege, we start imagining improvements that would help *everyone*.

The ramifications of improved mobility are felt far beyond the initial focus on freedom of movement for those whose mobility is most chal-lenged. We are able to see how redesign (and accommodation) can enhance the mobility of those pushing strollers and delivery dollies, those carrying lots of books, and those recovering from an injury. All are able to move more freely and safely. For example, parents with children in strollers can go to museums, which furthers their children's and their own education. However, curb cuts do not discriminate about the kinds of mobility they enable. Access ramps may attract skateboarders or facilitate cyclists' going on the sidewalk to avoid automobile traffic. In this way, curb cuts might *inhibit* the mobility of everyone. Attentiveness to all forms of mobility *can* yield design solutions that enable safe mobility and better living for all, but it does not necessarily.

It is not enough *that* we pay attention to invisible privilege and marginalization; it matters *how* we pay attention to them. In designing our architectural landscape, we could rely on ourselves to do our best to think about the needs of people with disabilities, or to develop specific guidelines (like the International Building Code). We could design for those with mobility privileges and accommodate others or we could design so as not to privilege certain groups. No matter our approach, we cannot be confident that our designs (or accommodations) insure that our curb cuts worked for those in wheelchairs or that they made conditions better for all. Architects and city planners seek out 'rules' to help guide their choices, yet the insights of users are still the most valuable for noticing privilege.

Rather than relying on our best efforts – which can be fruitless or even harmful despite our intentions – we should develop *a method of thinking* that is always informed by the experience of people with mobility disabilities. Rather than relying on ourselves to do our best in thinking about the challenges and opportunities of marginalized people which could end up reflecting our own epistemological myopia (that is, our own unexamined view of what constitutes knowledge and of what data constitute evidence), we need a *method* for thinking about lived experience and for thinking about what lived experience tells us for theory and conceptualization, epistemological and empirical assumptions, research design and methods choices, and data analysis and publishing decisions (Ackerly 2000; Sandoval 2000).

Insights from feminist curb cutting inform my research and reveal the hierarchies between me and my research subjects and among my potential research subjects. Such reflections can help me carry out a research project that is self-reflectively attentive to power, boundaries, and relationships throughout the process. Applying these insights helps us see the political, social, and economic processes of normalization that sustain hierarchies. All sorts of values, practices, norms, and institutions impede, exclude, ignore, or marginalize some women, but not all women, nor only women. Curb cutting assumes that identifying and analyzing the conditions of oppression provides greater insights than those possible from positions of relative privilege. For example, I discussed above that I did not want to rely solely on Internet-accessible research subjects or on women who were well integrated into transnational feminist networks.

Those who are 'most' or 'differently' oppressed may not be visible to the theorist or to the relatively powerful. Hence, for the follow-up interviews in 2005, I sought out women whom I perceived as silenced in the feminist meetings that preceded WSF 2005. Furthermore, the perspective not yet imagined is even more marginalized than the most marginalized perspective that one can imagine. I explored the silences in my own data: Who *was not* at WSF? What were my research subjects *not* telling me?

I put 'most' in quotes to indicate the need to reflect critically on the term. The point is not to privilege marginalization but to be self-conscious about the power exercised through marginalization and to be aware that the political claim to being 'most' marginalized can be used to challenge the patterns of hierarchy (Vélez-Ibañez 1983). As I describe in the preceding section, at every turn – from question through publication – the research needs to reflect on these power dynamics. Feminist curb cutting is a tool that any researcher can use to teach herself to be attentive to the politics of knowledge and to the power of privilege in her research practices. Attentiveness to these politics does not remove them, but it allows the researcher to unmask some and mitigate others, even as she enacts still others.

Conclusion

The methodological dilemmas I have discussed (and so many others) emerge as important in part because feminist theory says that the feminist researcher should worry about the ethical implications of the hierarchies of knowledge within which she works and to which she contributes. Attention to these requires not turning away from the discomfort associated with hierarchies of knowledge, but rather committing ourselves to looking for and to attending to them, always, already.

As I thought through these methodological dilemmas, I was working within and contributing to changing feminist theory. Feminists are appropriately worried about universalizing across differences. My work shows that we should be likewise worried about failing to work across differences because we are worried about universalizing. Feminism is hard work. Feminism cannot be a theoretical perspective that legitimates *not* attending to hard questions because the politics of epistemology are difficult to unmask. Feminist theory guides feminist empiricists to continue to seek out such dilemmas and to expose them.

Each research question is unique and each scholar will be faced with specific methodological dilemmas. I have offered my dilemmas and theoretically guided process of attending to and working within them as an outline in order to indicate the scope of feminist methodological reflection – from research question to publication. At no stage in the research process can the feminist, attentive to power, be confident that her research methodology has adequately interrogated the possibilities for absence, silence, difference, and oppression that the power of knowledge and research can conceal as well as reveal. However, that humility should not obfuscate her responsibility for the choices that she has made. Being 'in the field' brings ethical responsibilities. Taking that responsibility requires recognizing that 'getting it just right' is a privilege itself, one best shared. For many feminists, theory and empirical work is in the largest sense collaborative (Ackerly and True 2006). Such collaboration requires sharing our dilemmas, our imperfect efforts to work through them, and our partial insights.

4
Case Selection

Audie Klotz

For most researchers, case selection *defines* method: a few cases of a particular phenomenon make a study 'qualitative' but a lot of cases turns it into a 'quantitative' analysis. Usually a case is equated with a country, and there is often an implicit presumption that some sort of history will be traced. In International Relations (IR), qualitative method typically means a study of one or a few foreign policies, with a decision-making process to be traced at the micro-historical level (George and Bennett 2005). Yet for many questions, say, about globalization, countries are not necessarily the appropriate unit of analysis; economic systems might be. And historical evolution can happen at a higher level of aggregation, such as macro-historical changes in property rights.

Too often, the justification for a research design begins and ends with the rationale for the number of cases, obscuring key issues, such as the unit and level of analysis. In part, this is the result of the problematic conventional dichotomy between qualitative and quantitative methods. Would a project where the researcher uses statistical analysis *within* a single case study be qualitative or quantitative? From a comparative perspective, much of the work on American Politics looks just like that! Intensive analysis of a single case can employ all types of methodological tools without agreement on the degree of general, extensive, knowledge being sought.

Researchers need to remember that cases are cases *of* something. Well-crafted case selection takes into account the universe of possible cases and the logic of comparison implied by the research question. In this chapter, I will show how clarifying the overall purpose of the project and its theoretical framework broadens the rationales for single case studies, paired comparisons, and slightly larger studies. Often I will draw on guidelines by other researchers and suggest their publications for further reading. Most of my illustrations will come from my dissertation-based book, *Norms in International Relations: The Struggle against Apartheid* (1995), because I can delineate explicitly the sorts of trade-offs and choices that rarely appear in published work.

Cases *of what*?

Appropriate case selection depends first and foremost on ontology, because any research question relies on core concepts. That brings us to the starting point for case selection: a case *of what*? As Leander (in this book) underscores, questions and concepts remain embedded in theoretical presuppositions. Quite often, these assumptions and subsequent propositions would benefit from clarification. Vagueness is not always the result of sensitivity to context and complexity! What are the key concepts that define a 'case' and what are the key dimensions that should be compared? These are not simply questions of finding indicators, although definitional decisions do hold implications for that stage of research design (Adcock and Collier 2001; Goertz 2006).

When I was formulating my dissertation, for example, I confronted the question of how to conceptualize 'race' in global politics. Was it an ideology? While otherwise quite useful, I found that this standard conceptualization underplayed contestation, and I was intrigued by the international controversy over South African apartheid, particularly the policies of neighboring states. Out went ideology. Alternatively, should I analyze the word race as a linguistic signifier? I found semiotics too focused on specific words, leaving out the material and social dimensions that ideology did capture. Was racism cultural? Yes, in a general sense, but the term 'culture' implied a dense immutability inappropriate for studying IR. I was looking for something less monolithic. Each of these formulations had advantages and disadvantages, but none seemed to capture how the global politics of race appeared to me in the late 1980s.

In the end, I opted to define race in terms of contending 'norms' of racial equality and racial superiority, situating my study in the context of regime theory. Responses to South African apartheid became *a puzzling case of international consensus* that challenged prevailing theories of cooperation based on rational calculations of material interests: Why would racial equality trump domestic jurisdiction? Adcock and Collier refer to this as the shift from a 'background' concept to a 'systematized' one (2001: 530–1; Goertz 2006: 27–57), moving the researcher from abstractions toward measures.

Yet conceptualization is not simply a one-way process, from general to specific. The way the researcher narrows a general concept in order to do empirical research also affects the formulation of the main question – not solely the choice of 'indicators.' Had I defined race through a different theoretical framework, my key question (and subsequent case selection) might also have shifted substantially. More influenced by Michel Foucault and Edward Said, for example, Roxanne Doty (1996) pursued similar questions about race through an analysis of hegemonic discourses, rather than regimes. She queried the constitutive role of race (in the imperial relationships of the United States with the Philippines and of Britain with Kenya), whereas I concentrated on a moment of contestation over it. We started with similar frustrations with the omission of race in IR theories, but our alternative theoretical frameworks led to different key questions, core conceptualizations, and subsequent cases.

Because IR theory lacked any standard conceptualization of 'race' at the time, Doty and I each independently devised a definition to put into practice. That potentially leads to the commonplace critique that case study researchers define concepts idiosyncratically. But the tendency to contextualize concepts need not be an insurmountable problem for comparing across cases. For instance, even an elusive concept like 'regime' has fuelled reams of insightful research on international cooperation and global governance, despite abiding definitional disputes. And applications of constructivism and critical theory have advanced in the two past decades to the point that researchers should be able to find enough common ground in definitions of race (though Doty might not agree with me on this). Most qualitative researchers remain comfortable with a moderately flexible set of characteristics, and many acknowledge the danger of 'stretching' a concept to the point that it loses its essence (Sartori 1970; Collier and Mahon 1993).

Still, case study researchers should avoid undue vagueness and would benefit from the series of questions that Goertz poses (2006: 30–5). He starts with a very basic question: What is the *opposite* of the concept? For example, democracy might be contrasted to authoritarianism *or* monarchy, depending on the research question. The opposite of racial superiority (of which apartheid was one manifestation) might be non-racialism (not accepting the existence of race as a way to categorize people) *or* multiracialism (not privileging one race over another). Another useful suggestion is to pay attention to the use of adjectives that modify key nouns, such as 'parliamentary' or 'presidential' democracies, or racial equality versus racial superiority. Since I did not have Goertz to prod me before I got 'to the field,' I had to figure out some of these distinctions – and their *political* significance – as I parsed the sanctions debates.

How many *possible* cases?

After defining a case and the dimensions of comparison, the researcher needs to decide whether to analyze the full universe of cases or some subset. That requires identifying the 'universe' of cases. It may be small, such as 'world wars' or 'nuclear weapons laboratories' (Gusterson in this book) or large, such as wars or laboratories in general. Clarifying what would be a *non*-case helps for delineating possible cases. A non-case of a nuclear weapons laboratory could be a weapons laboratory or a civilian laboratory. A non-case of war might be violent conflict that remains within the territorial boundaries of one state, a militarized interstate dispute averted, or stable peace. It all depends on the formulation of the research question, although clarifying the universe of cases might, in turn, mean going back to reformulate the core research question.

In my efforts to understand how race affected policies toward South Africa, for instance, I had to decide whether to include all sanctions policies or select a few 'senders' (in the language of that literature). Initially, this task seemed straightforward: list the relevant international organizations and states, then decide the feasibility of including all of them in the analysis. I remain indebted to my dissertation committee for pointing out that only looking at those who adopted sanctions would have prematurely truncated the list of possible cases. My universe of cases quickly expanded, because I needed to include all the *debates* over sanctions to capture times when sanctions *might* have happened but were rejected. (Similarly, see Ackerly's discussion, in this book, of her difficulties trying to analyze marginalized and silenced discourses.)

The distinction between cases and non-cases may not be stark. And the gray zone may actually be more interesting (politically as well as theoretically) than the poles – Britain had mixed policies which critics did not consider sanctions at all – but we still need the full spectrum in order to identify its significance. In more formalized terminology, Mahoney and Goertz (2004) offer their 'possibility principle.' They rightly note that most non-cases are actually implausible and the subset of possible cases is much narrower. The trick is to figure out the difference. If you were lucky, like I was, you have a dissertation committee – or a colleague sufficiently informed but not vested in the outcome of the research – to keep you honest about plausibility. Those comfortable with the language of variables will also benefit from reviewing Mahoney and Goertz's rules of inclusion and exclusion (2004: 657–8).

Some studies go even further to analyze the non-cases, such as policies that are *not* adopted (Price 1997; Tannenwald 2007). Indeed, depending on how the research question is framed, one study's case may be another study's non-case. The use of counter-factual scenarios further expands the range of potential non-cases, although their use raises a whole host of additional issues (Fearon 1991; Tetlock and Belkin 1996). Indeed, I do wonder why post-modernists are derided for challenging the objectivity of historical narratives yet made up counter-factual scenarios can be taken so seriously by social scientists. I prefer to treat these as theoretical formulations or predictions, rather than cases *per se*, because all researchers employ hypothetical 'what if' and 'why not' scenarios, either implicitly or explicitly. And that leads us to the next step in case selection, sorting out the logic of comparison employed in the project.

Which logic of comparison?

Delineating a universe of cases (including non-cases) does not tell a researcher *how* to analyze them, beyond some notion of comparison. Even a single case is not unique, otherwise there is no basis for calling it exceptional. However, the comparison might be against an ideal type. There are diverse ways that researchers parse evidence within a comparative logic. The type of question the study seeks to answer, in turn, depends on its underlying logic.

For example, King, Keohane, and Verba's (1994) controversial advice to increase the number of observations applies a statistical logic of theory testing: the larger the universe (or representative sample), the more persuasive the hypothesized claims about patterns between variables. Yet, for better or worse, redefining a key concept in order to create more observations may fundamentally alter the research question. World wars are not the same thing as militarized interstate disputes. If the research question really is about *worldwide* war, or *nuclear* weapons laboratories, the change may be unwarranted, and a study of only a few events or locations would be appropriate regardless of what the statisticians might think. For questions looking at wars or laboratories in general, though, expanding the study could be beneficial, since it reduces over-generalization from the experiences of great powers or scientists working on secret projects.

Making a choice between, say, five cases that lack the ideal controls versus a near-perfect quasi-experimental paired comparison that shifts the main question depends on the researcher knowing the embedded logic of comparison. This *sounds* simple. Typically, social science projects seek to make somewhat general causal claims, while those drawing on post-modernism do not. Yet once we start delving into what exactly it means to make a causal claim, neither epistemological position proves to be so obvious.

There is no single 'scientific' logic. Some, inspired by physics, advocate deduction to generate hypotheses, usually followed by statistical testing. Others prefer focused comparison, because it mimics a test tube experiment in a chemistry laboratory. Biology and geology offer other templates. Policy-focused or intensive ethnographic research can also lead to general claims that might be reformulated as hypotheses to test and may convincingly disprove a prevailing theory in particular circumstances (see 'Single Case Studies' below; also Leander and Gusterson in this book). All researchers, therefore, would benefit from clarifying their analytical assumptions by asking themselves the following three general questions.

Does the study seek to test theories?

Avowed social scientists are not the only ones who put forth general claims; a study does not need to use the terms 'hypothesis' or 'variable' to offer theories that can be tested. Furthermore, theory-testing studies are only as good as their hypotheses. And as Ackerly underscores (in this book), there is no guarantee that factors, notably gender (and I would add race), have not been systematically omitted. Framing theoretical insights through the dominant scholarly discourse of testing propositions can lead to productive engagements, even if the initial studies do not use the vocabulary of variables.

For example, critical theorists have raised the visibility of 'omitted variables' such as gender and deserve credit for getting them into the 'equation.' See, for instance, Goertz's overview of how the addition of gender transformed the literature on the welfare state (2006: 88–93). In IR, Foucauldian notions of epistemic power have made in-roads in the past 20 years, as the limits of a materialist conception of power have become increasingly apparent. Not coincidentally, feminist approaches have gained legitimacy along with constructivism (Peterson *et al.* 2005). I adamantly refused to have variables in my dissertation, but these sorts of examples have mellowed me over the years, and therefore I encourage others not to react to scholarship based solely on differences in terminology (Klotz and Lynch 2006).

Are causal claims made in terms of conditions or mechanisms?

One of the most basic lessons about analytical inference is the differentiation between correlation and causation. Its application seems straightforward: use statistical analysis to identify patterns, and then select cases to illustrate which direction the causal effect runs (or figure out if another variable explains both). Case studies trace a causal process that links the proposed independent variable to the dependent one, in order to offer an explanation for why the pattern emerges. This research design has been the bread-and-butter model for mixing methods. More recently, the marriage of rational choice theory (which derives its hypotheses deductively, rather than observing statistical patterns) with historical narrative relies on the same process tracing approach to theory testing.

Elaborating on this as a social *scientific* basis for case studies, advocates of mechanisms have been contributing a lot to the burgeoning literature on qualitative methods (George and Bennett 2005; Gerring 2007). As with all approaches, a focus on mechanisms has its strengths and weaknesses (Checkel in this book). For example, such studies in IR usually demonstrate a chain of decisions by policy makers that presumably links the independent and dependent variables. But because any mechanism can be scaled up or down (Tilly 2001), no one can possibly test all the plausible alternatives. Once again, we are reminded that ontological assumptions about units and levels of analysis are critical.

Yet the problem runs deeper than researchers failing to test propositions about alternative processes. Causal chain narratives downplay contingency and contestation. Indeed, in his (otherwise quite useful) practical guidelines for historical research in IR, Trachtenberg (2006) *advises* writing historical narratives to emphasize the almost-inevitable nature of the outcomes, even if the preceding analysis does take into account alternative scenarios. But these chains of mechanisms, which focus on the presence or absence of factors, are not the only type of causal argument.

Probabilistic claims, articulated in terms of likelihoods, are based on conditions and the conjuncture of various factors at a particular point in time. This latter view shares a contingent quality that post-modernists favor. To see these distinctions in practice, note how Checkel and Dunn (in this book) employ documents and interviews in similar ways to different analytical ends. Checkel aims to create an historical narrative that positions social facts into a coherent story, whereas Dunn offers a genealogy that highlights contestation over meanings. (Little 1991 offers a succinct overview of different types of causal arguments.)

Are constitutive claims adequately distinguished from causal ones?

My suggestion that probabilistic causal claims may have something in common with genealogy, through their similar emphasis on complex conjunctures, makes it especially important to understand the distinction between a 'constitutive' and a 'causal' argument. In post-modern critiques of social science, these two components often get conflated. Yet even Goertz, a quintessential social scientist, acknowledges the constitutive side of causal theories: 'concepts are theories about ontology' because they are about 'the fundamental constitutive elements of a phenomenon' which play a critical role in explanation (2006: 5).

One might think of this as treating the independent variable in a causal study as the dependent variable in a constitutive one. Foreign policies may 'constitute' identities, by inscribing definitions of Self and Other. Those identities, in turn, narrow the range of conceivable options. Identities thus play a 'causal' role in the sense of making certain choices more likely (and inconceivable ones, extremely unlikely). Formulating constitutive claims as conditional or probabilistic makes them causal *in a particular sense*. This challenges both post-modernists' claims not to be offering explanations and mechanism-oriented social scientists' claims to offer the only true proof of causal connections. Certainly constitutive claims *do not need* to be formulated as causal arguments. But I do think it helps to avoid tautology, which is particularly prevalent in arguments about the 'mutual constitution' of structures and agents (also see Hoffmann in this book).

There is at least one other advantage of *trying* to think of constitutive claims in causal terms: it encourages the researcher to think about what it means for a proposition to be 'wrong.' I do not mean 'falsification' in the narrow sense of largely discredited positivist standards for refuting theories. By 'wrong,' I mean that researchers benefit from thinking about what sorts of evidence might make a particular claim untenable. For example, the role of identity in foreign policy is a common theme in critical security studies. Quite likely, identity is defined in a way that precludes the possibility that there is *no* identity. ('What is the opposite of the concept?') But the question could be reformulated to *ask whether specific interests conflict with specific identities, rather than presuming that the former derives from the latter.*

Similarly, if the researcher assumes *multiple* identities, then the question might revolve around what a *dominant* identity might look like

('What adjectives modify the concept?'). Evidence might lead to the conclusion that a particular identity is *not* dominant; it might be subordinate (Neumann in this book), marginalized (Dunn in this book), or silenced (Ackerly in this book). Similarly, if the boundaries of identities are posited to be fluid rather than fixed, another common assumption, what would a relatively stable identity look like (Hermann in this book)?

My point is that researchers from many positivist and post-modern perspectives do parse evidence along similar lines, despite dissimilar philosophical moorings. This suggests potential for complementary insights, if researchers are willing to focus on their logics rather than labels. Recognizing this, we can put pluralism into practice in the selection of cases.

Single case studies

Often single case studies emerge out of an empirical puzzle. We see something that does not fit our expectations based on prevailing theories or conventional wisdom. A researcher, already knowledgeable about a part of the world or particular issue, may have some hunches about what is happening and perhaps some critiques of dominant frameworks. For example, my dissertation built on the observation that materialist theories were of little use for understanding why Zimbabwe risked so much to condemn racial segregation in South Africa. Simply put, apartheid should not have been an international issue if the Realist building blocks of IR, such as sovereignty and balance of power, were accurate. That observation, however, did not tell me what an alternative theory might be, nor did it tell me whether this one anomaly justified the wholesale rejection of Realism.

As my research question emerged, I readily found theoretical arguments that offered a plausible alternative – ideational – framework in Kratochwil and Ruggie's (1986) critique of regime theory. However, this nascent constructivism did not offer a specific theory to test. Indeed, it resisted the whole endeavor of testing theories in the conventional sense! My research into why states and international organizations censured South Africa became a 'plausibility probe' to see if meta-theoretical arguments about the constitution of interests could be translated into empirical research. I presented Realism and Marxism as materialist foils to highlight key aspects of my alternative ideational framework, but the study itself was not designed as a *test* of any theory (evident to anyone who ventures back to read the dissertation's theory chapter).

Plausibility probes are certainly not the only option. Single case studies *can* be used effectively to test theories if they fall into one of two categories. Some cases should be 'easy' for a theory to explain, yet it falls short. Others are 'unlikely' for a theory to explain, yet it does surprisingly well. There are various labels out there but these are the two general logics. Not all single case studies will fall into one of these two categories. Just the opposite: rarely will such a crucial case be available, but its analytical usefulness can outweigh many large-*n* studies.

An easy case can readily be confused with a plausibility probe, but the distinction is significant because each relies on the opposite logic. The exact same empirical evidence can contain more than one theoretical implication, but not all are of equal significance. For example, imagine that the evidence I gathered did show that norms could reasonably be interpreted as justifications for the pursuit of deeper material interests. An ideational approach would not be a better explanation of the censure of South Africa for racial discrimination – there would be little reason to reject Realism in favor of a new (and barely formulated) alternative theory. Yet a conclusion that Realism indeed could explain the putative weakness of norms would also not, in any strong sense, confirm the theory because South Africa was not a 'great power' (among other issues). Simply put, apartheid was a trivial case for testing Realism.

The second type of theory testing based on a single case is a 'least likely' scenario. Again, this should be distinguished from a plausibility probe, because the two may look similar. Unlike the easy case, a plausibility probe may follow the same logic as a hard case; the difference is the relationship between the theory and the empirical evidence. For example, if constructivist theory had been articulated in a less meta-theoretical way when I plunged into my dissertation, I might have framed it as a 'least likely' study because of the substantial amount of evidence in favor of materialist arguments (strategic resources in southern Africa, markets, and such). Other studies around the same time did directly target those theories by focusing on actors and arenas that prevailing theories considered most important: the World Bank (Finnemore 1996) rather than the Commonwealth, for instance (also the contributions in Katzenstein 1996). Not coincidentally, it was the part of my study on the *United States* that got published in *International Organization (IO)*.

The value of single cases – perhaps more so than other selection rationales – depends in particular on the *status* of the theory that underpins it. In the late 1980s, constructivism had not been articulated to the point where, epistemological disputes aside, it could have been tested – those 'importing' frameworks from other disciplines may face a similar situation. When I revised my dissertation for publication, I sought in the conclusion to translate my framework into more detailed claims that others could subsequently probe. In retrospect, I might have formulated these suggestions in terms of interests or identities as the 'dependent variable,' had I felt more comfortable with that vocabulary.

Now, if someone were to do a similar study, I would expect to see a research design that is built on the logic of easy or least likely cases, because the basic insight that norms or identities 'matter' is no longer novel. With the plausibility of the theoretical claim established, the value of doing additional single case studies (aside from the inherent value of knowing more about a particular place or issue) diminishes. As the circumstances that warrant the use of a 'crucial' case are limited, the research design questions shift to consider carefully paired comparisons or a larger set of cases instead.

Paired comparisons

Experimental logic makes carefully paired comparisons most acceptable for 'positivists' who aspire to test hypotheses. Yet given the infinite number of hypothetically possible variables across diverse levels of analysis, even carefully paired comparisons are inevitably easy to challenge. Outside the laboratory, as social scientists readily admit, ideal conditions will rarely exist. I refrain from saying 'never,' in recognition of a growing interest in field experiments, but these would be tough to apply widely in the IR context. Simulations, either with people or with computers, also offer potential insights, but they remain heuristics (Hoffmann in this book).

The closest approximation is the exploration of a single case over time, sometimes called 'within case' comparison, because it enables a researcher to hold many potential variables relatively constant. What might initially appear as one case turns into a comparative study. The best way to make this longitudinal approach work is when an 'exogenous shock' – the dramatic shift in an independent variable – enables the researcher to track closely what else does and does not change. Otherwise, there is nothing truly *paired* about breaking one case into component parts over an extended period of time. Simply 'tracing' the 'history' of a single case over time does not really take the logic of comparison seriously.

Yet even when there is evidence of such a sharp break, establishing historical stages remains difficult. Questions include how far back to go and on what criteria to demarcate eras (see Neumann in this book). Quickly a comparison between two periods devolves into a longer study. And then researchers need to look beyond 'pairing' to tackle the difficulties of slightly larger small-*n* studies – the sorts of problems that George's notion of 'structured focused comparison' sought to alleviate (George 1979; George and Bennett 2005). I am not suggesting that we should abandon cross-temporal studies – we simply should not treat them as a special form of rigorous comparison.

The limitation which I find less frequently acknowledged in otherwise sensible discussions is whether paired cases are truly independent units or events. Tilly's (1984) notion of 'encompassing' comparisons comes close; some people use the phrase 'world time' to denote the importance of shared global historical context. Given increasing emphasis on 'globalization' across the social sciences, the question of inter-connections between cases (and not just variables) needs to be confronted explicitly. If countries, the most common unit of analysis, are not independent, then researchers need to figure out ways to control for external factors that may not appear as variables in the relevant literature. For instance, globalization has produced a new interest among comparative politics specialists in norms that diffuse to the local level, and they increasingly acknowledge significant cross-case interactions, such as emulation.

In this context, my South Africa study might be viewed as a study of the evolution of a particular norm (anti-racism). If there were a critical juncture, at which point one could claim that the norm emerged or consolidated, then a 'before' and 'after' study could be treated as a paired comparison, with most key variables either held constant or at least readily identified. In the United Nations debates over apartheid, 1963 marks such a turning point: the Security Council rejected a domestic jurisdiction defense in favor of a 'threat to peace and security' argument. However, in the Commonwealth, 1961 marks the key break: South Africa declared republican status and withdrew from the organization. We cannot do a structured, focused, *paired* comparison across these two organizations, because we cannot apply the same timeframe. Furthermore, the UN decisions took place in the context of prior Commonwealth debates, while those took place following earlier challenges to domestic jurisdiction by India going even farther back than the UN founding. We can learn a lot about, say, majority voting versus consensus by pairing these organizations, but they do not offer independent cases.

With few single cases passing muster as 'crucial' and so many inherent problems in paired comparisons, most qualitative studies fall into the murky range of small-*n* studies. This gray-zone of 'more than two' but 'less than whatever is statistically significant' presents difficult terrain for case selection. The demands for detailed evidence garnered by a solo researcher are still possible but the results are inevitably more superficial. Some of these constraints can be alleviated through collaborative projects, but dissertation writers are less likely to gain funding for that, unless they work as part of a supervisor's larger project. Therefore, I assume that the trade-offs are faced by individuals.

More-than-Two but Not-a-Lot

Clearly, there is no single formula for dealing with multiple cases. Particularly for studies that start with an empirical puzzle, rather than a theory to test, some of the parameters of case selection are dictated by social realities and historical circumstances (see Dunn in this book). Yet I fear that research designs too often reflect the typical structure of a book: a magic trinity of three case study chapters, along with an introduction and conclusion, comprise a readable and reasonably priced volume. My goal in this section, therefore, is to get away from that trinity without tossing out the possibility that three case studies may indeed be appropriate.

For instance, in my study of international reactions to apartheid, I *could* have analyzed a wide range of international organizations and foreign policies. Yet it made sense to focus on the three communities in which South Africa had historically played a role: the international community (represented by the United Nations), the Commonwealth (initially as a Dominion within the British Empire but then during decolonization), and Africa (as a result primarily of geography rather than choice). Within each of these three communities, I analyzed the collective decisions of an international organization (UN, Commonwealth, and Organization of African Unity) and a key state within each group (the United States, Britain, and Zimbabwe). The result was, indeed, a reasonably priced book that I have been told is readable, as well as fairly convincing to specialists of each of these communities. I cannot complain too much about the magic trinity. But the choice of three communities was primarily inductive, the result of the historical legacies of South Africa's origins as a state in the international system.

Yet, on closer examination, counting the cases in my study is tough. These communities, taken together, comprise a single case of international cooperation (to condemn institutionalized racism in South Africa). In that sense, these are *not* six independent cases of sanctions policies (in three instances across two types of actors). But if the theoretical focus were theories of decision-making, rather than regimes, they could be. In another sense, each pair of organizations and states could count as a case for tracing norm diffusion (but note the problem of interconnections discussed above). Going that route, the effects of sanctions on South Africa should also be considered a case, but it would not be a 'structured focused comparison,' because South Africa was the target while the other countries were senders of sanctions.

What is a confused researcher to do? My general advice, and my constant refrain in this chapter, is to remain mindful of the theoretical framework and core question, which do lead to reasonable conclusions about relevant cases at appropriate levels of analysis. And do not flee back to the world of single cases studies because they seem simpler; most of them lack analytical leverage. Yet that leaves my students profoundly unsatisfied, and I confess that I too remain uneasy. Other researchers (who also, notably, teach methods) have offered two directions for honing the selection of multiple cases: typologies and fuzzy sets. I am not yet convinced by either but both deserve serious attention from anyone trying to sort out this gray zone of Not-a-Lot of cases.

Typologies provide a fruitful path between the extremes of unattainable universal generalization and idiosyncratic contextualization. One of the advantages of a typology is that it offers an escape from the search for a crucial case or an elusive paired comparison by offering the possibility of comparing one or more cases against an ideal. Think about the adjectives often attached to concepts like democracy or war. These can easily be turned into descriptive or analytical typologies that differentiate forms of a phenomenon. And these typologies can be linked to constitutive or causal claims. One might explore a number of cases to illustrate the full range or concentrate on one cell, depending on the research question. (For elaboration and advocacy of 'typological theories,' see George and Bennett 2005: 233–53.) So far, so good.

Still, I advise caution, because it is seductively easy to draw up a two-by-two table for just about anything. That leads to a tendency to construct a dubious typology that justifies research that you already know you want to do or, especially for seasoned scholars, that relies heavily on research you have already done. I did just that for my dissertation: drawing on the sparse literature on pariah states, I identified two descriptive factors, which were only evident together in the South Africa case. I intended eventually to examine other historical examples (since

I claimed that none of the other contemporary cases were comparable). Although I dropped this convoluted foray into typologies for the book, I hesitate to dismiss the exercise completely. It prodded me to think more historically, which I generally was not inclined to do. And my favorite comparison, the Confederacy during the American civil war, inspired me to write a spin-off article comparing the abolitionists with the anti-apartheid activists (Klotz 2002). In the end, I still think that *insightful* typologies can help us avoid some of the difficulties of comparisons.

Another option gaining followers especially among those seeking to bridge quantitative and qualitative studies is Ragin's notion of 'fuzzy sets,' also known as 'qualitative comparative analysis' (Ragin 2000). Since his approach is full of technical terminology, I will simply mention here a few of the overarching goals that might encourage skeptics to take an initial look at some of his guidelines.

Rather than force complex concepts into rigid conceptual boxes, the notion of fuzzy sets accepts some inherent ambiguity. Concepts comprise a cluster of key characteristics, but no single feature is essential. Thus a 'case' of something includes some, but not necessarily all, of these core dimensions. Here is where the logic of Boolean algebra comes into play, and along with it, specialized terminology and formal notation. Anyone familiar with on-line library searches knows that typing 'and' gets a smaller number of hits than 'or' – it is the same logic. One might link this to typologies, for instance, by defining ideal types in terms of the most exclusive features ('and') while recognizing that cases will evince a subset ('or') of those characteristics (Goertz 2006: 84).

I find this logic appealing, because it helps me wrestle with a basic empirical question: should South Africa be considered a democracy? By the standards of the late 1700s, it certainly should – show me any political system based on universal suffrage at that time! By the standards of the late 1900s, its parliamentary elections without adequate representation clearly did not satisfy most definitions. Since electoral dynamics among white votes did play a significant role in the transition to inclusive democracy, the existence of certain features of democracy should not be overlooked. Also, there would not be much to the democratic peace literature if we used universal suffrage as a necessary feature for defining democracies in earlier times. Fuzzy sets move researchers away from essentialist terminology – which is also a major goal of constructivism and critical theory. Whether it can deliver on this potential for building conceptual bridges without getting mired in the jargon of its formal notation remains to be seen.

Conclusion

Perhaps because I grew up in a family of chemists, I never doubted the value of case studies. Paired comparisons come closest to controlled test tube experiments where one chemical agent (potentially) alters a reaction. No correlation will offer anything as compelling in terms of *causal* inference. Yet, I also never had illusions about the practice of science. For me, the laboratory was not the idealized space that philosophers contemplate; it emitted a distinctive aroma and was populated by human beings. And sometimes scientists – just like any other humans – have been extraordinarily successful in propagating ideas that subsequently appear quite ridiculous (Klotz 1986). I have never expected social reality to mimic molecules, because people are not objects. I also appreciate that scientists, like ethnographers, find some of their greatest insights while looking for something else.

Qualitative researchers of my generation had little to offer in terms of a methodological rationale. Scholars oriented toward theory testing easily dismissed our single case studies as 'thick description,' caricaturing Geertz's famous 1973 essay of that name. I distinctly recall an awkward job interview situation that followed along these lines. Fortunately, we have come a long way in the past 20 years. The significance of single case studies for theory testing is still debated, but it is better understood. And its significance for theory building is widely accepted. Greater attention can now be paid to the messy middle of more than two but less than whatever is statistically relevant. Let me reiterate that these are research design questions that barely begin to address subsequent methodological questions of how to do the actual empirical study within the cases. The remaining chapters in this book do that exceptionally well.

Acknowledgment

Wagaki Mwangi and Deepa Prakash provided insightful written feedback on a short turnaround, for which I am especially grateful.

Part II: Classic Qualitative Tools

5
Discourse Analysis

Iver B. Neumann

As a 22-year-old, I held a stray job fetching bundles of fur from minks, seals, polar foxes, blue foxes, and red foxes to show the buyers at Oslo Fur Auctions. The work altered the way I saw the world in other realms. Most striking was how one of my main interests at the time, looking at women, acquired a new dimension. Where I had previously focused on shape and movement, attire now became an important factor. My new interest in fur coats changed the way I sifted what I saw. Psychological experiments confirm my personal experience. For instance, children shown a cup with the handle turned away none the less drew a cup with a handle, because cups, by definition, are supposed to have handles. That is, the children drew the model, not simply what they 'saw' as a result of light waves hitting their optical nerves. People sort and combine sensory impressions of the world through categories (or models or principles). Language, as a social system with its own relational logic, produces reality for humans by mediating these sense data.

These examples highlight that perception is mediated by aesthetics, sexuality, morals, or other modes (Bauman 1992). In order not to forget that these meanings are socially reproduced, discourse analysts call them *representations* – literally re-presented. (I will concentrate on the precon-ditions for and jobs undertaken by representations; see Dunn's chapter in this book for more detailed discussion of analyzing the compon-ents of representations.) Representations that are put forward time and again become a set of statements and practices through which certain language becomes institutionalized and 'normalized' over time. They may be differently marked in terms of how influential they are. In the United States during the Cold War, 'dove' and 'hawk' representations of the Soviet Union were both institutionalized, but so was the (even less changing) representation put forward by the American Communist

Party. When people who mouth the same representations organize, they make up a position in the discourse. Like representations, positions may be dominant or marginalized in various degrees.

Demonstrating institutionalized discourse can often simply be done by proving that metaphors regularly appear in the same texts. In my study of European discourse on Russia, for example, I found a representation, which stressed that Russian females had been raped by Mongol and Tatar males for centuries, and that this had fostered a particularly wild and barbarous people ('scratch the Russian, and the Tatar will emerge'). This representation began to form fairly early, reached a peak in the inter-war period, and then lived a very submerged existence in European discourse. In the Baltic states, however, it was very strong indeed throughout the Soviet period and into the 1990s. The more such things may be specified empirically, the better the analysis. The ideal is to include as many representations and their variations as possible, and to specify where they are to be found in as high a degree as possible.

The first research task is to show the affinities and differences between representations in order to demonstrate whether they belong to the same discourse. But repetition does not preclude variation or gradual re-presentation, so discourse analysis also seeks to capture the inevitable cultural changes in representations of reality. For example, in the late 1980s, Russia was obviously heading for challenging times, and I reckoned that this would entail wide-ranging changes in relations with Europe. My basic idea was that, regardless of period, Russia's relationship with Europe had not been straightforward, yet it seemed set to remain central to Russian foreign policy as well as to Russian self-understanding. I wanted to be able to say something general about prerequisites for Soviet/Russian foreign policy in a situation where so many things seemed to be in flux.

Discourse analysis is eminently useful for such analysis, because it says something about why state Y was considered an enemy in state X, how war emerged as a political option, and how other options were shunted aside. Because a discourse maintains a degree of regularity in social relations, it produces preconditions for action. It constrains how the stuff that the world consists of is ordered, and so how people categorize and think about the world. It constrains what is thought of at all, what is thought of as possible, and what is thought of as the 'natural thing' to do in a given situation. But discourse cannot determine action completely. There will always be more than one possible outcome. Discourse analysis aims at specifying the bandwidth of possible outcomes. This works the other way, too; discourse analysis may also start with a specific outcome and demonstrate the preconditions for it happening, demonstrating concurrently that the outcome might have been different.

To map these patterns in representations, discourse analysts examine utterances. They may be texts (written statements that do some kind of work in a context). However, any sign – a semaphore, a painting or a grimace – may be analyzed *as* text, because it conveys meaning in a particular context. Since we 'read' societal processes as the functional equivalent of texts, one may, for example, cull data from ethnography (see Gusterson in this book). Due to limits on length, I will focus in this chapter on written sources. (For an example of discourse analysis of ethnographic data, see Neumann 2007.)

Acquiring a certain cultural competence is a prerequisite for discourse analysis, as for most qualitative methods. After discussing the need for basic language skills and historical knowledge, I divide my lessons for method into three concrete steps. First, one needs to delimit the discourse to a wide but manageable range of sources and timeframes. From these texts, the analyst then identifies the representations that comprise the discourse, taking into account censorship and other practices that shape the availability of text. Finally, to explore change, one uncovers layering within the discourse. The more actions that the analysis may account for by demonstrating its preconditions, and the more specifically this may be done, the better the discourse analysis.

Prerequisite: cultural competence

I always encourage students to draw on extant knowledge when they choose their topics; it saves time, and they start out with a competitive advantage. It also provides a degree of 'cultural competence.' For example, I had done my conscription at the Norwegian Army Language School, where I studied Russian. Then I lived in Russia for half a year and did university courses in its history and foreign policy. All this gave me a certain cultural competence when I set out to research Soviet discourse as a doctoral student at Oxford (later published as Neumann 1996). I knew the Russian language, genres of relevant texts, and something about the general social and political setting (such as when Russia was at war with other states that it considered to be European and the extent to which European history and language were taught in schools).

This cultural competence enabled me to use tools of discourse analysis to demonstrate variations in meanings and representations. The more in-depth the general knowledge, the easier the specific research. For example, I knew that many Russian newspaper articles were divided into two parts: a first part that repeated the so-called main line, then a part that dealt with new material that still had not been sorted in relation to and assimilated by that dominant representation. What is crucial for the discourse analyst is the separation of these two parts by *one* codeword, *odnako*, which is best translated as 'however.' If one knows such conventions, the reading of texts becomes easier: I could rush through part one, which is a simple re-presentation of an already known reality, and concentrate on part two. Similarly, the expression *en principe* in French signals that one is putting forth a representation which one generally shares, but from which one nonetheless is going to deviate.

Of course, some things may be learnt on the job. As a British-trained Norwegian Russian specialist, I needed to work at mastering phrases like 'to go' and 'drag it through the garden' to buy a hamburger in the United States. But there are other things that you have to know before you can start. When I turned to the analysis of discourse in the United States, it was inconceivable for me not to know references such as 'I have a dream' (a speech by Martin Luther King, Jr), 'beam me up, Scotty' (a line from the television show Star Trek) or 'I pledge allegiance' (to the flag). The point is that a researcher needs a basic level of cultural competence to recognize the shared understandings that create a common frame of reference, which makes it possible for people to act in relation to one another.

Let us not forget that the analyses we write up are written *for* some-body. What is adequate cultural competence for a specific discourse analysis hangs, among other things, on whether the resulting analysis may tell the intended readers something new. Ideally, a scientific text should tell every conceivable reader something new. That is a situation that is very rarely reached, however. The world is full of researchers who produce texts that do adequate jobs in adequate settings because they are new *in those settings*, and not necessarily anywhere else.

There is a trade-off with cultural competence. Culture appears to be shared. Close up, it turns out not to be. Phrases may mean a number of different things, or they may be used without the user knowing all their cultural references or implications. The challenge is not to get naturalized – not to 'become' part of the universe studied – but to denaturalize. If you are a native speaker and know a culture as only a native can, then you do not have that marginal gaze where things look strange enough to present themselves as puzzles. You will also lose touch with your own biases. You become what anthropologists call 'home blind.' For example, I once submitted an analysis of US foreign policy discourse which used a quote from the then chairman of the

Senate's Foreign Relations Committee, a key Republican senator of long standing, as representative of American discourse. The two reviewers, who wrote flawless American English, objected to my treatment of him as an elder on the grounds that they considered him out of touch and a crackpot, respectively! These readers were definitely 'home blind.' It is fully possible to do discourse analysis in the culture you know best, but you still need some kind of distance. You cannot be *too much* at home.

An historian or anthropologist would at this point ask, whose representations, whose culture? (See also Leander and Ackerly in this book.) We are talking about cultural competence regarding the culture that spawns the representations to be analyzed, not necessarily for other related cultures. When I was done with my discourse analysis of Russian representations of Europe, I noted that I had documented what I held to be so much arcane and downright silly Russian representations of Europe that I felt I owed it to the Russians to analyze European representations of Russia as well, presuming that just as much arcane and silly stuff would crop up. (It did; see Neumann 1999.) For that analysis, I needed neither Russian nor much knowledge of Russia. Instead, it was important to know German, French, and English. It was a problem that I could only cover Spanish and Portuguese representations in translations. But I still felt warranted in talking about European representations of Russia, for there were strong regularities between German, British, French, and Scandinavian representations of Russia at any one given time during the last 500 years that presumably could be generalized to 'Iberian representations.'

As in any other research, this lacuna has to be stated, and it will serve as a challenge to new researchers. (I have tried, so far unsuccessfully, to get a doctoral student to write about Iberian representations of Russia.) Methodologically, this points to the importance of being explicit about your sweep: the broader it is, the more general knowledge you need, and the less risky it is to leave lacunae. But great care should be taken here. No good Russianist would assume cultural competence about Serbia, and old cultural competence from the Soviet era may not necessarily be applied to Ukraine after its formal political separation from Russia. Knowing the ever-changing limits of your cultural competence may be as important as knowing its contents.

Step one: delimiting texts

Discourse analysts read texts. But what texts? In certain cases this is a simple question to answer. If one is to study party systems, then party programs, election laws, and articles as well as speeches by party leaders are typical primary materials. Still, the quantity of material is usually enormous, especially if one includes the secondary literature. It is crucial to draw some lines, but problems of delimitation are inevitable. The choices applied to each individual discourse analysis always have to be defended. For example, if one repeatedly finds statements such as 'scrape a Russian and the Tatar will appear,' it would be mistaken to omit representations of Tatars from an analysis of Russian identity.

A given discourse cannot be entirely detached from all other discourses. They are ordered and scaled in relation to one another. Russian identity, therefore, must be studied as something Russian and something non-Russian. However, which relation or relations to study – between Russia and Asia, Russia and Europe, Russia and Germany, Russia and Tatarstan, Russia and the Jews, Russia and the feminine – is not given. Ideally, all should be covered. In practice, that is rarely possible. The choice of which relation(s) to single out may be theory driven (let us see what happens if we bring a feminist standpoint perspective to the study of Russian identity and look at the constitutive role of gender), utilitarian (I need to illuminate the identity aspects involved before I can get a handle on Russian–German energy relations; how do Russians think of Germany in general?) or ludic (my own favorite: why is it that Russians treat me the way they do? This must have something to do with general Russian ideas about Europeans.).

Insofar as politics is a struggle between named groups and people, politics is conflict. Conflict should therefore attract the analyst of political discourse. One will often find direct references to texts that are being attacked. It is usually apparent who is attacking whom. When there is such a racket, it is because something new is happening, something that is meeting various attempts at limitation from those who dominate the discourse (see Lukes 1974).

However, the pursuit of commotion can be a methodological problem, since realities are maintained by the frequent repetition and confirmation of representations. The absence of commotion does not mean that the discourse in question is non-conflictual. One has to use more time and mental energy to work out how and why things remain unaltered. Concentrating on the texts that produce the greatest racket might mean that one automatically privileges the dominant representation, which usually will be the loudest (Wæver 1999). Some texts remain unpublished when censorship is successful. Challengers may remain undetected for other reasons, including socially distributed lack of writing skills. One may also turn this around: publications that only repeat or incrementally expand the main representation tend to pass relatively quietly. If one fails to detect these processes of power, then the analysis easily becomes a shallow one of the boundaries of the discourse and its domination.

Also, social and political life is full of cases where somebody writes something new and intriguing, with no immediate reception whatsoever. It may simply be that the text is so new or different in relation to what already exists that it goes unnoticed for this very reason. There are existing texts as well as future texts that will suffer this fate. If a text from a relatively obscure source becomes central – as did Francis Fukuyama's 'The End of History?' in *The National Interest* – then it is a research task to demonstrate how the text overcame the odds.

Some texts will show up as crossroads or anchor points, such as short government treatises outlining policy (called white papers in most English-speaking countries). These are called canonical texts or monuments (compare Laclau and Mouffe 1985 on nodal points). In my dissertation research, I was actually able to identify the textual canon by starting with the secondary literature, because it proved to be well informed. I took the 'monuments' to be the works that were generally cited in the secondary literature. I read these works, and indeed I found that they tended to refer to one another. This, as well as the negative finding that there were few additional central texts, confirmed them as monuments.

It is useful to select texts around these monuments, since monuments also contain references to other texts, which again pointed me to others that were related. One discovers that some texts are 'canonical,' in the sense that they have a broad reception and are often cited. If one identifies these texts, reads them, and then reads the central texts that these texts in turn refer to, soon one is able to identify the main positions and versions. In most contemporary Western nationality discourses, for example, the representation of history for political purposes is widespread.

However, it is not always possible to go back to antediluvian events, so one must delimit the timeframe. For example, once I had my dissertation topic, I read up on the secondary literature in order to identify cut-off points. An obvious one would have been the coming to power of the great Europeanizer Peter the Great in 1694. In order to trace discourse in more depth, I chose the Napoleonic wars that really brought Russia into the heart of European great power politics, and treated the period from 1694 to 1815 cursorily as a prehistory. The other cut-off point presented itself during the work, as the Soviet Union split up in the autumn of 1991.

In specifying the sweep of the analysis, it is also important to keep in mind your reader. I later did a discourse analysis in my native Norwegian on Norwegian representations of Europe (Neumann 2001). I tried to tackle the question of home blindness by going way back in time – who is really 'at home' in the Middle Ages? In this case, the main intended reader was an informed Norwegian. I therefore needed to be fairly detailed in drawing up representations from the last 50 years. Yet I did not present context that was already fairly well known, which would not be particularly interesting to the prospective reader. When I did a shorter version in English (Neumann 2002), the intended readers were different, so I dropped detail and filled in context. A doctoral student in Europe, who has little idea who his readers will be, will tend to write differently from an American student, who has a committee from the outset. And how do you weigh writing for your examiners against writing for a more general audience that may also be interested in the texts? There are authorial decisions to be made – different strokes for different folks; broader ones for non-specialist foreigners, dense professors and academics working in outer disciplines.

Participants themselves also delimit their discourses. For example, medical diagnosis relies upon the definition of diseases and syndromes, upon which doctors draw. Analyzing the struggles over these definitions, and the process of getting them registered as such, form part of the research. If the chosen discourse is *international* intervention (to distinguish from medical interventions), then the struggle over the characterization of certain policies as 'humanitarian' is decisive. The main task is to dig out the production of specialized knowledge. In analyzing Norwegian human rights law, for example, there will be a number of relevant texts in legal journals and government policy papers. One can compare related professional discourses in other countries. However, the connection to general political discourse may not be explicit.

Some texts can acquire importance from the medium through which they are published. For example, a private letter from the 1830s threatened the dominant Russian representation of Europe after it got a wide reception through the circulation of copies in the saloons of St Petersburg, even though the author was declared mentally ill and incarcerated. It is important to bear in mind the values which different media give texts. If one is to carry out a discourse analysis of peace operations in the 1990s, it is important to distinguish between those journals that aim at operative milieus (*Foreign Affairs* or *Survival*), those that are written for a more general audience (*International Affairs* in Europe), and those that are mainly read by academics (*International Peacekeeping*).

But what if there is a Russian letter or unpublished manuscript from the 1930s, unseen by more than a handful of people, which projects a representation of Europe that makes my analysis incomplete? In terms of the history of ideas this would be very interesting, precisely because of its originality and its lack of reception. Its discovery would provide a more accurate definition of the borderline between possible thought and the communication of that possibility. In terms of politics in the 1930s, however, it would be a non-event, because the analysis concerns texts that are socially communicated.

What if it turns out that there are a number of texts that are systematically overlooked, which jointly document that there was a main representation that previously had not been included in the analysis? In the area of women and war, one can at least imagine the possibility that a systematic reading of all available sources on the national service in Norway written by women would result in a revision of previous views of the national service institution (see Ackerly's chapter on subaltern discourses in this book). Mikhail Bakhtin's concept of genre is useful.

Genre carries its own memory, in the sense that every text relies on its predecessors and carries with it their echoes. If previous analysts have for some reason overlooked an entire genre, then it is an important research task to cast light upon how this has happened. This will change the way we remember a given historical sequence and is politically relevant to today's situation. Excavate one text on women and war, and you have an idiosyncratic voice and an indication that a group has not met the preconditions for action to make itself heard. Excavate many, and you have documentation that an entire group has been silenced. It is also possible that there are too few texts published, making it difficult to get started. One can carry out a discourse analysis of material that has not been in general circulation (for example, of classified material). If the reason for the lack of text is the novelty of the specific discourse, with, for example, only newspaper articles existing, it is possible to include a small text-based analysis of this material in an analysis that also draws upon other methods of data collection, for example interviews, surveys or participant observation.

When does one have enough material? The ideal situation is that one covers a maximum of eventualities, by reading as much as possible from as many genres as possible. Foucault insisted that one should 'read everything, study everything.' This is not feasible in practice, and there will therefore always be a risk that some relevant texts are not included.

However, almost regardless of the extent of the discourse, relatively few texts will constitute the main points of reference. Therefore at some point one has to be able to decide that one has read enough, even if one has not read everything. *Only* if a text emerges that cannot be subsumed under one of the main positions must the analysis be adjusted – or perhaps even rewritten entirely (see Hansen 1997).

Step two: mapping representations

A discourse usually contains a dominating representation of reality and one or more alternative representations. Discourse analysis therefore is particularly well suited for studying situations where power is maintained by aid of culture and challenged only to a limited degree, that is, what Gramscians call 'hegemony.' Structuralists and post-structuralists disagree over whether one can take a small part of the discourse and read it as symptomatic of *all* representations. Post-structuralists find the notion of a latent structure simply too deterministic. One must think flow, not control.

The task is to search out and identify these various representations and possible asymmetries between them. The analyst accepts and works with the inherent conflict between representations. Monuments frequently position themselves in the discourse by referring (adversarially or sympathetically) to texts that were previously considered monuments. Reading monuments in Russian foreign policy discourse, for example, helped me identify adversarial representations (for instance, 'Europe is vital, we should learn from it' versus 'Europe is rotten, we should isolate ourselves from it'), since these texts, often written at the same time, referred directly to one another. The advantage of a marginal position emerges clearly here for setting up an inventory of representations.

Researchers question how uncertain or challengeable a given representation is. The limits of discourse are inscribed with varying means and degrees of violence. If there is only one representation, the discourse is closed. This of course does not mean that it is not political, because it takes a lot of discursive work to maintain a situation where this representation cannot be challenged openly. If moves to do something new by the text-writer are not successful, it is not necessarily because the discourse is successfully policed. On the other end of the spectrum, the field can be said to be open if there are two or more representations and none of them are dominating. (See Leander's chapter in this book on the boundaries of Bourdieuan fields here; historically Bourdieu formulated his theory among other things as an extension and correction of

Foucauldian discourse analysis.) Yet it is difficult to imagine a discourse that is entirely open or closed over time. Social relations will always be in some degree of flux.

There is a second problem in addition to specifying the discourse's degree of openness. On the one hand, the number of permutations of relevant signs is endless, so the range of meanings is in principle infinite. On the other hand, politics involves contestation between relatively clearly defined positions, which compete to find resonance among a number of carriers. Thus it is desirable to identify these positions. Typically, one position will be dominant, and one or two other positions will challenge it on certain points. The dominant position will either present itself as being the way things have 'always' been (for instance, a democrat: humans are born free) or hark back to an idealized beginning (a democrat: Athenian democracy broke out of benighted despotism). Terms mean different things in different epochs, but carriers of a position will tend to tap the advantages of having a long (and presumably dignified) history by acting as if this were not the case (Koselleck 1988).

It is important that the discourse analyst start with the representations themselves – the stories of how things have 'always' been like this or that. For example, Athenian democracy was hardly a democracy by the lights of the 21st century. Neither was the ante-bellum United States. Arguing that every man is born free and has rights while having a number of living beings around who visibly are not born free and have rights (as slaves, or women, or children) reveals that the discourse is not open to the possibility that 'man' may be someone other than an adult, white male. Within the boundaries of his own political discourse, thus, it was not a problem that George Washington remained a slave owner throughout his adult life.

However, a good discourse analyst should also be able to demonstrate that where the carriers of a position see continuity, there is almost always change. Because of the nature of politics as a structured activity between groups, a discourse is politicized precisely through the evolution of two or a few patterns of meaning, which is the discourse analyst's task to uncover. It is possible to distinguish between the basic traits of such a meaning pattern (what unites the position) and varieties of it (what differentiate it).

In principle, the discourse will carry with it the 'memory' of its own genesis. Showing how each text is made possible by the preceding texts, often it is possible to find a prehistory to the main representation. It is, for example, hard to think of Stalin's funeral oratory for Lenin without having the model of the Russian Orthodox oratory in mind.

Methodologically, this is significant because, as a given representation establishes itself in the discourse, one should go back to find 'pioneer texts' that foreshadow it. This allows us to make a prediction: if a new main representation of Europe surfaces in Russian discourse during the next years, more likely than not it will be churned out of material that is already present in the discourse.

There are a number of formal and informal practices that determine which representations are allowed into the discourse, and that make it possible for the analyst to map meanings. Among the most obvious are legal systems and censorship, whereby sanctions against violating the boundaries of the discourse are threatened explicitly. An example: in Norwegian nationalist discourse of the 1990s just using the word 'race' activated a set of sanctions, foremost among which are laws that prohibit what Americans call 'hate speech.' The fact that there is no comparable Norwegian concept for the phenomenon, and that the American term is used regularly, are data for a discourse analysis of 'race.' (See also Klotz's discussion in this book of the concept of race in case selection.)

One can also examine what kind of self-censorship different types of mass media apply and what deviation it takes to provoke more formal sanctions. Legal verdicts on the borderline between incitement to violence and freedom of speech, and the debates surrounding it, would be one of several clues. To study nationalist discourse in the Soviet Union in the 1930s, where every newspaper, radio, and television station sifted what was printed and broadcast, one must start by examining the formal censorship instructions. Thereafter one might look at what unpublished and imported texts circulated, and what incidents resulted in Gulag sentences.

One should not overlook cultural artifacts with a widespread, so-called popular culture (see Dunn's chapter in this book). Discourse analysis is, for example, a useful way to examine film, understood as text. Rather than looking at museums, one can look at the reality production that happens in soap operas. If one is to examine the reality of 'Germany' in British discourse, then in addition to cases such as bilateral political discourse, EU discourse, and so on, it will also be of interest to look at representations of Germany in magazines, pulp fiction, and imported B movies (where it is still not unusual to find narratives where German Nazis are the crooks).

I would argue that the discipline of International Relations is not at present paying enough heed to artifacts of popular culture, but such an analysis must be situated, in the sense that one must be able to point out the inter-relation between representations of, say, Germany in popular culture and political discourse about Germany. How does popular culture appear in and relate to political discourse? To what degree do representations from the former result in truth claims in the latter? 'Situating' (showing where something can be found, where it is *in situ*, 'in place') can be specified as proving inter-textuality between expressions, texts, and discourses (see Neumann and Nexon 2006).

Ethnography and discourse analysis are similar in that they pay, or should pay, a lot of attention to how the analyst is situated in relation to the data. In the 1980s, a key development in ethnography was an intensified attention to the writing up of the ethnography, and this turn was directly inspired by discourse analysis (Clifford and Marcus 1986). Typically, however, discourse analysis would splice data collection methods such as fieldwork or memory work with the analysis of written texts. It would also typically turn to written texts first, and think of other data collection methods such as interviewing as complementary or substitutionary.

Certain analysts are more formal in their mapping than others. I see heuristic value in being stylized. When discourse analyses are highly formalized, however, I always ask myself whether the reason is a need to appear social science like in order to get published, or whether it is actually an urge growing out of the text itself, whether it is necessary, and whether it is a market-driven or a scholarly necessity.

Step three: layering discourses

Not all representations are equally lasting. They differ in historical depth, in variation, and in degree of dominance/marginalization in the discourse. The third task for the discourse analyst is to demonstrate this. The production of gender is an example. There are a number of biological and social traits (diacritics) that line the boundary between the sexes, from the presence of ovaries to ways of brushing hair away from one's eyes. Few can be counted as unchangeable. However, some are more difficult to alter than others. It is easier to neutralize the gender-specific aspect of the sign 'unremunerated domestic labor' than 'childbirth.'

At this stage, some discourse analysts would cry foul, because they would like to insist that everything is fluid, and that nothing should be reified in the analysis. I agree that everything is fluid in principle, but the point here is that not everything is *equally* fluid. Furthermore, it is impossible to analyze something without reifying something else. Indeed, as my initial example of the child perceiving the cup is meant to bring out, it is impossible to see and to live without reifying things.

We have to subsume new phenomena into already existing categories in order to get on with our lives. Arguing that everything is equally fluid makes it impossible to analyze something in its social context. It also goes against what seems to be the very physiological preconditions of our existence as *Homo sapiens.*

Certain representations in a discourse will thus be slower to change than others. Signs that are 'good to think with' (Lévi-Strauss 1963) and representations of material objects will often be among these. However, now physical reality turns up. Put in everyday speech: material objects are difficult (though not impossible) to 'explain away.' But for the study of human behavior, this is not a problem. As Laclau and Mouffe illustrate,

> An earthquake or the falling of a brick is an event that certainly exists, in the sense that it occurs here and now, independently of my will. But whether their specificity as objects is constructed in terms of 'natural phenomena' or 'expressions of the wrath of God' depends upon the structuring of a discursive field
>
> (Laclau and Mouffe 1985: 108).

Meaning and materiality must be studied together. It is possible to take as one's starting point for a reading of a social event, such as the reasons why Sweden went to war in 1630, that there are a number of material 'facts,' including archaeological objects. Any valid representation of the social event must relate to and at the same time study the various representations of the social event without having to hunt some kind of 'truth' about it *beyond* accounting for these objects (see Ringmar 1996; Neumann 1997). The question is what the scope or degree of social construction is in the relationship between 'fact' and 'representation.' We should expect greater 'inertia' in the representation of material objects than that of other things, but this still does not ensure the place of the objects in the discourse.

This issue also lays bare the metaphors on which the discourse approach rests. Foucault wrote about archaeology and genealogy, the basic idea being that of things emerging, with some things remaining the same, and others changing. An archaeological site will contain certain artifacts that tell of continuity – there will be shards of pottery and traces of funeral rites – and these will vary with the period. But, in a particular site, certain things will remain stable whereas others change. The key, in archaeology as in social analysis, is to specify what changes and what does not, and how. The same is true of genealogy, the basic meaning of which is that you start with one human and trace his or her ancestry. You will tend to find people who become less and less interrelated to one another the further back you go. At some stage, all they have in common is that they are all the ancestor of that particular human.

If some traits unify and some differentiate, it is reasonable to think that the traits that unite are more difficult to change. For example, if one chooses to study German identity, one will find endless variations on which things are thought to be German. If one looks at the question of how the state is related to the nation, the range of meaning will be lesser, perhaps only covering two possibilities: one, that the nation defines the state by being its cultural carrier, *Kulturnation*, or second, that nation and state are both anchored in citizenship, *Verfassungspatriotismus* (see Wæver 1999).

In my doctoral thesis, I approached this question of layering by postulating explicit and implicit family resemblances across time. The element of Europe as a place to learn from was in evidence at all points in time since the latter half of the 17th century, except for the High Stalinist period (two decades from the early 1930s onwards). In later work (Neumann 2004: 21), I formalized this step by drawing up a model of Russian discourse on Europe across time, using three layers: basic concepts (state, people, and so on), general policy orientation (isolation, confrontation, learning, and such), and concrete historical examples (pan-slavism, Bolshevism, early Yeltsin years, among others). At the level of the broad historical sweep, such a mapping of preconditions for action is the endpoint of discourse analysis. As should be clear by now from the discussions above, however, there remains endless work of specification on different constitutive relations, close-ups of specific time periods, tailor-making of the analysis to illuminate specific (types of) action, and so forth.

Conclusion: a discourse analysis toolkit

If one should fashion such a thing as a discourse analysis toolkit, it would perhaps look like this. Tool one would be a carver that would carve texts out of the social world. Tool two would be an equalizer that makes other phenomena (for example, a semaphore, an ad, a body) into material to be analyzed on a par with texts. Tool three would be something like a herding dog that would group these phenomena together based on them being about the same thing. Tool four would be a slicer, cutting the phenomena into different representations of the same thing. Tool five would be some kind of optic device that would make visible the meaning dimension of the material phenomenon to its users. It would come with a grading spectre that could demonstrate how easy it would be to change the different layers of a given phenomenon. And finally, the only one that I would really like to see on my desk, tool six would be a self-reflecting quill that accounted for my own weighting of the phenomena of which I wrote as I wrote.

The point of such a tool kit would be to help us understand how the seemingly unchanging and 'natural' stuff of which our social worlds actually emerged as a creation of human history. Discourse analysis makes the social world more transparent by demonstrating how its elements interact. By demonstrating that things were not always the way they appear now, discourse analysis makes us aware that they are most probably changing as we speak. In order to account for global politics, therefore, it is not enough to study what one clerk wrote to another, how statesmen pontificate about the policies they pursue, or the technological changes that make for different kinds of warfare. The study of the meaning which these different phenomena have to those concerned also has to be included, and this means that discourses should be accessed at many different points.

Representations are constitutive in determining what is sensed and communicated, but they do not necessarily come with 100 percent built-in guides for action. If one has, for example, mapped Russian discourse on Europe, one has demonstrated several preconditions for foreign polit-ical action, but one has not necessarily cast any light directly upon the specific processes in the determination of such action (see Neumann 1996). A representation can make room for several different actions, and its carriers can be more or less conscious in their relationship with this representation. An analysis of representations of Europe will thereby not constitute an exhaustive analysis of Russian foreign policy. To do that, one must not only systematize the analysis of those sanctions that follow deviance, as I have already mentioned, but must also look at a number of other aspects of the materiality of discourse.

To the extent that a fuller understanding of where we are and how we landed here is helpful in getting us somewhere else, discourse analysis may be 'useful' for solving problems. But it is not your first choice in a tightly scripted situation, such as answering why state X went to war against state Y at point Z in time. Rational choice may be fine for that, even though the assumptions of the two approaches are very different indeed. An analyst may use discourse analysis in order to study how structures produce agents, and then decide to 'freeze' agents at a specific point in time, for example at the outbreak of war. The analyst may then change tack and analyze the outbreak of war drawing on social choice theory. Such splicing of methods is highly unusual, among other things because few analysts are fluent in such diverse methods, but also since the analyst's own identity may be so tied up to one particular method as to make the very thought of mixing methods appear as sleeping with the enemy. To make a self-reflective point, why this is so may be studied by drawing on discourse analysis.

Acknowledgment

I thank Karen Allen, Stephanie Smith, my co-contributors and especially Audie Klotz and Deepa Prakash for a range of positive and productive comments on earlier drafts.

6
Historical Representations

Kevin C. Dunn

I am most interested in how certain social identities are constructed, and how they make certain practices possible but others unthinkable. Like Roxanne Doty, I examine 'how meanings are produced and attached to various social subjects and objects, thus constituting particular interpretive dispositions that create certain possibilities and preclude others' (1996: 4). I am less interested in 'what' questions, since these often prompt historical narratives that mistakenly assume a simple linearity of events. I am also less interested in 'why' questions, which tend to assume that a certain set of choices and answers pre-exist. Rather, we should investigate how those options and the larger possibilities of action get established. Doing so allows for greater understanding of the processes and interactions within international relations.

Choosing to explore these questions raises another fundamental 'how' question: How does one actually investigate structures of knowledge, such as social identities? How does one collect and analyze appropriate data? Because humans make sense of the world by navigating the social understandings that make reality knowable, researchers must employ interpretative methods. In doing my research on historical representations, I focus in various ways on language, ideas, and culture, particularly as they contribute to the creation of structures of knowledge during specific historical moments.

In this chapter, I discuss the various theoretical and methodological issues I encountered while researching my dissertation on representations of Congolese identity, which was later published as *Imagining the Congo* (2003). In the first section, I explain what I mean by historical representations, why it is important to study them, how they are linked to broader discourses, and why a deep historical analysis is needed. Employing a contextualized 'thick' description is useful for gathering and analyzing data, I argue, but not without limitations. The rest of the essay is dedicated to a frank discussion of how one does this type of research while avoiding possible pitfalls. To guide potential researchers, I focus on four issues in this final section: parameters, sources, data collection, and analysis.

Representation and interpretation

My interest in historical representations flows from my epistemological assumptions, which are grounded in post-modernist and post-structuralist thought. 'Reality' is unknowable outside human perception, and there is never only one authority on a given subject. As Friedrich Nietzsche noted, 'There are no facts in themselves. It is always necessary to begin by introducing a meaning in order that there can be a fact' (quoted in Barthes 1981: 15; see also Leander and Neumann in this book). This position does not deny the existence of reality but suggests that the 'true' essence of the object is always unknowable to us. Therefore we must interpret representations of it.

By historical representation, I refer to how the object of an inquiry (X) has been represented over time and space. X can be anything at all: a country (the Congo), a nation or community (the Kurds), a person (Saddam Hussein), or a concept (sovereignty). Societies discursively produce, circulate, and consume representations of X, constructing what are often called 'regimes of truth' or 'knowledge.' These discourses are comprised of signifying sequences that constitute more or less coherent frameworks for what can be said and done. Perhaps the best-known example of this approach is Edward Said's *Orientalism* (1978), in which he exposed how British and French societies constructed 'truth claims' about the supposed innate and inferior qualities of non-white, non-Christian, 'Oriental' people.

Informed by Said and other like-minded scholars, numerous international relations (IR) scholars have studied historical representations. Roxanne Doty's *Imperial Encounters* (1996) compares asymmetrical encounters between Great Britain and colonial Kenya with representations of the Philippines by the United States within its own imperial project. Cynthia Weber's *Simulating Sovereignty* (1995) traces how the meaning of sovereignty has shifted over time within discourses of intervention. Her later book *Faking It* (1999) playfully explores the representation of the Caribbean region in US foreign policy discourses. I will discuss my own work on contested meanings of the Congo in more detail below. One of my current research projects uses African national parks as its object of inquiry.

All of these studies, and many more, reveal how certain structures of knowledge have been produced and some of their political consequences. Unlike other structural approaches to IR (either Neo-Realist or Marxian), this discursive approach rejects the idea that resources can be explained outside of their discursive context. Rather, social interaction is influenced by cognitive scripts, categories, and rationalities (see Torfing 1999: 81–2). Power is the *practice* of knowledge as a socially constructed system, within which various actors articulate and circulate their representations of 'truth.'

Since representations of reality and their sequences within discourses are what we work with to understand power, I am primarily concerned with how names, meanings, and characteristics are attached to the world around us. I focus on the *mechanics* of knowledge and identity, and how they differ across time and space. For instance, understanding that this is a 'tree,' that is a 'book,' and I am a 'man' presumes access to commonly shared structures of knowledge about objects such as trees, books, and men. But these naming practices might mean something different (or perhaps nothing at all) to people living in different cultures or historical eras. A tree might be a natural resource to be preserved, a commodity to be harvested, a living soul force to be honored, or an embodiment of the spirits of the dead to be worshipped. So it becomes important to understand that representations are historically and contextually contingent. Specifically, I am looking for the ways that actors represent the object of inquiry. What adjectives, illustrations, or comparisons do they use?

Representations are inventions based on language, but they are not neutral or innocuous signifiers. Because they enable actors to 'know' the object and to act upon what they 'know,' representations have very real political implications. Certain paths of action become possible within distinct discourses, while other paths become unthinkable. For example, two photos circulated in the media in the aftermath of the August 2005 flooding in New Orleans. The first showed a couple chest-high in the water with bags full of groceries. The caption stated that this couple had 'found' food in the wake of Hurricane Katrina. The second photo was of a similar scene, a woman chest-high in the water with a bag full of groceries, but she was identified as a 'looter.' This disparity generated much attention because the 'finders' were Caucasian while the 'looter' was African-American. But even beyond the racial elements at work here, these representations enabled and justified certain actions. Police, for instance, would be expected to assist the couple and to arrest or even shoot the single woman. Thus discursive practices created a truth-effect – 'a doing, an activity and a normalized thing in society, one enjoining activity and conformity' (Brown 2005: 63) – that shaped the possibilities for action. Or, as Iver Neumann states, 'Because a discourse maintains a degree of regularity in social relations, it produces preconditions for action' (in this book: 62).

Since some representations become accepted as 'true' and others do not, it is important to ask how certain structures of knowledge become dominant. Particular meanings and identities are widely accepted, or 'fixed,' not because of any inherent 'truth' but because of the strength of that specific representation. The production and circulation of discourses are politically contested, and which discourse will gain social acceptance will depend in large part on the distribution of power (see Leander's discussion of symbolic power and power relations). Representations are rarely the exclusive product of the object itself, even if it has agency, such as a state or an individual. One must do more than merely examine the utterances of Congolese political leaders or of Saddam Hussein. In both cases, a number of external actors have had greater success in establishing 'truth' and 'knowledge.'

We must ask, Who constructs knowledge and truth claims, for what purposes, and against what resistance? For example, Saddam Hussein may have produced a specific image of himself and his history as Iraqi leader, but his ability to circulate this image and have it gain social currency was limited during his incarceration. In contrast, George W. Bush and his administration had far greater power within the international community to ensure that their representation of Hussein became socially dominant. I suspect that most readers would give little credibility to the representations of Hussein's identity and history, despite the fact that those discourses have had tremendous salience for Iraqi lives and people elsewhere.

One can investigate the workings of power in the production of discourses by exploring the struggle over who gets to speak authoritatively. External forces are constantly at play, seeking to select, plot, and interpret the events and meanings by which identities are represented. As Said noted, the dominant knowledge of 'the Orient' was a creation of the European imperial imagination. With its representations repeated over and over again in Western literature, government publications, and advertisements, Orientalism became *authoritative* knowledge. This helps a researcher disaggregate actors. My research on representations of the Congo led me to investigate the discourses of non-Western actors and, more significantly, forced me to unpack 'the West' by focusing on specific discursive agents and their struggle to gain hegemonic represent-ation. I had to distinguish between Western governments (particularly the United States and Belgium) and explore important divisions within those governments (such as between the White House, CIA, and State Department).

Power is also exercised through the circulation process as competing discourses jockey for greater social acceptance and reproduction. There are often multiple and complex reasons for certain discourses gaining hegemony, and I believe it is important that a researcher be sensitive to these issues. Indeed, while discourses shape power, power also shapes discourse. Power, like discourses, is never totally centralized. A primary goal of this approach is to explore the relationship between discourse and power as they relate to representation (see also Ackerly in this book). The significant points I would underscore here are the multi-plicity and contestedness of discourses; the complicated ways in which power works through the production and circulation processes; and the recognition that researchers are not neutral observers, but often are intimately related to the power hierarchies at play.

With regards to agency, this approach assumes that people are guided to act in certain ways, and not others, by their discursively produced understanding of the world and their place in it (see Ringmar 1996). It rejects arguments that actors are motivated by inherent (universal) interests, rational means-ends preferences, or even internalized norms and values. As a fairly macro-level approach, it is admittedly limited in its ability to investigate issues of agency (again, see Leander's employ-ment of Bourdieu). But I am skeptical that micro-level attempts at causal explanation offer better analyses because micro-level analyses usually ignore the effects of discourses as structures of meaning (contrast with Checkel's claims in this book).

So how does one study representations? My own work on the Congo assumed that representational practices are embedded in historical social narratives. Therefore, I combined discourse analysis and historical research to examine struggles over the articulation and circulation of competing narratives. Each of these actors claimed dominant author-ship, but obviously, some of these voices were reproduced more than others, giving them greater 'weight.'

Exploring the complexities of this discursive production required me to engage with a wide and diverse spectrum of sources and authors. During the 1960s, for instance, the Congo was rewritten on the floor of the UN General Assembly by representatives from the Soviet Union, newly independent African states (most notably Ghana and Guinea),

Belgium, and the United States, all competing to present their narrative of events. Within the Congo, multiple voices – President, Prime Minister, future coup leader, secessionist leader, local media, citizenry groups, members of the army – articulated either a Congolese national identity or a regional, sub-state identity. Competing narratives also circulated in international and regional media, pamphlets and fliers passed around at political meetings across the globe, government pronouncements from Western and African capitals, best-selling novels, fictional and documentary films, and the 'bush' of the Congolese jungle. As I discuss in the next section, I found it necessary to engage in a wide variety of sources when researching, in part to explore the multiplicity and contestedness of discourses, to disaggregate actors, and to explore the complicated ways discourses were circulated and achieved social dominance.

Interpretation requires not just a description of these particular representations and representational practices but a deeper contextualization within the larger structures of meaning of which they are a part. Without going into the theoretical and philosophical debates within the discipline of History (see White 1978; Barthes 1981), let me merely point out that I believe historians produce their own 'regimes of truth,' not objective 'truth.' History produces its own discourses. Research is highly contested, and the historian is not neutral. This means that both primary and secondary sources should be treated as texts to be decoded and deconstructed. Moreover, this requires a distinction between empiricism as a *method* (skills of verification, close textual attention, proper sourcing, referencing, and so on) and as a *philosophy of knowledge* (the illusion of delivering fact, truth, and a knowable reality). While I (and other 'post-modern historians') value the former, we reject the latter.

I find Clifford Geertz's 'thick description' (1973) a useful label for this type of deeply contextualized historical analysis. In particular, I have found the 'long conversation' concept of historical anthropologists Jean and John Comaroff to be a useful way of understanding the historic contestation over representations. In their work on the colonial contact between the Tswana peoples of South Africa and the British Christian missionaries, the Comaroffs define the 'long conversation' as 'the actions and interactions that laid the bases of an intelligible colonial discourse' (1991: 198–9). They argue that there were two faces to this conversation between colonizer and colonized: what was talked *about;* and the struggle to gain mastery over the *terms* of the encounter. I believe that representations are historically produced within similar 'long conversations,' where multiple actors come together to contest the meanings of those identities and the terms in which they are expressed.

Drawing from my research on the Congo, one can see such a conversation taking place at the time of Congolese independence. What was under discussion was the extent that the Congolese were 'civilized,' 'developed,' and 'mature' enough to enjoy the 'gift' of independence and sovereignty. One can recognize how various actors struggled to establish both what was talked about and the terms of that conversation.

However, there is a third dimension to the 'long conversation' overlooked by the Comaroffs: the struggle over finding and creating an acceptable position or space within the conversation. Specifically, this refers to the ability to access 'discursive space' within which to engage in the conversation – as Foucault noted, discourses empower certain people to speak (and act). Delineating and policing discursive space has been an important element in international relations, especially for disadvantaged Third World states like the Congo. At times, international discursive space has been actively closed off to competing and counter-hegemonic discourses. For example, immediately after independence, Western governments not only intervened directly to deny the seating of Prime Minister Patrice Lumumba's United Nations delegation, but also his access to the radio station in his country's capital. Both of these actions effectively limited his ability to articulate and circulate his narratives of Congolese identity within the 'long conversation' at the moment of Congolese independence.

Let me reiterate that I am not arguing that the existence or absence of a specific historical representation offers a causal explanation, largely because these representations are historically contingent (see Hermann's discussion of content analysis and Duffy's application of pragmatic analysis, both in this book). For example, the image of Congolese 'inherent savagery' (a familiar Western trope) engendered intervention and colonial conquest in the late 19th century: 'bringing civilization to the savages.' But this same representation enabled Western policies of inaction and indifference to the Congo a century later: 'violence is due to their innate barbarism and tribalism, so there is nothing we can do about it.' Representations do not cause policies, such as intervention, nor do they explain choices, such as whether to intervene at one time rather than another. Representations cannot determine action completely. As Neumann notes, 'Discourse analysis aims at specifying the bandwidth of possible outcomes' (in this book: 62).

I maintain that structures of knowledge establish preconditions and parameters for the possibility of action, rather than explaining why certain choices are made. For example, it helps a researcher understand the range of options imaginable to President John F. Kennedy during the Cuban Missile Crisis, but it does not explain why he made specific decisions (Weldes 1999). To examine individual decision making, one would need to employ other methods. But while there might be methodological compatibility, one should be sensitive to the possible existence of an epistemological divide on the issue of causality. Personally, I remain unconvinced that we as scholars can offer causal explanations, only reasonably informed conjectures. The world is far too complex and contingent to be studied with any degree of certainty. My postpositivist approach is based on 'a logic of interpretation that acknowledges the improbability of cataloguing, calculating, and specifying "real causes"' (Campbell 1993: 7–8; also see the significant differences between Gusterson and Checkel in this book).

Practical advice for dealing with data

There are several steps to this method, each with its logistical challenges. I will discuss some of these along four general lines: establishing the parameters of a doable project, selecting appropriate sources of data, collecting that data, and analyzing it. But let me preface those comments by pointing out that there is almost always an arbitrary element in case selection (even more than Klotz suggests in this book). Many cases may actually work just as well as the ones you end up choosing. It is always useful to keep in mind that your project should be relevant, enjoyable, and doable.

Simple logistical issues will determine some parameters of your research. For example, basic language limitations matter: if you do not speak or read the language that most of the data is in, you should probably find another case. Or there simply might not be enough information out there to find. But you do have to make others choices for yourself, and you should be honest about why you make them. My comments here aim to help researchers understand the intellectual justifications that underpin the choices involved in historical analysis of representations.

Establishing parameters

It is easy to get overwhelmed by a topic that is just too unwieldy. I find it useful to pick a very narrow, specific topic that allows me to explore much larger issues (note Leander's similar advice). For my dissertation, I chose to examine how the Congo had been represented within the international community, beginning with its colonial conquest up to the current civil war. This case study let me explore not only issues of colonialism and neo-colonialism, but the social construction of sovereignty, the performativity of stateness, repression, and resistance, and the decline of the Westphalian state system.

However, telling the definitive story of how the Congo has been imagined over the past century would be an overwhelming task, filling numerous volumes. To make my project doable, I focused on four historical moments: the colonial 'invention' of the Congo at the end of the 19th century; its decolonization in 1960; its re-invention as 'Zaïre' during the 1970s; and the 'return' of the Congo at the end of the 20th century. (For more guidance on demarcating such historical periods, see Neumann's discussion of 'monuments.') During each of these four periods, the identity of the Congo was being contested, with numerous forces attempting to produce and attach meanings to its territory and people. These forces sought to create 'regimes of truth' about the Congo by defining and inscribing its identity.

I originally wanted to have six historical moments but found that would require more time and effort than was reasonable. Likewise, I wanted to have one of my historical moments focus on the Ali-Foreman 'Rumble in the Jungle,' and I soon realized that there were a few strong intellectual reasons to include that case beyond it simply being cool – if there had not been a larger justification, being 'cool' would not cut it. When examining historical representations, what matters most is selecting points where forces are seeking to create regimes of truth about the object of inquiry, representation X, by defining and inscribing its meaning. This type of approach stresses historical contingency with a focus on ruptures and disjunctures rather than continuities. In researching the Congo, I chose four moments that seemed to involve the greatest degree of contestation over the Congo's identity and that were historically varied, spanning over a century. Admittedly there can be a bit of arbitrariness to the selection of historical moments, but one should acquire a certain level of background knowledge on the subject in order to identify empirically rich moments of historical rupture.

Sources of data

When I talk about 'data,' I am first and foremost referring to textual representations: attempts to fix the meanings of my object of inquiry, representation X. This tends to be done by numerous actors. Discourse analysis requires employing multiple texts given that 'a single source cannot be claimed to support empirical arguments about discourse as a social background' (Milliken 1999: 233). When researching the construction of Congolese identity, I engaged empirical data from a broad array of sources. While the majority came from the 'official' realm of governmental reports, speeches, and documents, I also drew from journalism, travel literature, academic treatises, fiction, film, museum displays, art, images, maps, and other 'popular' texts. These texts often provide the most vivid and potent examples of the techniques through which Third World subjects have been narrated by Western hegemonic powers. For many outside observers, including politicians, these are the sources that have provided the primary framework within which the Congo has been made 'knowable.' As David Newbury (1998) pointed out, many Westerners are intellectually uninformed about the Congo but are so inundated by stereotypical images that they feel they have a well-defined cognitive framework. Novels such as *Heart of Darkness*, films such as *Congo*, and cartoons such as *Tintin in the Congo* constitute the basic discursive structure through which many Westerners view the Congo even today.

Different topics will, of course, mean engaging in different sources of data. But I firmly believe in casting the net wide, mainly because our structures of knowledge derive from a variety of sources. Therefore, possible sources include (but are by no means limited to): speeches by political leaders and elites, government records and public announcements, private writings of political elites, popular fiction, non-fiction, newspapers, magazines, music, cartoons, music, television, and the Internet. I will discuss the 'weighting' of various data below, but for now I think it is important to begin with an open mind (see also Ackerly and Neumann). A popular text (that is, a text with wide circulation such as a presidential speech, popular movie, or well-known photograph) will clearly be important in the process of structuring meaning. But more obscure texts (those that have a much more limited circulation, like an academic article or poem by an unknown writer) are often still important, if for no other reason than they represent an alternative to the dominant discourse.

Collecting data

I often combine archival work in historical records with interviews and investigations of popular culture texts. These three sources can each provide their own unique problems. Despite my emphasis on narrowing down potential sources, scarcity of data can also be an issue, since gaining access to data can be challenging.

While I regard the distinction between 'official' and the 'popular' data to be a fiction of the discipline, I employ the distinction here in order to highlight different ways of collecting data for each. The 'official' is what has traditionally been treated by the political science discipline as 'legitimate' source material: government documents, speeches by state leaders, the writings of political elites, and so forth. What I am calling the 'popular' can be considered the non-traditional: literature, movies, music, cartoons, and so forth. This has generally been designated at the realm of 'popular culture' as opposed to 'political culture.'

The 'official' data relevant for an examination of historical represent-ations are found in a number of places, from libraries and the Internet, but most often in government archives. Without meaning to state the obvious, not all archives are the same. For example, the British National Archive is extremely well organized, with the entire catalog accessible from the Web. But some countries have, shall we say, a different culture about sharing state records. The Belgian archive was very difficult for me to access, and I was denied entry on several occasions. Or it may be that no organized archives exist to house the historical material you are interested in investigating. For example, King Leopold II burned almost all the documents associated with his rule in the Congo immediately before handing control over to the Belgian government. Fortunately, the Belgian foreign ministry had their own copies of many of the torched documents.

Archives in the developing world often are not as organized, access-ible, and user-friendly as those in the developed world, possibly for good reasons – ranging from a healthy (and sometimes well-founded) suspicion of Western researchers to neglect and mismanagement to the impoverishment of state infrastructures due to global inequalities. Some-times state officials might not even be aware of the existence of archives even though they may be in the same building – an experience I have encountered on more than one occasion. It is usually safe to assume that your time in the archive will take longer than you expect. My experience has been that a personal contact at an archive (no matter where it is) is an invaluable asset for the researcher.

Access to popular culture can also be difficult or simply impossible. For example, I have no idea how I would go about accessing texts from Congolese society in the late 18th century. Therefore, I only examined examples of Western fiction and non-fiction writing, from travelogues by colonial explorers and tourists to popular novels by Conrad and Graham Greene. I examined the ways the Congo was discursively repres-ented: As an empty landscape waiting for Western conquest (Stanley)? As a primordial 'heart of darkness' that corrupted civilized Europeans (Conrad)? These were powerful and evocative images that have been re-employed and circulated frequently over time. I also looked at the representations of the Congo in the popular press. I focused on the major newspapers in Belgium, the United States, and France, including major magazines of the day, such as *Time, Life,* and *Newsweek.* I also found it useful to examine how the Congo was portrayed in music, movies, television, and cartoons (a highly fruitful source of data for multiple reasons). Museums, world exhibitions, and public spaces (such as public statues and commemorative arches in Brussels) provided additional rich source material. While by no means a comprehensive sample of how the Congo was portrayed in the Western popular imagination, drawing on the myriad of textual and visual forms by which actors attempt to articulate, circulate, and fix meanings compensates for inevitable limitations in any particular source of data.

A potential limitation is language proficiency. The representations of the Congo exist in numerous languages. For example, there are several major languages in the Congo itself (including French, Lingala, Kiswahili, Kikongo, and Tshiluba), while its colonial ruler, Belgium, has three official languages – none of which are my native tongue. This has meant that countless relevant texts went unstudied by me simply because I could not understand them. And even when I could, I suspect my language skills were not proficient enough to capture subtle meanings, allusions, and jokes. This is a serious problem (see Neumann's observations about 'cultural competency'). Focusing on material only available in your native tongue greatly limits your observations. In the end, I tried to acknowledge these limitations, avoid any overly grand claims, and recognize the narrow focus of my work.

Interviews provide more challenges than I have room here to discuss fully (see Gusterson for elaboration). Gaining access to subjects can often be difficult. Again, language limitations can also be problematic. For instance, I often use an interpreter and rely on him to accurately translate the words and meanings of the speaker, which is often extremely difficult to do. My being a white male also raises gender and racial problems that can often color the exchange, and often in ways that I am unaware. And, of course, interview subjects may simply be untruthful for numerous reasons.

In many cases, the researcher may be faced with data overload, a problem I frequently encountered when doing my Congo research. For example, when investigating historical representations of the Congo at the time of independence, I was simply swamped with what often seemed to be relevant data – from *National Geographic* articles to innumerable political cartoons from the European press to an endless slew of official pronouncements from various governments. If I did not make hard decisions about what counted and what would not (such as limiting my review of newspapers and news magazines to a handful), I have no doubt I would still be researching today – and in some ways I still am! This gets back to my earlier point about setting parameters: I had to make tough decisions in order to make my project doable, and I had to have solid intellectual reasons for making those decisions. I tried to be as honest and transparent about those decisions as I could (see both Leander and Ackerly on reflexivity). As a result, all my conclusions are tentative and tenuous at best. But I believe that is the nature – and value – of doing qualitative research.

Analyzing data

So what do you look for in the data? Even as I am gathering data, I begin analyzing it. First, I try to identify the different discourses engaged in representing X at a given moment. In what ways do these actors represent the object of inquiry? What type of language do they use when referring to it? For example, at the time of Congolese independence, how did Western leaders in Belgium and the United States portray the country, its inhabitants, and its leaders?

Second, I chart the contestation of these discourses. For instance, why did the Belgian and American presses portray the Congo in different – though equally negative – ways at independence? Who is engaged in the articulation and circulation of these alternative discourses? What is potentially at stake for these actors? Why do certain discourses emerge as socially dominant but others do not? What are the social and political strategies involved in that contestation? How are these discourses being consumed, and by whom?

Third, I historicize and contextualize these representations and discourses within the larger structures of meaning of which they are a part. For example, American representations of the Congo during its independence were situated within a larger Cold War discursive frame-work, while Belgian representations were part of a longer colonially inspired framework. Sensitivity to history and context allowed me to observe how portrayals of the Congo changed over time. Here is where I also realized how much the 'official' sources were informed by 'popular' structures of knowledge. During the 1960 crisis surrounding Congolese independence, Western political elites frequently employed texts, meta-phors, and images from popular culture, ranging from *Tarzan* movies to Joseph Conrad's *Heart of Darkness* and H.G. Wells' *War of the Worlds* to contemporary magazines and cartoons. The reason for this is simple: the structures of knowledge in a society are as much a product of 'popular' culture as they are of 'political' culture. The dichotomy between the two is an illusion that obscures more than it reveals.

Finally, I explore how the dominant discourses enable certain policies and practices to become possible. That is, what becomes thinkable and what does not? For example, the Eisenhower Administration's eventual declaration that there was a Congolese problem, and that Lumumba was the source of that problem, had clear political implications: namely, the authorization of his assassination by the CIA. This action was only thinkable because of the representations generated during this time (with their strong historical roots).

Obviously, my approach produced copious amounts of notes (always written on just one side of the page so as to make it easier to find missing quotes or pieces of information later). In this work, I try to track the development of representations and assess their intensity in terms of circulation and social acceptance. I try to structure a narrative of these events – the production, circulation, and contestation of discourses and the range of possible actions they engender. Admittedly, the narrative I produce is an artificial and subjective creation that I use to impose order. Since I am interested in examining historical contingency by focusing on ruptures and disjunctures, I eschew the impulse of traditional historical narratives to portray continuity. In the end, I try to write a convincing narrative that provides an understanding of the 'how' questions which initiated my research.

Conclusion

As I noted at the outset, I do not believe that the world presents itself to us as self-evident. I believe our engagement with it is based on interpretation. As human beings, we make sense of the world around us through the social construction of the meanings, characteristics, and 'truth' that make reality 'knowable.' There is no way to step outside of interpretation. There is no objective Truth to discover, only competing interpretations to navigate.

Since my epistemological position is open to the criticism that it leads to relativism and raises questions about the role of the researcher in the interpretive process, let me respond. I do not believe it is possible to strive for some mythical goal of objectivity, since no such *terra firma* exists. Therefore, I recognize I am not neutral, and I am not too concerned with charges of interpretative bias. But are there ways to decide what counts as 'good' analysis? I believe there are. For me, there are two important issues to consider when judging the validity of one's interpretation.

First, is there supporting evidence to back up my claims? As a researcher, it will often seem obvious to us that the bulk of our data is pointing to a certain set of interpretations. Of course, our interpretation of that data is what is leading us to our concluding interpretation. But I believe it is important to have supporting evidence. If I claim that the US government portrayed the Congo as Y, which thus enabled it to act in Z manner, I need to provide evidence of both Y and Z. If I cannot, then my claims should be taken as highly speculative. I would argue that this is the reason one needs to do as much historical research as possible. But am I slipping rationality and empiricism back in? I reiterate my distinction between empiricism as *method* versus *philosophy of knowledge*. The value I place on the former does not make my claims 'true,' but it does strengthen my ability to argue for their validity.

This leads to my second point: that the validity of one's interpretation can be measured by its logical coherence does not imply that there is an objective measure of logical coherence (in contrast to a rational choice approach, for instance). Put simply, I am interested in whether or not my conclusions make sense to me, and if they are convincing to others. Do they provide a reasonable answer for the questions I was trying to answer? If not, then I try again. Does such a position lead to relativism? Absolutely. My goal as a researcher is to provide an argument about why my interpretation is valid, so that I can convince others that mine is one of the best interpretations out there. In a very real sense, I am constructing my own representation of the representations I am studying – I am very much part of the process of knowledge construction that I am investigating. Being self-reflexive and honest, I admit that I, like all other researchers, am motivated by an array of personal, political, and intellectual agendas. With my work, I am constructing my own discourses. And because I want them to gain social dominance, I am concerned that my conclusions convince other people.

7
Ethnographic Research

Hugh Gusterson

> The anthropologist is always inclined to turn toward the concrete, the particular, the microscopic. We are the miniaturists of the social sciences, painting on Lilliputian canvases with what we take to be delicate strokes. We hope to find in the little what eludes us in the large, to stumble upon general truths while sorting through special cases.
>
> Clifford Geertz (1968: 4)

James Clifford (1997: 56) has, in a much cited locution borrowed from Renato Rosaldo, theorized the methodology of ethnographic research – my craft – as 'deep hanging out.' This perverse phrase captures nicely the improvisational quality of fieldwork, the confusing overlap between informal streetcorner conversation and the serious inquiry embodied in ethnographic fieldwork, and the profound level of understanding of the other for which ethnography aims through apparently casual methods.

This phrase 'deep hanging out' also hints at a contrast between the methodologies of cultural anthropology (which inclines toward the informal) and political science (which is more tightly buttoned). It is my impression, based on limited observation of the training of graduate students in international relations, that political scientists are expected to go into their dissertation research with well-honed hypotheses that aim to prise open crevices in the existing literature based on a careful parsing of independent and dependent variables and a shrewd selection of case studies that might illuminate the relationships between those variables. Political Science graduate students often seem to know what their dissertation will argue, and what the chapter outline will look like, before they have got deeply into the research. While anthropology graduate students spend years acquiring language skills, working on pre-dissertation literature reviews and writing dissertation proposals, these proposals often focus more on broad questions suggested by the existing literature than on hypotheses to be tested. Meanwhile dissertation committees in anthropology departments tend to expect student research plans to shift as they encounter the vicissitudes of the fieldwork environment: bureaucratic difficulties in accessing a particular site, research subjects disinclined to discuss the topic that seemed so crucial in the student's literature review, research subjects passionately interested in discussing issues the student had not thought to inquire about, and unpredicted events (riots, protests, scandals, conflicts, funerals, celebrations, and so on) that provide unforeseen but compelling windows onto an unfamiliar cultural world.

Moreover, although there are stories of anthropologists such as Melville Herskovits insisting that his students mail their fieldnotes to him from the field for review, most anthropologists report that they received minimal guidance about fieldwork from advisers and disserta- tion committees either before they went to the field or while they were there. I myself, for example, have never seen another anthropologist's notes, and I am far from unique in that regard (see Sanjek 1990). Anthro- pologists often assume that each fieldwork situation is different, and that researchers will have to improvise accordingly. Furthermore, first fieldwork is a 'rite of passage' (turning graduate students into mature anthropologists), and it is part of the ritual testing to throw students on their own resources.

In this chapter, stressing the simultaneous informality and rigor of ethnographic fieldwork, I shall take the reader through the key components of 'the ethnographic method.' Although anthropologists often use methods that overlap with those of other disciplines – archival research, written questionnaires, and formal interviews, for example – I focus here on methodological concerns more unique to the ethnographic encounter: gaining access to the field; doing semi- structured interviews and what anthropologists oxymoronically refer to as 'participant observation'; navigating the ethical obligations of fieldwork; and writing up research first through fieldnotes and, later, in ethnographies. (The word 'ethnography,' confusingly, refers both to a method of research and to the finished literary product.) Until the upheavals in anthropology of the late 1980s and 1990s, anthro- pologists were most likely to study non-Western cultures rather than Western, metropolitan cultures; to study a single localized site; and to focus their studies on those subordinate in status. Recent years, by contrast, have seen the increasing legitimacy in the anthropology of 'repatriated anthropology,' 'multi-sited ethnography,' and 'studying up' (Nader 1974; Clifford and Marcus 1986; Marcus and Fischer 1986; Marcus 1995).

I shall draw opportunistically on the relatively small methods literature in anthropology and on what I know of others' fieldwork, but I shall also draw considerably on my own experience doing ethnographic research among American nuclear weapons scientists and, to a lesser extent, antinuclear activists. My original dissertation fieldwork in the San Francisco Bay Area in the late 1980s, part of the disciplinary transformation, was on the Lawrence Livermore National Laboratory, the nuclear weapons laboratory that designed the warheads for missiles (Gusterson 1996). I was trying to understand how scientists came to feel that they had a vocation to design nuclear weapons; I also wanted to describe the phenomenology of weapons work, the effect of weapons work on marital and family relationships, the relationship between the weapons laboratory and local institutions ranging from churches to the town council, and the impact upon the laboratory of the sizeable antinuclear protests of the early 1980s. I interviewed many of the protestors as well, and at one point accompanied a group of anarchists from the Bay Area on a weeklong protest trip to the Nevada Nuclear Test Site.

More recently, for a follow-up book, I have been doing multi-sited fieldwork among weapons scientists at both the Livermore and the Los Alamos nuclear weapons laboratories; among antinuclear activists in California, New Mexico, and Washington DC; and sporadic interviews with senior bureaucrats from the nuclear weapons complex wherever I can find them. If my earlier fieldwork focused largely on rank-and-file weapons scientists, this research has been more centered on senior managers of the weapons laboratories and on major players in the Washington defense bureaucracy – busy decision-makers who are not easily accessed. The purpose of this research is to trace the process by which the national security bureaucracy (especially the nuclear weapons complex) came to acquiesce in the suspension of nuclear testing and the negotiation of the Comprehensive Test Ban Treaty in the early 1990s (Gusterson 2004). If the first research project was anchored to a single, localized site – the Livermore Laboratory – the second project has, in keeping with a more general anthropological evolution away from a preoccupation with the local, focused much more on diffuse networks, structures, and processes that are both national and international in scale.

Accessing the field

Like the space shuttle entering the earth's atmosphere, the ethnographer entering the field must get the angle of approach just right, or the resultant friction may burn up the mission. Unlike shuttle astronauts, ethnographers have widely varying missions, each with different optimal angles of approach. Sometimes what opens the village doors can be quite unpredictable, especially to an outsider. Paul Stoller (1989: 40–1) reports that he made little headway in penetrating the world of sorkos – magician-healers in Niger – until the day a bird defecated on his head. This was taken by a sorko who witnessed it as sign that Stoller was chosen for apprenticeship.

What works for one ethnographer seeking entrée to the field may prove disastrous for another. Margaret Harrell (2003), for example, is an anthropologist who studied US military families. She reports that a letter from a commanding officer directing military personnel to cooperate with her was indispensable to her fieldwork. By contrast, the anthropologist Philippe Bourgois (1995), who did fieldwork with crack dealers in New York's Spanish Harlem, would have been crippled by the endorsement of uniformed authorities and, in his case, being mistreated by the police on one occasion helped his fieldwork considerably. In general, ethnographers entering the field seek to ally with gatekeepers who will vouch for them and to avoid falling in with the wrong crowd – the only problem being that, as you enter an unfamiliar cultural situation, it can be quite hard to tell which is which.

Ethnographers are inevitably marked in the field by their race, class, gender, education level, nationality, and other characteristics. In some contexts, aspects of the researcher's own identity may play a facilitating role; in others they may be crippling. It is hard, for example, to imagine a woman doing Loic Wacquant's (2003) research with boxers in Chicago, or a man doing Elizabeth Fernea's (1969) research among the wives of a sheikh in Iraq or Stephanie Kane's work with female prostitutes (1998). Ethnographers inevitably have to decide which aspects of a field environment are more or less accessible or closed off by virtue of their own identity.

In my own case, when I decided to do an ethnography of the Lawrence Livermore National Laboratory, my problem was that I was a foreign (British) citizen attempting to study a top secret military facility where I knew nobody and to which access was largely forbidden for those without clearances. I thought of making a formal approach to the Laboratory's management for permission to study the facility, but decided the likelihood was low that such permission would be granted and, once denied, it was not inconceivable that Lab management would actively obstruct more informal approaches to their weapons scientists. In the end, I tried a scattershot approach of three simultaneous entry strategies, only one of which was truly fruitful and one of which was nearly quite damaging.

The first strategy, joining my practical need for accommodation with my interest in meeting laboratory employees, was to look for a room in a house occupied by lab employees. Over the course of 2 years of field-work, I lived in three different houses with different kinds of laboratory employees – a technician, a computer programmer, and an engineer. Over time, I heard a lot of gossip about the Lab from these employees, who I got to know well as individual friends. However, they did not introduce me to many other lab employees, and it is dangerous to rely on single sources to understand a complex institution employing over 8000 people. I felt as if I were slowly developing a deep understanding of very tiny and isolated pockets of laboratory life from my roommates.

Roommates were, however, a particularly good source of basic orientation information. Disorientation is one of the strongest sensations of the ethnographer newly arrived in the field. Consequently, the beginning of field research is often dominated by an attempt to simply get one's bearings by asking lots of very basic questions. In my case, these questions included the following: Why do some people have red and others green badges? How many directorates are there at the Lab, and what do they all do? What is that tall building in the middle of the Lab I can see from the perimeter? What kinds of clothes do people wear to work at the Lab and how should I dress when meeting them? Is it alright to talk about 'bombs' or should I call them 'devices'? What is a CAIN booth? (It regulates access to restricted areas of the Lab for those with clearances. An employee stands in the booth and swipes a card, as if at an ATM, entering a secret code, and is then granted admission.)

My second strategy was to make use of one chance contact I had made at a party a few weeks before coming to Livermore. At this party I met a woman and her husband, who worked as a scientist at the Lab. They both lived in Livermore, and the wife was especially interested in my research. She invited me to lunch with a promise that she would provide me entrée to a wider network in Livermore. I noted that she brought her teenage daughter to lunch and seemed uncomfortable. I was fortunate to discover from a friend of the couple that her husband (who was not keen on talking to me) was concerned that my interest in his wife was not purely academic, so I moved on. As my research unfolded, I observed that scientists were happy to talk to me when I was introduced through networks of scientists at the Lab, but often resisted talking to me if the introduction came through their spouses.

The approach that worked, my third strategy, was the result of extraordinary serendipity. My graduate student advisor mentioned to me that he was supervising an undergraduate thesis on the town of Livermore by a student who grew up there. I contacted the student and found that his father worked at the Lab. The son arranged for me to go and visit his father. I anticipated discussing with the father the feasibility of my study and getting his advice on how to approach people. Instead, when I arrived at his home at seven o'clock one evening, he said, 'Take out your notebook. I will tell you my life story.' I said very little for the next 2 hours, at the end of which I had pages of fascinating material about a man who had fled North Korea as a teenager, come to the United States with nothing, trained as a physicist, and sought work as a weapons scientist because of what he referred to throughout the interview as his 'monolithic anticommunism.' He demonstrated for me that evening that the way to understand lab employees was not to ask a series of abstract questions about their ideological beliefs but to elicit life histories that crystallized their commitments in narratives of the events through which they were enacted – a technique whose power has been beautifully demonstrated in Faye Ginsburg's (1989) ethnography of pro-life and pro-choice activists in the Mid-West, published just 2 years after my conversation with the Korean scientist in Livermore. At the end of our encounter, the scientist offered to put me in touch with five more lab scientists if they agreed. They did. Each of them referred me to still more colleagues, and the rest was history.

This technique of building an exponentially increasing network of research subjects from an original subject zero is referred to in the methodological literature, for obvious reasons, as the 'snowball technique.' Its strength is that people who trust one another trust those referred to them through the network. Its weakness is that it does not operate through random sampling, and there is an obvious danger that the ethnographer will get trapped inside the network's echo chamber and will be confused by what he or she hears there for the wider discourse of an entire institutional setting (see also Ackerly in this book). In my own case, I was confident that I was reaching a wider sample partly because my collection of interviewees was so large, and partly because I deliberately pushed interviewees to refer me to others chosen to diversify my sample.

I also, over time, further diversified my pool of subjects by searching for interlocutors in other settings too. In a context where about three quarters of weapons scientists identified themselves as active Christians, church attendance proved an important way of getting to meet them as well as building relationships with their pastors, who also became interview subjects. I joined a softball and a basketball team at the Lab; I joined the Lab singles group (more of a Friday evening and weekend outings club than a dating arrangement); I hung around bars in town, and I sometimes went for lunch to the Lab cafeteria, which was open to the public and proved a good place to cajole scientists I already knew into introducing me to others.

The pool of interlocutors I developed through these techniques has been important also for my newer research on the weapons laboratories' adaptation to the end of nuclear testing. I have gone back to some of these interlocutors to explore their reaction to life in a weapons laboratory without nuclear testing. However, my new research has focused much more on very busy senior managers than my earlier research did. In securing interview access, I have been fortunate to be able to build on the success of the first research project: that research secured me a professorship at MIT, which is a highly respected institution at Livermore and Los Alamos. Senior managers there will usually make time to talk to an MIT professor. Beyond that, my original research has now been widely profiled in local newspapers, it produced a book that many lab employees have read, and I have written a number of articles for local newspapers. This has given me a measure of legitimacy around town, and it gives potential interlocutors a sense that I am a known quantity who can be trusted as much as any outsider can. One lesson to draw is that when anthropologists' relationships to research sites carry on across a decade or more, as they often do, they deepen over time, opening up new vistas of understanding.

Participant observation

If you asked an older generation of anthropologists to define 'the ethnographic method,' they would put 'participant observation' at the center of it. Participant observation, the essence of the 'deep hanging out,' denotes a method of research in which ethnographers join in the flow of daily life while also taking notes on it (either in real time or shortly afterwards). If the locals went hunting, harvesting, drinking, feasting, or pilgrimaging, the anthropologist tried to go with them, often to do it with them, and to record as accurately as possible what was said and done.

There are many obvious benefits to participant observation. First, this level of sustained contact with research subjects helps to build relationships of trust and intimacy with them. Second, seeing for oneself what people do and choosing what to record of it is surely far better than learning about it after the fact in a fragmentary fashion from documents or informant interviews. It is the difference between sitting in someone's living room with them and peeking in through a keyhole. Finally, participant observation is a particularly effective way of exploring the difference between the 'frontstage' and 'backstage' – between formal, idealized accounts of a culture and the messy divergences of actual practice. Imagine what a Martian ethnographer would believe about the way an American university works if they relied on formal interviews with faculty and staff, and then imagine what they would learn instead if they went to faculty meetings and gossipy lunches with the staff while living in a student dorm in the evenings, and you will get my point.

Some of my favorite ethnographies use participant observation for particularly good effect. In *Peyote Hunt*, Barbara Myerhoff (1976) accompanies a group of Huichol Indians led by Ramon, a shamanic figure, on a long pilgrimage into the Mexico desert to the Huichols' original mythic home and home still to their gods. Their pilgrimage culminates with the sacred ingestion of peyote and with the harvesting of the hallucinogenic buttons for rituals for the coming year. Her participation in the pilgrimage and its visionary culmination enables her to get inside Huichol cosmology and mystical religious experience as much as any outsider can. Myerhoff's narrative has a cinematic quality. As she relates, with a novelist's eye for detail and drama, the pilgrims' jokes, the reader feels that he or she is alongside the Huichols in their journey. *Of Two Minds*, by Tanya Luhrmann (2001), looks at the socialization of American psychotherapists and psychiatrists. Her description of the way medical residents learn their trade and internalize diagnostic categories of mental illness is particularly enlivened by the fact that she put herself through the same apprenticeship in order better to understand it.

Participant observation has been especially important in ethnographic investigations of American poverty. This is because there is often a sharp divergence between, on the one hand, judgmental assumptions about the poor that circulate in the media and among policy makers and, on the other hand, the lived experience of poverty. In books such as Carol Stack's *All Our Kin* (1997) and Philippe Bourgois' *In Search Of Respect* (1995), privileged white ethnographers reposition themselves by living in the midst of poor black and Hispanic communities. More effectively than any dry, statistics-laden policy study, these ethnographies build a picture of the exhausting daily grind of lives lived in poverty, of creative adaptations to poverty that are also entrapping (such as crack dealing), and of the barriers to escaping the ghetto that are so much more clearly visible from within than outside. But the ultimate exercise in participant observation in poverty was conducted not by a professional ethnographer but by the journalistic public intellectual Barbara Ehrenreich. In her justly celebrated book, *Nickel and Dimed* (2002), she goes undercover, working as a low-end waitress, a hotel maid, and a Walmart worker. Ehrenreich records not only the mass of petty brutalities against the poor in the workplace but also keeps an exact ledger of the financial costs faced by low-income workers versus the income they can secure. By the end of the book, one thinks it a miracle anyone moves up from this life at all.

Given the insights participant observation facilitates, I regret the limited role it played in my own fieldwork among weapons scientists. Although I spent as much time as possible simply 'hanging out' with Lab employees in church, in their homes, and on hikes, I sometimes wonder what I might have seen had I been allowed to come into the Lab day after day with my notebook and fade into the background. Anthropologists of science who have been given full access to scientific laboratories have often written ethnographies that focus on the microprocesses through which scientific facts are constructed (Latour and Woolgar 1986; Fujimura 1996; Knorr Cetina 1999). I suspect that, had I engaged in participant observation within the Lab itself, I would have written an ethnography more focused on disputes over weapons design details, the bureaucratic relationships between different ranks and categories of employees, and the phenomenological disconnect between small daily tasks within the laboratory and the laboratory's larger project of developing a massive arsenal of weapons of mass destruction capable of liquidating hundreds of millions of people. As it was, my enforced positioning on the margins of laboratory life produced an ethnography that foregrounded secrecy practices within the Laboratory and the Laboratory's relationships with other institutions, and my residence outside the Laboratory fence but within the homes of weapons scientists made me particularly sensitive to the role and experience of laboratory spouses.

Despite the circumscribed role participant observation played in my field research, there are still things I would not know without having engaged in it. For example, I recall being in the cafeteria of the Livermore

Laboratory when CNN started to broadcast the story of the Oklahoma City bombing. As I watched weapons scientists around me turn up the volume on the cafeteria TV and, using CNN's details about blast damage, rush to calculate the power of Timothy McVeigh's bomb on the backs of their white paper table napkins, I viscerally understood something about the phenomenology of their craft. Other informal interactions have also been instructive. By befriending a new Lab employee and watching her mounting anxiety as her investigation for a security clearance dragged on for months, I came to understand, better than I could through interviews, the indispensability of a clearance, the petty humiliations of life without a clearance, and the terror an employee feels at the prospect of denial. Taking a long and beautiful dog-walk with another employee, I was stunned by a torrent of criticism of the Director of Los Alamos that he (and his colleagues) had held back in other interactions. I have also found that rank-and-file weapons scientists talking over a beer joke to the detriment of their managers and evince much more skepticism about the new simulation technologies being developed at the weapons labs than similar scientists do in tape recorded interviews or than managers in any context I can access. Rank-and-file weapons designers' informal narratives of the origin of these simulation technologies are more likely to stress pork barrel deals in Washington, whereas more formal interviews with managers accent the scientific and technical logic of the technologies and the overall rationality of the program of stockpile stewardship. In other words, my ability to 'hang out' with ordinary weapons scientists gave me special insight into the gulf between 'frontstage' and 'backstage' narratives of the stockpile stewardship program, between what is said in public and what is whispered or said jokingly in private.

A second example comes from my parallel fieldwork among antinuclear activists. As these activists prepared to go on a week-long protest to the Nevada Nuclear Test Site, I attended their preparatory workshops where I heard first-hand about people using sick days and vacation time to keep their jobs while they went on the protest. I joined with them as they role-played being arrested and subjected to police brutality, and having their planning meetings infiltrated by undercover police officers. Then I traveled with them to the Nevada Desert, where I lived in a tent for a week with no running water and was taught by those around me how to deal with the extremes of heat and cold in the desert in spring. Finally, I shared their experience of civil disobedience. Without having gone through all this myself, I do not think I could so easily grasp the extraordinary sense of community among the activists, the sacrifices many of the protestors made to be there, or the relationship between the privations of protest and the strange rush of euphoria from civil disobedience. Nor, without my time amongst the protestors, would I have recognized with such clarity the mistaken nature of comments made by members of the Livermore community characterizing the protestors as communists and unemployed folks who had nothing better to do.

A final contribution made by participant observation is more amorphous and mysterious, but no less important for that. It concerns the reformation of my own emotional relationship to nuclear weapons. When I arrived in Livermore in the mid-1980s, I did so as someone who had been deeply concerned about the possibility of superpower nuclear war to the point of even having occasional nightmares about it. By the time I left Livermore 2 years later, I had lost my subjective fear of nuclear weapons and have never been able to recover it. It just disappeared! I am unable to give a precise account of the processes involved here but it is clear that, in some way, living amongst people who joked about nuclear weapons and took for granted the human ability to control these weapons, I absorbed their sense of ease – or, if you prefer, their ability to live in denial.

Semi-structured interviews

The core of my research consisted of semi-structured interviews organized around the elicitation of life histories. I collected well over a hundred of these interviews, which were almost always tape-recorded. This was important because I was interested in the exact language scientists used to describe their beliefs and experiences, and because my interlocutors attached great importance to precise quotation of their remarks. In my original research it was through such semi-structured interviews that I came to understand how weapons scientists understood the ethics and politics of their work, how they reconciled their weapons work with their religious commitments, how they experienced the weapons design process emotionally, and how weapons work affected family life. In my more recent research, I have used such interviews to reconstruct negotiations about the end of nuclear testing at the higher levels of the weapons bureaucracy, to understand the purpose of new simulation technologies being built at the weapons labs, and to elicit the response of rank-and-file weapons scientists to the end of nuclear testing and the emergence of virtual nuclear weapons science.

Many social scientists, less interpretively focused than I, are deeply concerned about the exact comparability of their subjects under the research microscope. Sociologists devising questionnaires, for example, seek to ensure that, however diverse their pool of research subjects, they are responding to the same questions. Here it is the consistency of the questions posed to different individuals or populations that enables the sociologist to make differentiating generalizations: everything comes back to the way different people respond to the same questions. If each interview or questionnaire is different, then comparison is clouded.

While the benefits of such a research protocol are obvious, it also acts as a straitjacket. If, as Sharon Hutchinson (1996) says, ethnography is 'the fine art of conversation,' individuals like to talk about different things and, by insisting on precise comparability, this research methodology prevents the detailed exploration of individuality. It also tends to bore research subjects, forcing them into a kind of mass-produced superficiality. In my interviews there was a core set of questions I asked everyone: where were you educated? To what level and in what subject? What are your religious commitments? What is your work at the Lab or in the antinuclear movement? How did you come to decide to do weapons work? Has anyone in your family or beyond given you a hard time for working on weapons? Such questions, as well as producing a matrix for comparison, served as icebreakers and orienting probes for deeper conversations that followed. But beyond this elementary set of common questions, my interviews with different research subjects diverged quite substantially as I followed strategies I call 'branching' and 'building.'

My interviews followed a 'branching' pattern as I tailored them to individual interests and identities. Interviews followed different trajectories for physicists and engineers, for the elite weapons designers and the scientists who worked under them, for Christians, Jews, and atheists. Interviews also branched in different directions as my line of questioning responded to what individual scientists showed particular interest in discussing.

As for 'building,' each interview built upon earlier ones as my understanding of the Lab deepened and expanded over time, and interviews I did at the end of the research project were quite different from those conducted at the outset. I came to think of myself as having conversations not just with unique individuals, each fascinating in his or her own right, but also with a single entity: a discourse community. As these unfolding conversations suggested recurrent discursive themes, new avenues of inquiry, or newly evident lacunae in my own understanding, so the questioning shifted, each conversation establishing a new beachhead as I probed more deeply into the culture of the Lab or, sometimes, circled back recursively to check anomalies and uncertainties.

Researchers who subscribe to more positivist understandings of the world than I do assume that research subjects have stable 'values,' 'preferences,' 'beliefs,' 'ideologies,' or 'cultures' and that it is the researcher's job to find out what they are as cleanly as possible (to some extent, Checkel and Hermann, in this book). But I soon noticed that subjects I interviewed more than once might contradict themselves in interesting ways, or that some interviewees presented themselves quite differently to journalists and to me. Positivists would see such fluctuations as 'noise' to be eliminated in order to ascertain what the informant 'really' thinks. I came, instead, to see these instabilities of discourse as themselves part of informants' cultural identities. And if, for example, a scientist's statements about the Russians showed little fluctuation while his or her comments about the ethics of weapons work were variable, this variability was itself an important ethnographic datum.

Just as Lao Tzu said that no two stones can be thrown in the same river, so I would say that it is not possible to interview the same subject twice. Thus, rather than thinking that I was sampling or eliciting a stable, pre-existing reality as objectively as possible, I began to think of interviews as dynamic events through which the identity of the subject was performed and even co-constructed by the interviewer and interviewee. In these conversations, interviewees did not so much manifest an unchanging essence there, like some geological pattern, plain for any researcher to see if they knew how to scrape away the surface. Instead they drew on the complex repertoires of their speech community to perform themselves in response to particular lines of questioning (How is your work ethical? Do you think nuclear war will happen? How do you deal with antinuclear activists?) that often reflected my own past in the antinuclear movement. A different interlocutor with different preoccupations would have provoked different performances of self since, as Renato Rosaldo (1989: 19) observes, 'the ethnographer, as a positioned subject, grasps certain human phenomena better than others. He or she occupies a position or structural location and observes with a particular angle of vision.' And, of course, as my earlier discussion of the way my interviews built upon one another makes clear, I was changed by each interview too: no two interviews were done by the same interviewer.

At their worst, these interviews produced the ethnographic equivalent of American Presidential debates: stale performances using rehearsed lines and recycled snippets from the Laboratory's public relations campaigns. At their best, the interviews produced performances of self in modest kitchens and living rooms around Livermore that were profound, touching, revelatory, funny, counter-intuitive, and educative. The role of interviewer affords a license to ask questions of a kind that would not normally be permitted for strangers – indeed, even for friends in most contexts – while the act of sustained, attentive, supportive listening can be powerfully enabling for the person being heard (and indeed, in a different way, for the listener as well). This kind of listening – accompanied by requests to clarify apparent contradictions, to tie emotions to recalled events, or to address narrative gaps – can induce a creatively reflective state of mind as interviewer and interviewee move into a zone of interaction that hybridizes therapeutic encounters and journalistic interrogations.

Some of my interviews lasted 4 hours. One lasted for 15 hours, spread over a series of sessions, which a retired scientist taped as a bequest for his daughter. (When I attended his funeral after he died of Alzheimers a few years later, I felt a secret and special bond to him.) I began to realize that, as scientists reflected on the ethics of their work, reconstructed their decisions to come to the laboratory, and recalled their emotional responses to nuclear tests they had experienced, they were sometimes opening spaces they shared with few others. One wife, eavesdropping on my interview with her husband, interrupted to say, 'How come you told him that? You've never told me that!' Many scientists told me that they thought about the ethics of their work but none of their colleagues did – a clear indication that everyone was thinking about nuclear ethics, but quietly and in private. The interviews, then, generated articulations not only of fiercely public ideologies, but also of the private, the whispered, the half crystallized on the edge of consciousness. And once these articulations became public, as they were pushed back into the community through my writing, then in a modest way they changed the field of discourse I had come to study.

Inscriptions

In earlier generations, anthropologists passed many of their evening hours typing up index cards. These cards enabled them to store and sort information they had gathered on, say, patrilateral cross cousins, funeral rituals, or witchcraft beliefs. Doing fieldwork in the computer age, I use the cut-and-paste function of Word to do some of the work for which those anthropologists used index cards. However, I mainly organize my notes around interviews and interactions with individuals, recording their exact words whenever possible. The fundamental organizing principle of my notes, then, is the individual biography, though I do also sort information on my hard drive and in manila folders around themes. Sometimes I take a pair of scissors to printed transcripts of interviews, scattering textual shards to differently themed manila folders. Clearly there is a relationship between the organization of my notes around individuals and the fact that my writing often makes use of long quotes from individual informants and, on occasion, features extensive profiles of individual research subjects (Gusterson 1995a,b).

How do ethnographers know when it is time to leave the field and start writing? Often, they have no choice: their research funds dry up or their sabbaticals end, and they go home with whatever notes they have. In my own case, I felt that fieldwork was getting stale when I found myself often able to predict how research subjects would answer my questions. While I was still learning new things, this meant that my understanding of the culture was achieving a certain depth and stability and was, to some degree, plateauing. It was time to stop talking and start writing.

In preparing to write, I read my notes on interviews with individual interlocutors, as well as transcriptions of them, flagging recurrent patterns, variations on themes, and quotable passages. The recurrent patterns have ranged from noting that Livermore scientists are more optimistic about simulation technologies than Los Alamos scientists to observing the use of similar metaphors by different people, often people who do not know one another. Examples include the use of birth metaphors to describe the process of designing and testing a nuclear weapon, the use of machine metaphors to describe the human body, and the use of anthropomorphic metaphors to describe machines.

Ethnographers of my generation, often influenced directly or indirectly by the writings of Michel Foucault, tend to see human cultural worlds as constructed by the intersecting power of ingrained cultural practices and the discourses through which people speak about their world. When we do fieldwork we note these practices and we record as much of the discourse as we can, looking for recurrent patterns. Just as psychotherapists have to talk to people at the conscious level in order to deduce what is happening in their unconscious worlds, so anthropologists have to observe and talk to individuals (or groups of individuals), but are really interested in the practices and discourses that transcend the level of the individual and, to put it in Foucauldian terms, provide the social material from which their individuality is constructed.

(See Neumann and Dunn, in this book, for examples of finding such discursive patterns at other levels of analysis.)

Writing this up as ethnography poses its own set of challenges since, compared to political science monographs, the criteria for writing and judging ethnography are much looser and more heterogeneous. Ward Goodenough (1981), likening culture to language, said that an ethnography was a sort of cultural grammar book, and that, just as a grammar book would teach you how to speak a language, so an ethnography should teach you how to behave appropriately in a particular culture. Clifford Geertz (1973), seeing culture as a text to be interpreted rather than a set of rules to be followed, thought good ethnography gave deep insight into the nuances of an alien lifeworld and into the meanings by which its adherents struggled to live. Carolyn Nordstrom (2004: 14) meant something similar when she said 'ethnography must be able to bring a people and a place to life in the eyes and hearts of those who have not been there.'

Such descriptions imply that the goal of ethnography is just particularistic description. However, as the quote by Clifford Geertz at the front of this chapter makes clear, the point of ethnography is to describe the particular in order to illuminate 'general truths' – the functioning of capitalism, the nature of ritual, the experience of oppression, say. In general, anthropologists would agree that good ethnography gives a rich evocation of the cultural world it describes while also contributing something to theory and being of interest to those who are not specialists on the culture area described. They would also say that it should 'feel right' to those other area specialists – though not being without surprises – and that it should give a thick enough description that readers could draw their own inferences about the culture being described.

The index card generation of anthropologists often said in their writing that 'the data suggest' and 'it was observed that...,' but who collected these data and by whom was it observed? References to 'data' and the use of the passive voice – the hallmarks of what Donna Haraway (1988) calls the 'God's eye view from nowhere' – are the familiar tropes of phony objectivism. Of course, we check our facts, quote people accurately, and do our best to make sure we know what people mean by what they say, but in the end 'data' are collected and written up by individual researchers who have their own concerns, insights, and blind spots. For this reason, as I have done throughout this chapter, I use the first person in my writing, in order to remind the reader that the 'data' have been collected, sifted, organized, and represented by a particular individual who readers have to decide whether or not they trust. As a way of helping readers to make up their minds, at the end of my first book, *Nuclear Rites*, I also gave a page each to a handful of key informants to comment on the book.

Human subjects and ethics

In the United States, government agencies such as the National Science Foundation (NSF) and the National Institutes of Health (NIH) require that research they fund be approved by university panels for the protection of human subjects and refuse to disburse money until these review boards have approved it. In the wake of scandals such as the death of Jessie Gelsinger, a healthy 18-year-old killed in 1999 by poorly conceived gene therapy research at the University of Pennsylvania, universities are also increasingly concerned to review the safety of human subjects in research conducted by their students or faculty (Stolberg 1999). (For an example of a human subjects tutorial and exam, see http://web.mit.edu/committees/couhes/.) While the process of human subjects review gives universities more control over research for which they may be legally liable, it can also benefit researchers, since the university effectively legitimates the research it has approved and indemnifies researchers in the event of legal action.

Many anthropologists see human subjects review boards as, at best, institutions that slow research with unnecessary red tape and, at worst, the preserve of curmudgeonly bureaucrats from other disciplines who do not understand the unique exigencies of ethnographic fieldwork. In the past, conflicts have focused in particular on consent forms. Human subjects bureaucracies like consent forms because they clarify the contract between researchers and subjects while providing tangible evidence that subjects agreed to be studied. Anthropologists often dislike consent forms, first, because their subjects may not be able to read and are often suspicious of people bearing bureaucratic paperwork and, second, because in many Third World countries (especially those with overly energetic police forces) the quickest way to lose a subject's friendship and cooperation is to ask them to sign a form saying they agree to inform on their country to a foreigner. Consequently, anthropologists are sometimes tempted to engage in research under the human subjects bureaucracy radar or to diverge from written protocols in research practice.

Readers should not infer from this that anthropologists are indifferent to the well-being of their subjects. In my experience, the opposite is true.

But, in keeping with the informality of anthropology, it is often assumed that human subjects are best protected not by inflexible bureaucratic codes but by ethnographers who think situationally about an internalized mandate to 'do no harm.' Such a perspective is affirmed by the current language in the American Anthropological Association (AAA) ethics code (http://www.aaanet.org/committees/ethics/ethcode.htm (See also Fluehr-Lobban 1998, 2003)), which states,

> [I]t is understood that the informed consent process is dynamic and continuous; the process should be initiated in the project design and continue through implementation by way of dialogue and negotiation with those studied. Researchers are responsible for identifying and complying with the various informed consent codes, laws and regulations affecting their projects. Informed consent, for the purposes of this code, does not necessarily imply or require a particular written or signed form. It is the quality of the consent, not the format, that is relevant.

The 1971 version of the AAA ethics code took a particularly strong stance against secret consulting by ethnographers. Reflecting general disapproval of anthropologists who secretly consulted for the American national security state during the Vietnam War, it said,

> 'In accordance with the Association's general position on clandestine and secret research, no reports should be provided to sponsors that are not also available to the general public and, where practicable, to the population studied ... Anthropologists should not communicate findings secretly to some and withhold them from others.'

In response to lobbying from anthropologists who consult for the private sector and are concerned about proprietary data, that language has now been watered down. The current AAA ethics code merely says that anthropologists 'must be open about the purpose(s), potential impacts, and source(s) of support for research projects with funders, colleagues, persons studied or providing information, and with relevant parties affected by the research.'

Still, even in its contemporary weakened version, the ethics code stresses the importance of obtaining the informed consent of those being studied:

> 'Anthropological researchers should obtain in advance the informed consent of persons being studied, providing information, owning or

controlling access to material being studied, or otherwise identified as having interests which might be impacted by the research.'

This is quite different from the ethics code of, say, the American Psychological Association, which allows for the routine deception of subjects in psychological experiments, provided this deception has been approved by human subjects review boards and as long as it is explained to research subjects after the completion of the experiment.

Two famous scandals in anthropology underline the ethical dangers of the ethnographic method. In 1983, Stanford University (the department in which I was trained) denied a PhD to Steven Mosher on ethical grounds. Among the concerns, he was accused of taking photographs without their consent of women undergoing abortions and of endangering research subjects who criticized China's birth control policies by not concealing their identities (Sun 1983; Turner 1983; Lee 1986). And the journalist Patrick Tierney (2000) unleashed the biggest controversy in 30 years by claiming that, in the 1960s, James Neel had exacerbated a deadly measles epidemic among the Yanomami of Venezuela through his inappropriate use of a flawed vaccine and that Napoleon Chagnon, complicit with Neel, staged fights among the Yanomami to make his documentary films more interesting, among other charges. In the confusing debate that followed, Tierney softened some of his allegations, and over time the charges against Neel began to look much weaker than those against Chagnon (Sahlins 2000; Borofsky 2005).

Such scandals aside, most anthropologists do show concern for the well-being of the human subjects with whom they work. If one listens to corridor talk among anthropologists, they tend to be concerned about protecting the confidentiality of their interlocutors and about advocating for underprivileged communities they study. Many anthropologists donate book royalties or other income to communities with whom they may have a lifelong research relationship, and they often go to special lengths to secure medical or educational help for individual interlocutors with whom they have particularly close relationships. One of my colleagues at MIT recently paid for the medical care of an ailing informant, for example, and then for his funeral.

Anthropologists who work in war-torn parts of the world also fret that their work might inadvertently facilitate government repression, the maneuvers of death squads, and so on. It is said, for example, that some anthropological work on Mayan textile patterns may have helped Guatemalan death squads identify indigenous communities for liquidation. The French anthropologist Georges Condominas was horrified to learn that the US government had (illegally) translated and distributed his ethnography of a Vietnamese people to Green Berets during the Vietnam War and that his research subjects were subsequently tortured (see Berreman 1980). There are even instances of anthropologists who have left book manuscripts unpublished out of such concerns. Ever since the AAA was torn apart in 1968 by revelations that some anthropologists were secretly consulting on counter-insurgency in Southeast Asia for the US national security state, most anthropologists have kept their distance from such agencies as the CIA, the Department of Defense, and even USAID that might be interested in their knowledge of populations around the world (Berreman 1974; Wakin 1992; Price 2000, 2004). After 9/11, some suggested that anthropologists should contribute their expertise to the war on terror by working more closely with US national security agencies, but this suggestion has been more condemned than approved within anthropology (Gusterson 2003, 2005; Wax 2003; McFate 2005; Moos 2005a,b; Price and Gusterson 2005).

As for my own research, I have had to make sure that my interlocutors understood why I was interested in talking to them. Most of them had PhDs and worked in bureaucratic contexts; they were reassured by a consent form stating that a university Institutional Review Board (IRB) had approved my research, that I was funded by a well-known foundation, and that set forth the contractual terms of our conversations. The most reassuring of these contractual terms was that I promised not to quote them by name – an easy commitment for me to make since it is conventional for anthropologists to invent pseudonyms for those they portray in their writing. The only exception I have made to this rule has been for very senior officials in the weapons bureaucracy who are often quoted in the newspaper and who give explicit permission to be quoted by name.

There were three respects in which my fieldwork relationship with human subjects was unusual for an anthropologist. First, most of the people I interviewed had top-secret clearances and I had to take special care not to jeopardize those clearances. In some cases that has meant not using information people have shared in indiscreet moments; in others it has meant taking particular care to obscure the source of information that, whether or not it is officially secret, does not usually circulate in the public sphere. Second, the antinuclear activists I studied are subjects not only of my inquiring gaze but also, often, of government surveillance. I have been acutely aware that it is difficult to draw a clear line between writing that explains the cultural logic of the antinuclear movement in ways activists themselves might appreciate and writing that might feed into the intelligence-gathering of government agencies that do not wish these activists well. I have tried to write about the symbolic and ideological systems of activists rather than about their operational procedures, though this skews my writing on this subject. Third, my commitment to fieldwork among both weapons scientists and activists – two communities deeply antagonistic to one another – poses a special burden. I have had to make sure that each community understood that I was also talking to their antagonists, but also to take care not to let either community use me as an intelligence agent against the other.

Conclusion

At the outset, I emphasized that ethnographic methods are simultaneously rigorous, informal, and improvisational. There is, obviously, a tension between these three descriptors, but I believe it is a creative one. While I have benefited enormously from reading the work on my research specialty, nuclear politics, and culture, by scholars from other disciplines, I am struck that no other research methodology enables the investigator to grapple with the lived experience of people in the way that ethnography does. Historians are confined by the documents they can find or by the decades-old memories of interviewees; psychologists only access the minds of their subjects through questionnaires or highly staged interviews; while political scientists often reify their material through the deployment, unpersuasive and metaphysical to this analyst, of assumptions about the rational calculations of human actors or the methodological separability of so-called 'dependent' and 'independent' variables. Ethnography is always in danger of lapsing into memoir or journalism at one extreme or obscuring the human beings it studies with relentless theorization at the other, but its creative stew of investigative techniques also holds the promise of a human(e) science that seeks objectivity without objectifying its subjects, that balances rigor with reflexivity, and understands that human action cannot be investigated apart from the local meanings attached to it.

Acknowledgment

My thanks for helpful feedback to Audie Klotz and the students in her graduate seminar on methods at Syracuse University. I also received valuable comments from my MIT colleagues Rufus Helmreich, Stefan Helmreich, Jean Jackson, Philip Loring, Heather Paxson, Susan Silbey, Susan Slyomovics, and Chris Walley. Special thanks to Heather and Stefan for excavating information about the Steven Mosher case and for inquiring into the archeology (or is it genealogy?) of the phrase 'deep hanging out.'

8
Process Tracing

Jeffrey T. Checkel

'This argument is too structural. It's under-determined and based on unrealistic assumptions. Moreover, it tells us little about how the world really works.' Among many scholars – the present author included – this is an oft-heard set of complaints. Consider two examples. The central thesis of the democratic peace literature – that democracies do not fight other democracies – is hailed as one of the few law-like propositions in international relations. Yet, as critics rightly stress, we know amazingly little about the mechanisms generating such peaceful relations (Rosato 2003: 585–6, *passim*; Forum 2005; Hamberg 2005). And scholars have for years debated the identity-shaping effects of European institutions. One claim is that bureaucrats 'go native' in Brussels, adopting European values at the expense of national ones. Yet, here too, critics correctly note that we know virtually nothing about the process and mechanisms underlying these potentially transformative dynamics (Checkel 2005a,b).

So, to paraphrase a former American president, 'it's the process stupid.' To invoke process is synonymous with an understanding of theories as based on causal mechanisms. To study such mechanisms, we must employ a method of process tracing. Process tracers, I argue, are well placed to move us beyond unproductive 'either/or' meta-theoretical debates to empirical applications where *both* agents and structures matter. Moreover, to capture such dynamic interactions, these scholars must be epistemologically plural – employing *both* positivist and post-positivist methodological lenses.

But realizing this epistemological–methodological promise is not easy. Proponents of process tracing should be wary of losing sight of the big picture, be aware of the method's significant data requirements, and recognize epistemological assumptions inherent in its application. To develop these arguments, I provide first the basics of a process- and mechanism-based approach to the study of international politics. The next section draws upon my own experience as an inveterate process tracer to outline how the technique works in practice. I then assess the method and, finally, conclude with several reflections on the epistemological challenges of this focus – challenges that should push process tracers to evince a new level of pluralism in their work.

Causal mechanisms and process tracing

Mechanisms operate at an analytical level below that of a more encompassing theory; they increase the theory's credibility by rendering more fine-grained explanations (Johnson 2002: 230–1). According to one widely cited definition, a mechanism is 'a set of hypotheses that could be the explanation for some social phenomenon, the explanation being in terms of interactions between individuals and other individuals, or between individuals and some social aggregate' (Hedstroem and Swedberg 1998: 25, 32–3; see also Hovi 2004). As 'recurrent processes linking specified initial conditions and a specific outcome' (Mayntz 2003: 4–5), mechanisms connect things.

For example, in a recent project on international socialization (Checkel 2005a,b), our objective was to minimize the lag between international institutions (cause) and socializing outcomes (effect) at the state or unit level. To this end, I theorized three generic social mechanisms – strategic calculation, role playing, and normative suasion – which allowed me to posit more fine-grained connections between institutions and changes in state interests and identities.

How does one then study these causal mechanisms in action? Process tracing would seem to be the answer as it identifies a causal chain that links independent and dependent variables (George and Bennett 2005: 206–7; Odell 2006: 37–8). Methodologically, process tracing provides the how-we-come-to-know nuts and bolts for mechanism-based accounts of social change. But it also directs one to trace the process in a very specific, theoretically informed way. The researcher looks for a series of theoretically predicted intermediate steps.

Conceptually, when talking of mechanisms and process tracing in this chapter, I have adopted a micro-perspective. Theoretically, this means I examine what are sometimes called 'agent-to-agent' mechanisms (George and Bennett 2005: 145). Empirically, I focus on specific decision-making dynamics (see also Hermann and Post in this book). However, this is merely a pragmatic choice, not an ontological claim.

I know this micro-level best, theoretically and empirically. Not all mechanisms need to be linked to individual decisions. Others have argued for a macro-focus in the study of causal mechanisms (Tilly 2001; Katzenstein and Sil 2005). Whether the specific lessons I offer can be scaled up to a more macro-level is a question for future research. Epistemologically, process tracing is compatible with a positivist or, to be more precise, scientific realist understanding of causation in linear terms.

In sum, process tracing means to trace the operation of the causal mechanism(s) at work in a given situation. One carefully maps the process, exploring the extent to which it coincides with prior, theoretically derived expectations about the workings of the mechanism. The data for process tracing is overwhelmingly qualitative in nature, and may include historical memoirs, expert surveys, interviews, press accounts, and documents (see Gheciu 2005a,b for an excellent application). Process tracing is strong on questions of interactions; it is much weaker at establishing structural context. Logistically, the greatest challenge is the significant amount of time and data that it requires.

In principle, process tracing is compatible with, and complementary to a range of other methods within the empiricist/positivist tradition. These include statistical techniques, analytic narratives (Bates *et al.* 1998), formal modeling (Hoffmann in this book), case studies (Klotz in this book), and content analysis (Hermann in this book). Process tracing is utilized by both empirically oriented rational-choice scholars (Schimmelfennig 2005) and conventional constructivists (Lewis 2005).

Process tracing in action: the case of European institutions

To illustrate this micro-level process tracing tool kit, I assess the causal impact of international socialization. In Europe, there are numerous tantalizing hints of such dynamics, for example, in the EU's Convention on the Future of Europe (Magnette 2004) or in the European Commission (Hooghe 2005). There are also ongoing, contentious, and unresolved policy disputes (*Economist* 2002, 2003) and academic debates (Laffan 1998; Wessels 1998) over the extent to which European institutions socialize – that is, promote preference and identity shifts. Moreover, with its thickly institutionalized regional environment and a supranational, polity-in-the-making like the EU, Europe seems a most likely case for socialization to occur (Weber 1994; Zürn and Checkel 2005).

Socialization refers to the process of inducting new actors into the norms, rules, and ways of behavior of a given community. Its end point is internalization, where the community norms and rules become taken for granted (Checkel 2005a). One way to reach this end point is via persuasion, which I define as a social process of communication that involves changing beliefs, attitudes, or behavior, in the absence of overt coercion. It entails convincing someone through argument and principled debate (Zimbardo and Leippe 1991; Perloff 1993: 14; Brody *et al.* 1996; Keohane 2001: 2, 10). To employ my earlier language, it is a social mechanism where the interactions between individuals may lead to changes in interests or even identities.

Persuasion may thus sometimes change people's minds, acting as a motor and mechanism of socialization. However, the key word is 'sometimes.' The challenge has been to articulate the scope conditions under which this is likely to happen. Deductively drawing upon insights from social psychology (Orbell *et al.* 1988) as well as Habermasian social theory, recent work suggests that persuasion (and its close conceptual relative, arguing) is more likely to change the interests of social agents and lead to internalization when: (H1) the target of the socialization attempt is in a novel and uncertain environment and thus cognitively motivated to analyze new information; (H2) the target has few prior, ingrained beliefs that are inconsistent with the socializing agency's message; (H3) the socializing agency/individual is an authoritative member of the in-group to which the target belongs or wants to belong; (H4) the socializing agency/individual does not lecture or demand, but, instead, acts out principles of serious deliberative argument; and (H5) the agency/target interaction occurs in less politicized and more insulated, in-camera settings (see Checkel 2005a for details).

This theorizing – done before I began my research – structured everything that followed. Given that persuasion was the causal mechanism whose effects I sought to explain, process tracing was the obvious methodological choice for studying it. How I studied persuasion and the kinds of data I needed to collect were dictated by these five hypotheses. Specifically, H1 and H2 required detailed knowledge of the target, his/her background, and beliefs on the subject at hand. In a similar fashion, for H3, I needed to collect data on the individual/agency doing the socializing – and especially his/her perceived status. Interviews were crucial for gathering these kinds of data; I then used secondary sources (media appearances, memoirs) as a supplement.

For H4 and H5, the data collection was more demanding as these hypotheses capture the interaction context of the attempt at socialization. In my case, this context was a series of committee meetings in an international organization. Obvious data sources would be interviews with committee members and minutes of the committee meetings. If the latter are unavailable, interviews with the secretary or administrative person in charge of the committee's operations would be a second-best proxy.

With my theory, hypotheses and ideal data sources now specified, I turn to the example: process tracing socialization dynamics in the Council of Europe as it debated issues of citizenship and nationality in the early and mid-1990s. The Council is a pan-European organization whose mandate is human rights. When it confronts a new issue, it sets up committees of experts, composed of representatives from Council member states as well as academic and policy specialists. Their mandate is to think big in an open way. In the early 1990s, two such committees were established: a Committee of Experts on National Minorities and a Committee of Experts on Nationality. If new norms were these committees' outputs, then the issue for me was the process leading to such outcomes. In particular, what role was played by persuasion?

For the committee on national minorities, there were few attempts at persuasion throughout its five-year life. Rather, committee members were content to horse-trade on the basis of fixed positions and preferences. Key in explaining this outcome was the politicization of its work at a very early stage (H5). Events in the broader public arena (the Bosnian tragedy) and within the committee led to a quick hardening of positions. These political facts greatly diminished the likelihood that the committee's formal brainstorming mandate might lead to successful acts of persuasion, where Council member states might rethink basic preferences on minority policies.

The story was quite different in the committee on nationality. Through the mid-1990s, nationality was a rather hum-drum, boring issue, especially compared with the highly emotive one of minorities. Initially, much of the committee's proceedings were taken up with mundane discussions of how and whether to streamline immigration procedures and regulations. In this technical and largely depoliticized atmosphere, brainstorming and attempts at persuasion were evident, especially in a working group of the committee. In this smaller setting, individuals freely exchanged views on the meaning of nationality in a post-national Europe. They sought to persuade and change attitudes, using the force of example, logical argumentation, and the personal self-esteem in which one persuader was held. In at least two cases, individuals did rethink their views on nationality in a fundamental way, that is, they were convinced to view the issue in a new light (Checkel 2003).

That last sentence, however, raises an important methodological issue. How does this tracing of the process allow me plausibly to assert a causal role for persuasion as a mechanism of socialization? Put more prosaically, how would I recognize persuasion if it were to walk through the door? I employed multiple data streams, consisting of interviews with committee members (five rounds spread over 5 years), confidential meeting summaries of nearly all the committee's meetings and various secondary sources, and triangulated across them (see also Pouliot 2007: 19; Dunn in this book).

In the interviews, I asked two types of questions. A first touched upon an individual's own thought processes and possibly changing preferences. A second was more intersubjective, asking the interviewee to classify his/her interaction context – a step dictated by hypotheses H4 and H5 above. I gave them four possibilities – coercion, bargaining, persuasion/arguing, and imitation – and asked for a rank ordering. Interviewees were also asked if their ranking changed over time and, if so, why (Checkel 2003).

These methodological injunctions aside, how did I really know that two individuals 'did rethink their views on nationality in a fundamental way?' How did I know these two were persuaded, and not strategically dissimulating or simply emulating others? I began with before and after interviews of the two individuals concerned – that is, interviews just as the committee started to meet and then again after one of its last sessions. I asked specific questions of their views on nationality, why they held them, if those views had changed, why they had changed, and what role(s) coercion, bargaining, persuasion, or imitation had played in the process.

Of course, one should never simply rely on what people say, so I triangulated. This meant that I cross-checked the story related by the two interviewees with other sources. The latter included interviews with other individuals who had observed the first two in action and an analysis of the committee's meeting minutes. The latter are typically not verbatim transcripts; moreover, they are highly political documents as committee members must approve their content before release. Members could – and did – have items (attributions of particular views, say) deleted from the summaries. To mitigate this (potentially huge) source of bias, I took the additional step of interviewing and getting to know the committee secretary, whose responsibility was to write up the minutes.

Collecting data in this theoretically informed way allowed me to reconstruct committee deliberations, building a plausible case that: (a) the views of the two individuals concerned had indeed changed; and (b) that persuasion (as opposed to imitation or bargaining) was the motor driving such shifts. I then further bolstered this claim – derived from my process tracing – by asking the counterfactual: absent these persuasive dynamics, would the outcome have been any different? In fact, the regional norms to emerge from the committee's deliberations were different from what otherwise would have been the case. For example, on the question of dual nationality, a long-standing prohibitionary norm was relaxed, thus making European policies more open to the possibility of individuals holding two citizenships (Council of Europe 1997, 2000).

Finally, moving outside the bounds of the case summarized above, my findings are consistent with insights drawn from laboratory experiments in social psychology on the so-called contact hypothesis (Beyers 2005) and from work on epistemic communities in IR theory (Haas 1992). Of course, ultimately, one can 'never know' as we are not privy to private thought processes. However, the step-wise, cross-checking procedure outlined here sharply bounds and minimizes the danger of erroneous inference.

Assessing process tracing: the good, the bad and the ugly

What have I learned from more than a decade of using process tracing as my method of choice? I offer 12 lessons – four good, five bad, and three ugly. The good is the value added that comes from applying the method – how it advances the state of the art methodologically, theoretically, and meta-theoretically. The bad are issues and failings of which to be aware before starting a research project with this method. The ugly stand out as 'red flags' – questions in need of attention. Addressing the latter will require process tracers to transgress both meta-theoretical (agents *and* structures) and epistemological (positivism *and* post-positivism) boundaries. In discussing the lessons within each category (good, bad, and ugly), I proceed from the practical (method) to the conceptual (theory) to the philosophical (meta-theory).

Lesson #1 (Good – Method): coming to grips with first mover advantages

Process tracing can minimize the problems of the so-called first mover advantage (Caporaso *et al.* 2003b: 27–8). If they are honest, most scholars will admit to having favorite theories. In empirical research, the tendency is first to interpret and explain the data through the lens of this favored argument. By encouraging researchers to consider alternative explanations, the positivist–empiricist tool kit has built-in checks against this first mover advantage. And process tracing can make such checks stronger. Predicting intermediate steps between independent and dependent variables essentially produces a series of mini-checks, constantly pushing the researcher to think hard about the connection (or lack there of) between expected patterns and what the data say.

Lesson #2 (Good – Method): answering 'how much data is enough?'

Process tracing makes it easier to address a question that often plagues qualitative researchers: 'When is there enough data?' My work on socialization in European institutions provides a case in point. After two rounds of interviewing, I took a break from data collection. Writing up the results – connecting the data to the causal story I was attempting to tell – allowed me to see where my data coverage was still weak. This suggested the kinds of data I would need to collect during future field work. Especially with interviews, I employed what is sometimes called a branching and building strategy, where the results of early interviews are used to restructure and refocus the types of questions asked at later points (see also Gusterson in this book).

After two more rounds of field work, I again wrote up the results, seeking 'to fill in the blanks' in my causal-process story. This time, I also circulated the draft to several colleagues. Based on their input and my own, I came to a determination that I had indeed collected enough data. More specifically, I felt that my story was now plausible in that a rigorous but fair-minded reviewer would read the analysis and say 'yeah, I see the argument; Checkel has made a case for it' (see also Dunn on establishing valid interpretations).

Lesson #3 (Good – Theory): helping to bring mechanisms back in

A very diverse set of social theorists now call for more attention to mechanisms (compare Elster 1998; Wendt 1999: ch. 2; Johnson 2006). There are good and sensible reasons for this trend. Most important, it moves us away from correlational arguments and as-if styles of reasoning toward theories that capture and explain the world as it really works. Less appreciated are the methodological implications. Simply put, if one is going to invoke the philosophy-of-science language of mechanisms, then process tracing is the logically necessary method for exploring them (see also Drezner 2006: 35).

Lesson #4 (Good – Theory): promoting bridge building

Process tracing has a central role to play in contemporary debates over theoretical bridge building (see Adler 1997). To make connections between different theoretical tool kits – rational choice and social constructivism, most prominently – scholars have advanced arguments on temporal sequencing and domains of application. Implicitly or explicitly, the method on offer is typically process tracing, as it is extremely useful for teasing out the more fine-grained distinctions and connections between alternative theoretical schools (Fearon and Wendt 2002; Caporaso *et al.* 2003a; Kelley 2004; Checkel 2005b).

Lesson #5 (Bad – Method): proxies are a pain

Process tracers often decry the unrealistic proxies that quantitative researchers employ in the construction of data sets (for example, Hug and Koenig 2000, 2002). But qualitative researchers, including process tracers, face similar problems, albeit at a different level. A central concern in my own work has been to theorize and document the causal mechanisms of socialization, such as persuasion. Did I ever actually see somebody persuaded? Did I see a decision-maker change his or her mind? No, I did not. I was not a fly on the wall, secretly observing these individuals. Participant observation was not an option. I, too, was therefore forced to rely on proxies – before and after interviews, documentary records of the meetings, and the like. At an early point, the process tracing, qualitative scholar thus needs to think hard about the conceptual variables at play in his/her project, and ask what are feasible and justifiable proxies for measuring them.

Lesson #6 (Bad – Method): it takes (lots of) time

Process tracing is time intensive and, to put it ever so delicately, 'can require enormous amounts of information' (George and Bennett 2005: 223). Researchers need to think carefully about their own financial limits and temporal constraints. My studies of socialization included five rounds of interviews spread over 5 years and a close reading of numerous documents (both public and confidential). In large part because of its methodology, the project has taken a long time to bring to fruition. While all scholars face trade offs when thinking about productivity, research endeavors, and methods, these dilemmas may be particularly acute for process tracers.

Lesson #7 (Bad – Theory): just how micro to go?

Process tracing and the study of causal mechanisms raise a difficult 'stopping point' issue. When does inquiry into such mechanisms stop? How micro should we go? In my project on socialization, I took one mechanism – socialization – and broke it into three sub-mechanisms:

strategic calculation, role playing, and persuasion (Checkel 2005a). Why stop at this point? Persuasion, for example, could be further broken down into its own sub-mechanisms, most likely various types of cognitive processes. My justification has two parts, neither of which has anything to do with process tracing. First, the state of disciplinary knowledge told me that it was a concept like socialization – and not persuasion – that was ripe for disaggregation into smaller component mechanisms (see also Alderson 2001). Second, a growing and increasingly sophisticated array of qualitative techniques (cognitive mapping, interview protocols, surveys) made it possible for me to craft reliable proxies to measure persuasion's causal effect (see also Johnston 2001, 2007).

Lesson #8 (Bad – Theory): non-parsimonious theories

Process tracing is not conducive to the development of parsimonious or generalizable theories (see also Drezner 2006: 35). In part, the reasons for this are social theoretic. As I argued earlier, process tracing is synonymous with a mechanism-based approach to theory development, which, as Elster correctly argues, is 'intermediate between laws and descriptions' (Elster 1998: 45). However, in equal part, the reasons are human and idiosyncratic. The typical process tracer is a scholar driven by empirical puzzles. He/she is happy to combine a bit of this and a bit of that, the goal being to explain more completely the outcome at hand. The end result is partial, middle-range theory (George and Bennett 2005: 7–8, 216). If one is not careful, middle-range theory can lead to over-determined and, in the worse case, 'kitchen-sink' arguments where everything matters. Early attention to research design can minimize such problems (Johnston 2005).

Lesson #9 (Bad – Theory): missing causal complexity

Like any method, process tracing abstracts from and simplifies the real world – probably less than many others, but abstract it still does. By tracing a number of intermediate steps, the method pushes a researcher to think hard about the role played or not played by a particular mechanism. Yet in many cases, the outcome observed is the result of multiple mechanisms interacting over time. Process tracing can help deal with this challenge of causal complexity, as can creative applications of agent-based modeling (Hoffmann in this book; see also Cederman 2003: 146). For instance, process tracing helped me establish when persuasion was present and when it was absent. The latter 'non-finding' then suggested a role for additional causal mechanisms, such as bargaining (Zürn and Checkel 2005: 1052–4).

Lesson #10 (Ugly – Meta-Theory): losing the big picture

In making a methodological choice to examine questions of process, it is all too easy to lose sight of broader structural context. For example, when I presented my findings on individual decision-makers and the social-psychological and institutional factors that might lead them to change their minds in light of persuasive appeals, interpretative scholars noted that I had no way – theoretically or methodologically – for figuring out what counted as a serious deliberative argument. I had just assumed it adhered to the individual, but it was equally plausible that my persuader's arguments were legitimated by the broader social discourse in which he/she was embedded. In positivist–empiricist terms, I had a potential problem of omitted variable bias, while, for interpretivists, the issue was one of missing the broader forces that enable and make possible human agency (compare Neumann and Dunn in this book).

There are two ways of responding to such a problem. One is to deny its validity, along the lines of 'Nobody can do everything; I had to start somewhere.' A second is to view such problems – and their resolution – as a chance to promote geniune epistemological and methodological pluralism within the community of process tracers, a point to which I return below.

Lesson #11 (Ugly – Meta-Theory): losing the ethics

Process tracers may be particularly prone to overlook normative-ethical context. In my collaborative project on socialization and European regional institutions, all participants adopted a mechanism-based approach, and many combined this with a process tracing method (Gheciu 2005a; Lewis 2005; Schimmelfennig 2005). Yet, while we were tracing such dynamics, we forgot to ask important normative-ethical questions. Is it legitimate and just that West Europe – through the EU, NATO, and the Council of Europe – imposes norms and rules on applicant countries from East Europe that in some cases (minority rights) are flagrantly violated by those very same West European states? What are the implications for democratic and legitimate governance if state agents acquire supranational allegiances and loyalties?

Lesson #12 (Ugly – Meta-Theory): the dreaded 'E' word

Most process tracers are empirically oriented scholars who just want to conduct research on the fascinating world around us. On the whole, this is a healthy attitude. Especially for rational-choice scholars who adopt process tracing (Schimmelfennig 2003; Kelley 2004), variable-oriented language fits well with their positivist–empiricist epistemological orient-ation. But constructivist theorists are split, with some explicitly (Wendt 1999: 82; also George and Bennett 2005: 206) or implicitly (Ruggie 1998: 94) endorsing the method, while others appear much more skeptical (Adler 2002: 109). Still others advocate a so-called bracketing strategy for capturing such dynamics (Finnemore 1996).

Yet, it is unclear if process tracing in general or bracketing as a specific strategy for implementing it are consistent with the mutual constitu-tion and recursivity at the heart of constructivist social theory (see also Pouliot 2007). Process tracing only works if you hold things constant in a series of steps: A causes B; B then causes C; C then causes D; and so on. Bracketing means, first, to hold structure constant and explore agency's causal role, and, then, to reverse the order, holding agency constant while examining structure's role. These are very linear processes. Indeed, those interpretative constructivists who do employ process tracing are careful to separate it from the discursive and narrative techniques at the heart of their approach (Hopf 2002).

To (begin to) address this state of affairs, the dreaded 'E' word must be revisited. As some have noted (Zehfuss 2002: chs 1, 6; Guzzini 2000), constructivists – and especially those who endorse methods like process tracing – do need more carefully to explicate their epistemo-logical assumptions. And such a rethink will likely require a turn to post-positivist philosophies of science.

Conclusion

After the numerous criticisms in the preceding section, readers may be surprised by my bottom line: Process tracing is a fundamentally important method – one that places theory and data in close proximity (see also Hall 2003). One quickly comes to see what works and – equally important – what does not. This said, process tracers need to think harder about the logical and philosophical bases of this mechanism-based approach. Positivism as a philosophy of science will not do the trick, given its correlational view of causation, instrumental use of theoretical concepts, and narrow methodological writ (Wight 2002).

One possible post-positivist starting point would be scientific realism, which is the 'view that the objects of scientific theories are objects that exist independently of investigators' minds and that the theoretical terms of their theories indeed refer to real objects in the world' (Chernoff 2005: 41; see also Wendt 1999: ch. 2; George and Bennett 2005: 147–8, 214). For many scientific realists, these 'real objects' are precisely the causal mechanisms of the process tracing studies highlighted in this chapter.

Scientific realism is also inherently plural in that 'no one method, or epistemology could be expected to fit all cases' (Wight 2002: 36; more generally, see Lane 1996). With such qualities, it would seem ideally placed to give process tracing conceptual grounding, and allow process tracers not just to triangulate at the level of methods, but across epistemologies as well. Indeed, my own decade-long, hands-on experience as a process tracer suggests that if we want to offer better answers to the questions we ask (Lesson #10 above), then such epistemological and methodological boundary crossing is both essential *and* possible (see also Hopf 2002; and the excellent discussion in Pouliot 2007).

Given such foundations, process tracers can then begin to ask hard questions about their community standards – standards anchored in a philosophically coherent and plural base. What counts as a good mechanism-based explanation of social change and what counts as good process tracing? How can discourse/textual and process tracing approaches be combined?

Building upon but going beyond – epistemologically – the 'process tracing best practices' advocated by Bennett and Elman (2007: 183), I would argue that good process tracing adhere to the following core maxims.

- *Philosophy*: It should be grounded, explicitly and self-consciously, in a philosophical base that is methodologically plural, such as that provided by scientific realism or other post-positivist epistemologies, including analytic eclecticism (Katzenstein and Sil 2005), pragmatism (Cochran 2002; Johnson 2006), or conventionalism (Chernoff 2002, 2005), for example.
- *Context*: It will utilize this pluralism both to reconstruct carefully causal processes and to not lose sight of broader structural–discursive–ethical context.
- *Methodology I*: It will develop and carefully justify a set of proxies that will be used to infer the presence of one or more causal mechanisms.
- *Methodology II*: It will take equifinality seriously, which means to consider the alternative paths through which the outcome of interest might have occurred.

While positivists have avoided such issues by focusing excessively on correlation and design at the expense of causation and method (King *et al.* 1994; see also Drezner 2006: 35; Johnson 2006), too many interpretivists for too long have simply sidestepped methodological questions altogether (Checkel 2006; Hopf 2007). The goal ought to be to give IR process tracers a middle-ground philosophy and epistemology that can fill the vast methodological space between positivism and post-structuralism. This chapter, the edited book of which it is a part, and other recent endeavors (Lebow and Lichbach 2007) hold out the promise of correcting this truly odd state of affairs.

Acknowledgment

For comments on earlier drafts, I am grateful to Hannah Allerdice, Petra Hejnova, Dick Price, the students of Political Science 694 at Syracuse University (Fall 2005), and, especially, Audie Klotz and Deepa Prakash.

Part III: Boundary Crossing Techniques

9
Political Personality Profiling

Jerrold M. Post

The Political Personality Profile was developed in order to provide senior policy makers with a comprehensive psychological representation of leaders in context. It describes the life course that shaped key attitudes, and specifies aspects of behavior especially relevant to policy makers dealing with leaders in summit meetings and other high-level negotiations, as well as in crisis situations. The approach asks two general questions: What were the events and experiences that helped shape the leader's personality (psychogenesis)? And what are the psychological forces within a personality that drive political behavior (psychodynamics)? We never can know for certain what drives an individual, but the more solidly we understand these foundations of the leader's psychology, the more confidently we can infer influences on – and patterns of – political behavior.

The Political Personality Profile characterizes the leader's core political personality. With its emphasis on the life course, it integrates longitudinal and cross-sectional analyses. In addition to traditional elements of clinical psychological assessment, elements of the profile include management style, negotiating style, strategic decision-making, crisis decision-making, rhetorical style, cognitive style, and leadership style. By combining them and specifying the political context in which the leader is operating, the Political Personality Profile produces a fuller picture, which identifies how the leader's core personality influences these important leadership characteristics. Another major difference is that the clinician interviews the subject directly, whereas leader assessments are developed indirectly. The interview of individuals who have met personally with the subject has been found to be extremely valuable in remedying this shortfall, and by interviewing a number of informants, one can reduce the likelihood of observer bias. In my profile of

Saddam Hussein, for instance, I was able to interview, either directly or by telephone, six former diplomats and business executives who had had personal contact with him.

The term 'personality' connotes a systematic pattern of functioning that is consistent and coherent over a range of behaviors and over time. To identify these deeply ingrained patterns, it is essential to integrate the life experiences that gave form to that political personality. But not all political situations engage the political personality, so the Political Personality Profile also seeks to identify which political issues are especially salient. The task is to identify which issues 'hook' the leader's political personality, but in so doing one must always analyze the leader in context. We must go beyond the family environment to encompass the historical, political, and cultural context as well.

Since the method I will be describing modifies the perspective of clinical psychology and psychiatry, the aspiring profiler may well ask: does this mean I have to be a psychologist or a psychiatrist to employ this method? The answer is distinctly No. I have been teaching the craft for some 35 years now, and most of the students have a background in political science and history, having taken few or no psychology courses. What is necessary is psychological mindedness. What I teach is the manner in which the life course influences the development of personality and how to draw psychological inferences from behavioral observations.

Let me give an example. A number of years ago, I was asked to develop a profile of the president of a Latin American country. In developing the psychobiographic study of the subject, his prior academic career was a rich source of psychologically relevant material. The Latin American president under my lens, during his academic career, had written extensively, and I had read all of his writings that I could get my hands on. In his major work, even his footnotes had footnotes, and there was an introductory note to one chapter, which was quite remarkable: 'The reader is advised to skip this chapter. It is dull and boring to the extreme. But for the sake of completeness, I must include it.' This punctilious concern for thorough scholarship to the point of perfectionism, even to the point of tedium, had alerted me to pursue behavioral observations that might confirm my hunch that the president had significant compulsive features in his personality. On my visit to the capital city to debrief key informants, I met one afternoon with the deputy chief of the US mission (the DCM), who had met frequently with the president under study. When I interviewed him, he was still fuming. The notoriously gridlocked traffic was particularly bad that day, and although he had left in what he thought was plenty of time for his one o'clock appointment with the president, he arrived at 1:03, by which time the agitated president had already called the embassy to complain about the DCM's lateness.

Primed by my working hypothesis that the subject of the study was probably quite compulsive, and struck by the exaggerated emphasis on punctuality in a country where time was usually treated very casually, my first question was, 'Describe his desk.' 'Interesting you would ask that,' the DCM responded. 'The president had two neat piles in front of him, which he kept straightening to ensure they were perpendicular to the desk's edge. And, in the midst of our conversation, he looked at the wall, leapt up, saying, "Excuse me, but that picture is tilted," and proceeded to straighten out a picture on the wall that was no more than a quarter of an inch out of kilter.'

The combination of punctilious scholarship, identified in the prior psychobiographic research, and the president's emphasis on punctuality and neatness suggested to me significant compulsive features in his personality, which could have important implications for negotiations. He could be expected to be conscientious and live up to his commitments. Moreover, his written words probably could be taken to reflect his dominant political goals, including the probability of nationalizing his nation's natural resources.

Most personality assessment systems attempt to assess three different dimensions: cognition, affect or feelings, and interpersonal relations. Different theorists will emphasize different dimensions, but understanding all three dimensions is important to addressing political personality. One distinction between the Political Personality Profiling method and the other profiling methods is the emphasis on psychogenesis and psychodynamics; it seeks to answer questions about both events that shape personality and psychological forces within personality that drive political behavior. The framework described is neither strictly Freudian, Jungian, Adlerian, nor Lacanian; it strives to help the policy consumer understand 'what makes this leader tick?'

In this chapter, I will first describe the manner in which a psychobiography is developed. I will then describe aspects of the personality study, emphasizing three political personality types. Two are quite common among political leaders: the compulsive personality, referred to above, and the narcissistic personality. The paranoid personality is much rarer but can be extremely dangerous when it occurs. Because of space limitations, I will only provide examples from profiles of how inferences can be drawn both from life course events and from behavioral observations.

More details on each element of constructing a Political Personality Profile can be found in the outline at the end of the chapter.

The psychobiography

The leader can be envisaged as residing within a series of fields, the cultural, historical, and political context of his country, the specific aspects of the leader's background, which shaped the individual, and the nature of the current political situation. The importance of that context cannot be overestimated. There is a profound difference in how personality will affect political behavior between a leader functioning in a collective leadership and a dictator in a closed system. The manner in which culture shapes expectations of the leader also shapes the formation and selection of the leader. The political leader who violates cultural norms will not long survive. In constructing a Political Personality Profile, the degree of constraint upon the political behavior of the leader by his role, the culture, and the nature of the political system is regularly examined.

The psychoanalytic framework of Erik Erikson (1963), which relates personality development to the cultural context, is extremely helpful as a model. It emphasizes the intimate dynamic relationship between the developing personality and the environment, and highlights the importance of the context in which the leader develops. Leader personality does not exist *in vacuo*; it is the leader *in context* that is our focus, both the context that shaped the leader's development and the contemporary context that continues to shape and influence behavior and decision-making. Thus, before even considering the particular circumstances surrounding the development of the future leader, one must understand thoroughly the culture, especially the political culture, in which the family was embedded.

The Political Personality Profile draws on the clinical case study methodology known as the anamnesis, which combines a psychobiography with a cross-sectional personality analysis. But the goal of the psychobiography developed to analyze political figures differs significantly from the analysis of the life course that psychiatrists develop to understand the traumatic events which predispose a patient to illness, for the goal is to understand how key life events have shaped the leader's personality, attitudes, and political behavior. Similarly, in the cross-sectional personality study of a political leader, the goal is not to specify dimensions of psychopathology, but rather to identify characteristic adaptive styles and those aspects of cognition, attitudes, affect, and interpersonal relations which bear on specific elements of leadership functioning.

The manner of writing the psychobiography should prepare the reader for the detailed description of the political personality and analysis of leadership to follow. The psychobiography is a collapsing and expanding profile rather than a linear and chronological depiction of life events. It may be that one sentence captures years, while the details of a key afternoon may require several pages. The primary focus is on shaping events and experiences. Early leadership successes and failures are particularly important to identify and analyze in detail, as they are often endowed by the leader with exaggerated importance in guiding the leader's future political decisions.

Sources of identity

In the psychobiographic reconstruction, particular attention is given to specifying the sources of political identity. Erikson's emphasis on the formation and vicissitudes of personal identity is especially helpful in reconstructing the lives of political leaders, for as personal identity is consolidating, so too is political identity. This requires careful research into the preceding generations. For example, the influence of King Abdullah, the grandfather of King Hussein of Jordan, was profound. A charismatic man of towering political stature, Abdullah was ashamed of his son Talal, who suffered from chronic paranoid schizophrenia, so he started shaping his grandson to the role of future king. Young Hussein was at his grandfather's side on the steps of the Al Aqsa Mosque when Abdullah was struck down by an assassin's bullet. The 15-year-old boy too was struck by a bullet, but was reportedly saved from death by the medal on his chest that his grandfather had given him earlier that day – probably a powerful determinant of Hussein's sense of destiny.

Indira Gandhi recounted in her autobiography the influence of her grandfather Motilal Nehru, Congress party leader and prominent nationalist leader, and her father Jawaharlal Nehru, prime minister of India, who continued his father's struggle for Indian independence. When her parents were away in prison, as they often were during her politically tumultuous childhood, Gandhi indicated she did not play with dolls, but rather with toy metal soldiers. At the head of the column of soldiers was one with a white shield on which there was a red cross, suggesting her identification with Joan of Arc. She marched the clumsy soldiers into a fire again and again, suggesting the early foundation of her career long bent for conflict, and perhaps presaging her assassination by her bodyguards. It is instructive to observe that she was characterized as 'the goddess of destruction' by her political opponents and was seen as a leader who regularly promoted political conflict, lacking her parents' conciliatory skills.

Key life transitions

Erikson follows the course of personality over the lifecycle, identifying the major crisis associated with each developmental epoch. Drawing on Erikson, Dan Levinson's work on the life course, *The Seasons of a Man's Life* (1978), is instructive in focusing on the three major life transitions: the Young Adult Transition, the Mid-Life Transition, and the Late Adult Transition. He emphasizes that the successful negotiation of each life transition requires successfully weathering the challenges of the previous life transition. I have developed the implications of Levinson's work for the influences of the lifecycle on the leader's political behavior (post 1980).

For example, Saddam Hussein's traumatic beginnings can be traced back to the womb. In the fourth month of his mother's pregnancy with him, his father died, probably of cancer. In the eighth month, his older brother died while undergoing surgery. His mother, understandably severely depressed, tried to abort herself of the pregnancy with Saddam and to commit suicide. She would not accept her newborn son in her arms, another sign of a grave depression. He was raised for the critical first years of life by his Uncle Khayrallah. When he was 3 years old, his mother remarried. Saddam went to her home, where his new stepfather abused him physically and psychologically. It is difficult to imagine more painful early years, which were the foundation of the wounded self, which underlay Saddam's grandiosity. I would submit that without understanding the magnitude of the traumas of Saddam's early years, it is simply impossible to understand the powerful forces within his political personality.

Childhood heroes and models are important to identify in the search for the foundation of political ambition, what Levinson has called the Dream: the crystallization of political ambition in adolescence that can serve as a lodestar. Young Anwar Sadat, for example, identified with Mohandas Gandhi and would cloak himself in a sheet, leading his goat around while on a self-imposed fast. I see this as the early foundation of his later role as peacemaker between Egypt and Israel that won him the Nobel Peace Prize.

The Dream may spur future greatness, but reactions to frustrated dreams of glory have led to intemperate acts that have been destabilizing as well. For instance, the Shah had written of his goal to transform Iran into a modernizing Middle Eastern country. When he was informed in 1973 that he was ill with a slowly developing malignancy, he accelerated dramatically the pace of his efforts. Breaking with OPEC, he quadrupled the oil revenues pouring into the country's poorly developed infrastructure. This led to a revolution of rising expectations, which destabilized the social structure, leading to profound discontent, setting the stage for Khomeini's Islamic revolution. In his rush to accomplish his dreams before he died, he superimposed his personal timetable on the political timetable.

The role of the mentor is also extremely consequential. Young Iosif Dzhugashvili (who assumed the pseudonym Stalin 20 years later), oppressed by the rigors of the Orthodox seminary in Tbilisi, rebelled by smuggling in the works of Karl Marx and Vladimir Lenin. He came to idealize Lenin through his revolutionary writings and left the seminary to serve the cause of the revolution. But the contrast between Lenin as idealized model at a distance and the personal relationship to Lenin as mentor was striking. Initially a loyal protégé, increasingly Stalin became restive under Lenin's leadership, seeking power and authority for himself, leading up to a powerful confrontation between them when Stalin was in his early 40s, the height of the mid-life transition. Lenin subsequently suffered a disabling stroke, and Stalin went on to consolidate his power.

Psychologically salient issues

It is important to distinguish between those political behaviors deriving from the leader's role and those that engage his political personality. Discriminating which issues can be considered objectively and which strike deep psychological chords is crucial. For instance, President Chiang Ching Kuo was judicious and objective in his considerations of economic policy to create the economic miracle of Taiwan. His primary political mentor was his father, Generalissimo Chiang Kai-shek, ensuring that the issue of relationships with Mainland China could never be considered with the same rational objectivity. Progress towards ameliorating that conflicted relationship would have to await his death.

The leader who cannot adapt to external realities because he is rigidly adhering to an internally programmed life script has, in the terms of Harold Lasswell (1936), displaced his private needs upon the state and rationalized it in the public good. Inevitably the gap between the private needs and the public needs becomes the source of ineffective and/or conflicted leadership.

The political personality study

The goal of cross-sectional analysis is to identify and characterize the nature of the subject's political personality. The term 'personality' implies a *patterned relationship* among cognition, affect, and interpersonal relationships. Accordingly, the concept links belief systems, value systems, attitudes, leadership style, and other features. The nature of personality puts constraints upon the range of beliefs and attitudes, and the nature of relationships with the leadership circle, including who is chosen to serve as closest advisors, all of which influence political decision-making.

As with the longitudinal analysis in psychobiographic reconstruction, careful attention is given to all of the traditional elements considered in the clinical case study. These include the following: Appearance; Level of Activity; Speech and Language; Intelligence; Knowledge; Memory; Thought Content and Delusions; Drives and Affects (such as Anxiety, Aggression, Hostility, Sexuality, Activity and Passivity, Shame and Guilt, Depression); Evaluation of Reality; Judgment; Interpersonal Relations (such as capacity for Empathy; Identity and Ambivalence); and Characteristic Ego Defenses. Additional elements particular to political leadership are examined as well, including the following: Health (energy level, working hours, drinking, use of drugs); Cognitive/Intellectual Style, and the drives for power, achievement, and affiliation. The latter are important in attempting to identify whether the leaders sought their roles in order to wield power, to be recorded on the pages of history, or merely to occupy the seat of power with the attendant place in the limelight.

Ego defenses and personality types

It is particularly important to identify the characteristic pattern of ego defenses, for it is this repetitive manner of mediating between the subject's internal and external worlds that is at the heart of personality. The identification of patterns of ego defenses is not a matter of intuition but of recognition. Well-trained clinicians reliably identify the same characteristic ego defenses, but it does not require clinical training to be sensitive to and identify these patterns.

Each particular personality type has a characteristic array of ego defenses mediating between inner drives and the external world, and each has its own cognitive, affective, and interpersonal style. In evaluating ego defenses, it is useful to discriminate a hierarchy from primitive through mature. Vaillant (1992) has identified four levels of defensive organization. The Psychotic Triad of Denial, Distortion, and Delusional Projection represent the most primitive level of psychological organization. The Immature defenses include the following: Projection, Passive Aggression, Acting Out, and Fantasy. The Neurotic (intermediate) defenses include Dissociation, Displacement, Isolation (or intellectualization), Repression, and Reaction Formation. Mature defenses include Suppression, Sublimation, and Altruism. Defenses do tend to aggregate, as exemplified by the so-called Psychotic Triad. This seriously disordered pattern is associated with paranoid psychoses and severe paranoid disorders. In contrast, the obsessive-compulsive personality pattern, which will be described in detail shortly, is associated with a much healthier array of Neurotic ego defenses.

Identifying a characteristic pattern of ego defenses is especially helpful in predicting behavior under stress, when these coping mechanisms can become exaggerated. This is particularly true in the face of serious illness and with increasing age. Thus the somewhat compulsive individual whose decision-making was unimpaired can become paralyzed by indecision, and the suspicious individual can become paranoid. Personality colors interpersonal relationships and thus can significantly distort relationships within the leadership circle. For instance, Beria was able to manipulate Stalin's paranoid tendencies to eliminate his own rivals. The fragile narcissist whose ego is intolerant of criticism may be impelled to surround himself with sycophants who can distort his appreciation of political reality.

In exaggerated form, each of these patterns can be psychologically disabling, at which time they would be considered as *personality disorders*. According to the standard psychiatric diagnostic reference, the Diagnostic and Statistical Manual of the American Psychiatric Association (DSM IV), the essential features of personality disorders are deeply ingrained, inflexible, maladaptive patterns of relating to, perceiving, and thinking about the environment and oneself that are of sufficient severity to cause either significant impairment in adaptive functioning or subjective distress. Thus they are pervasive personality traits and are exhibited in a wide range of important social and personal contexts. Since the stable pattern of defenses is also known as *character*, or the character armor (Reich 1933), personality disorders are also called character disorders.

Prominent examples of leaders with the full-blown disorders are found in the pages of history, particularly in closed societies led by dictators. Severe personality disorders are inconsistent with sustained political leadership in democracies, but, as noted above, under the stress of crisis decision-making, personality patterns can temporarily show features of a disorder. Therefore, a number of the features in the following summary descriptions of the Narcissistic, Obsessive-Compulsive, and Paranoid personalities have obvious potential relevance to the decision-making and behavior of political leaders.

The narcissistic personality and its implications for leadership

It is probably not an exaggeration to state that if narcissistic characters were stripped from the ranks of public figures, those ranks would be significantly thinned. This label covers a broad range of behaviors. At the healthiest end of the spectrum are egotistical individuals with extreme self-confidence. But primitive narcissism, so-called malignant narcissism, represents an extremely severe and dangerous personality disorder. In addition to extreme self-absorption with an associated incapacity to empathize with others, it is characterized by a paranoid outlook, absence of conscience, and willingness to use whatever aggression is necessary to accomplish personal goals (Post 1993).

The essential features of the narcissistic personality disorder are a grandiose sense of self-importance or uniqueness. This tends to be manifested as extreme self-centeredness, egocentricity, and self-absorption. There is also a preoccupation with fantasies involving unrealistic goals, such as achieving unlimited power, wealth, brilliance, beauty, or fame, leading to an exhibitionistic need for constant attention and admiration and more concern with appearance than substance. These fantasies frequently substitute for realistic activity in pursuit of success. Even when the goals are satisfied, it is usually not enough; there is a driven quality to the ambitions. Abilities and achievements tend to be unrealistically overestimated, but minor setbacks can give a sense of special unworthiness.

The interpersonal relationships of narcissists are regularly and characteristically disturbed, vacillating between the extremes of over-idealization and devaluation. There is a constant need for reassurance and an exaggerated response to criticism or defeat. Because these individuals are so self-absorbed, they fail to empathize with others, who are seen as extensions of the self, there only to supply admiration and gratification. They regularly ignore the rights and needs of others. An individual is no longer perceived as psychologically useful can be dropped suddenly. Often extremely charming, the narcissist surrounds himself with admirers and requires a constant stream of adulation from them. They expect special treatment from others, expect others to do what they want, and will be angered when people fail to live up to their unreasonable demands. There is accordingly a major inability to sustain loyal relationships over time.

A notable aspect of the narcissist in power is the manner in which this type of person seeks to gratify psychological needs through the exercise of leadership. Despite the apparent sustained devotion of their energies to socially productive endeavors, and 'selfless' rationales, the primary goal is actually to gain recognition, fame, and glory. This search for recognition and adulation springs from excessive self-absorption, intense ambition, and grandiose fantasies. But underlying and impelling this quest is an inner emptiness and uncertainty.

Kim Jong-il of the Democratic Peoples Republic of Korea demonstrates the impaired empathy of the narcissistic personality disorder. The average annual income of a North Korean is between $900 and $1000, and millions have starved in famines. Yet while Kim asks his people to sacrifice, he lives a remarkably hedonistic lifestyle in Pyongyang. According to the Hennessey Fine Spirits Corporation, in the 1990s, Kim annually spent between $650,000 and $800,000 on their most expensive cognac. Each grain of rice for 'Dear Leader' is inspected, and any with a minor defect is discarded. That he is insecure beneath his grandiose face is clear. Only about 5 feet 2 inches tall, he wears 4-inch lifts in his shoes and wears his hair in a pompadour to conceal his short stature.

The mirror image of the quest for adulation is sensitivity to slight and criticism. The narcissist is vulnerable and goes through complicated maneuvers to avoid being hurt. If the narcissist's self-concept of perfection and brilliance is to be sustained, no one can give him new knowledge, and no aspect of his understanding is to be faulted. Dogmatic certainty with no foundation of knowledge is a posture frequently struck. This profoundly inhibits acceptance of constructive criticism and leads to a tendency for the narcissistic leader to be surrounded by sycophants. The narcissist tends to devalue or even eliminate those who threaten his fragile self-esteem and, in subtle fashion, often plays one advisor off against another, to ensure that he is the major domo. This is particularly apt to stimulate the collective decision-making malady of 'groupthink.'

A vivid example is provided by Saddam Hussein, who demonstrated all of the characteristics of malignant narcissism. In 1982, when the war that he had initiated with Iran in 1980 was going very badly, he proffered a cease-fire to Iran's leader, Ayatollah Khomeini. But Khomeini said there would be no peace with Iraq until Saddam was no longer president. Saddam called a cabinet meeting and presented this dilemma. His sycophantic cabinet said in effect that 'you must stay on as president,

Saddam. Saddam is Iraq, Iraq is Saddam.' Saddam then went on to say, 'no, no, no, I want your frank, candid, and creative suggestions.' His Oxford educated minister of health Dr Ibrahim took him seriously and said, 'Well Saddam, you could withdraw from the presidency temporarily until our goal of peace is achieved, and then resume the presidency.' As the story goes, Saddam gravely thanked Ibrahim for his candor and arrested him on the spot. The minister's wife went to Saddam that night and pled with him, saying that her husband had always been loyal, and begged him to return her husband to her. The next morning he returned her husband to her in a black canvas body bag, chopped into pieces. This powerfully concentrated the attention of the remaining ministers who insisted that Saddam stay on as president of Iraq, and the war went on for another bloody 6 years.

The only central and stable belief of the narcissist is the centrality of the self. What is good for him is good for his country. It is hard to identify any consistent beliefs about the world because these tend to shift. Additionally, more than any other personality type, what the narcissist says should be viewed as calculated for effect. Accordingly, to place great weight on the analysis of core determining beliefs from speeches is apt to lead the unwary political analyst far astray, because words do not convey deeply held beliefs. Their only use is instrumental, to enhance personal position, to gain admiration and support. This attitude goes beyond 'naked' self-interest. The individual comes to believe that the national interest and national security are in fact crucially contingent upon his reelection or reappointment. For the narcissist, the problems are not threats to his country and what can be done to meet these threats but 'how can I use this situation to either preserve or enhance my own reputation?'

The obsessive-compulsive personality and its implications for leadership

The obsessive-compulsive (O-C) personality is frequently encountered in government and business executives, scientists and engineers, academic scholars and military leaders. Its strengths – organizational ability, attention to detail, emphasis on rational process – all can contribute to significant professional success. The O-C will have a sharp focus in examining the situation to get the facts but this preoccupation with details may show an inability to focus on 'the big picture.' Their everyday relationships tend to be serious, formal, and conventional, lacking charm, grace, spontaneity, and humor. There is an excessive devotion to work to the exclusion of pleasure. Wilhelm Reich (1933) described these individuals as 'living machines.'

This personality places heavy reliance on the ego defense of intellectualization, emphasizing rationality and abhorring emotionality, which implies lack of control. Individuals with the O-C disorder tend to be preoccupied with matters of rules, order, organization, efficiency, and detail. This derives from an inordinate fear of making a mistake, for the goal of the O-C personality is to leave no room for error, to achieve perfection. Efficiency and perfection are idealized but, of course, never attained. Time is regularly poorly allocated, with the most important tasks left to the last moment. Decision-making is avoided, postponed, or protracted, with characteristic indecisiveness.

Usually such individuals are excessively conscientious, moralistic, scrupulous, and judgmental of self and others. Location in the interpersonal hierarchy is of great importance to individuals with this character type, who are preoccupied with their relative status in dominant–submissive relationships. Although oppositional when subjected to the will of others, they stubbornly insist on others submitting to their way of doing things and are unaware of the resentment their behavior induces in others. Relationships are serious and formal, demonstrating a restricted ability to express warm and tender emotions. Rigidity leads them to be described as dogmatic or opinionated. Such individuals are perceived as uninfluenceable.

The preoccupation with productivity and concentration imparts a special cast to the cognitive style and lifestyle of these individuals. They are immensely productive and show impressive abilities to concentrate on their work, often cranking out huge volumes of work, especially in technical areas. But everything seems laborious, determined, tense, and deliberate; there is a quality of effortfulness, leading to the frequent characterization of them as 'driven.' But the driver for the O-C is his own harsh taskmaster. He regularly tells himself (and others) what he 'should' do; the language of 'want' is alien. While these directives are burdensome, they also provide clear guidelines for behavior. The guarded state of attention, the inability to relax, the preoccupation with 'should' are all in the service of avoiding losing control. There is a tight lid on feelings, an avoidance of impulse or whim.

This has major consequences for decision-making. The preoccupation with doing what is right places a premium on avoiding mistakes. Yet the O-C personality tends to see a world in shades of gray, characterized by complexity and subtlety. Accordingly, O-Cs often have difficulty in making clear choices and reaching closure, searching for additional evidence to ensure that they are not making a mistake. They follow the imperatives to 'act only after gathering as much information as possible' and 'preserve one's options as long as possible,' preferring procrastination to the dangers of hasty action or premature closure. This agony can be forestalled if there is a rule that can be applied. If there is no formula, however, the O-C will become quite anxious. New and unanticipated situations are particularly threatening.

The O-C will want to receive raw data, to see the minutiae about almost everything, and to become immersed in as many details as possible in a quixotic quest to somehow fully understand the issue. They have a great deal of difficulty delegating and relying upon subordinates, who, after all, might make a mistake. Crisis decision-making, where there is uncertainty or ambiguity, is especially difficult. Eventually, the O-C becomes overwhelmed and begins to think of issues in terms of data.

During an impasse in the Camp David negotiations, President Jimmy Carter made effective use of the profiles of Menachem Begin and Anwar Sadat that my unit at the CIA had prepared for him. Begin, who had been characterized as a compulsive tending to become preoccupied with details, was being intractable and refusing to compromise. Carter brilliantly exploited his understanding of Begin as an O-C personality, stating to him, 'Your excellency, President Sadat is concerned that we will become so bogged down in details that we'll lose sight of the big picture.' As reported by Carter, Begin drew himself up stiffly and responded, 'I too can focus on the big picture. We'll leave the details to our subordinates.' And they got past this impasse.

Dominated by a strong conscience, the O-C personality is a man of his word, like the Latin American leader I characterized at the start of this chapter. When he has made a commitment in negotiations, he can be relied upon, in contrast to the Narcissistic Personality, who can reverse himself as circumstances dictate. Moreover, to the extent that he has committed to writing his policy goals and preferences, these can be taken as a reliable map of intentions.

The paranoid personality and its implications for leadership

The essential features of the paranoid personality disorder are a pervasive and long-standing suspiciousness and mistrust of people in general. Individuals with this disorder are hypersensitive and easily slighted. They continually scan the environment for clues that validate their original suspicions and dismiss evidence that disconfirms their fearful views. A striking quality is pervasive rigidity. The suspicious person searches repetitively only for confirmation of danger, whereas the psychologically healthy individual can abandon suspicions when presented with convincing contradictory evidence. Attempts to reassure the paranoid or reason with him will usually provoke anger and the 'helpful one' may become the object of suspicions as well. This is because the paranoid position is restitutive, that is, designed to compensate for feelings of loss or insignificance. It is preferable to be the very center of a conspiracy than to be alone and insignificant. Theirs is a world of hidden motives and special meanings. They have a readiness to counterattack against a perceived threat, and can become excited over small matters, 'making mountains out of molehills.'

The paranoid is hyper-vigilant, ever alert to a hostile interpersonal environment and ready to retaliate. Always expecting plots and betrayal, his antennae constantly sweep the horizon for signs of threat, often generating fear and uneasiness in others. This requirement for enemies explains why paranoia is the most political of mental disorders. The only defense in such a dangerous world is to rely on no one, leading to an exaggerated emphasis on independence and autonomy. In a new situation, paranoids intensely and narrowly search for confirmation of their bias with a loss of appreciation of the total context. They usually find what they anticipated finding. Insofar as the paranoid intentionally seeks out only data which confirms his premise of external danger, and systematically excludes evidence to the contrary, his evaluation of reality is often skewed by the ego defense of Projection – the attribution to external figures of internal motivation, drives, or other feelings that are intolerable and hence repudiated in oneself.

Paranoids tend to be rigid and unwilling to compromise. Priding themselves on always being objective, unemotional, and rational, they are uncomfortable with passive, soft, sentimental, and tender feelings. They avoid intimacy except with those they absolutely trust, a minute population. The paranoid guards against losing control of his feelings. Being on guard at all times blocks spontaneity, and the absence of spontaneity clearly inhibits creative expression. There can be no humor or playfulness. Keenly aware of rank and power, superiority or inferiority, they are often jealous of and rivalrous with people in power. They avoid participating in a group setting unless they are in a dominant position. There can be no yielding to pressure or authority. The exaggerated need for autonomy has significant implications for leadership style but also affects cognitive style.

Thus the paranoid is simultaneously defending himself against external danger and against internal impulses, a burdensome and exhausting psychological war on two fronts. As internal tension builds, suspiciousness grows, and through the process of projection a *more manageable* external threat is constructed. The internal persecutor is infinite in quantity. The external enemy is finite and can be destroyed. The individual then has a state of heightened alertness, a state of continuous guardedness against the *now external* danger.

Of all the personality types, this is the one most motivated to maintain internal consistency among cognitive beliefs, often at the expense of an 'objective' examination of new information. The paranoid typically holds a very strong, rigidly entrenched belief system with a vivid and central image of the adversary. As one might suspect, the adversary is seen as inherently and pervasively evil and an incorrigible threat to one's own personal/national interest. The paranoid personality, by definition, sees the world in polarized terms, as a Manichean universe divided into two camps – allies and adversaries. Neutrals are impossible.

There is a powerful tendency to exaggerate greatly not only the hostile nature of the adversary's intentions but also the adversary's political and military skill. The paranoid personality tends to view the adversary as highly rational, highly unified, in total control of all his actions. People or nations are never compelled to do things by virtue of circumstances or by accident. War would never emerge in a crisis for inadvertent reasons. Actions are always a product of the adversary's negative qualities; war occurs because of nefarious, aggressive motivations. There is no such thing as a defensive action by the adversaries – all their actions are necessarily aggressive. One can never safely assume that the adversary's military potential is so small that it will never become a threat, even if it is not one now. The world is a conflictual place and the source of conflict is the evil nature or character of other nations or people.

Precisely because of the rigidity of these beliefs and the central importance of this image of the adversary, the paranoid's worldview is heavily biased in favor of worst-case analysis. Faced with the need to make a decision, the paranoid personality will manifest a strong tendency to act sooner rather than to procrastinate and has a strong preference for the use of force over persuasion. The paranoid may even initiate a crisis or a war out of the belief that preventive action against the adversary is necessary. The point is to alter leadership or capabilities rather than try to alter behavior. In fact, the information search pattern will be exclusively tactical in nature because the long-term objectives of the adversary are already known. A related topic of interest will be information relating to the 'enemy within' or 'fifth column activity.' The adversary is believed to be very creative and devious in this sort of covert subversion, and people of one's own country who do not fully share the views of the paranoid leader are believed to be either suspect themselves or, at best, naïve.

The paranoid will tend to adopt a management style that rests on the assumption that one cannot trust any one source of information or any one concentration of power. So to garner diverse information and, most importantly, to prevent the rise of any potential internal threats, the paranoid leader plays one advisor or one bureaucracy off against another one. They will typically not be satisfied with the analyses and conclusions of people working under them. The manipulative subordinate can take advantage of the paranoid leader's suspiciousness to plant suspicions concerning bureaucratic rivals, as did Beria with Stalin.

Conclusion

Case studies of individual leaders provide a particularly valuable longitudinal perspective that offers a framework for understanding the manner in which previous life experiences influence political behavior and for distinguishing between political behaviors, which are role dependent and those which reflect strong personality influences. The Political Personality Profile identifies enduring aspects of leader personality, including cognitive, affective, and interpersonal elements. A key aspect is the combination of psychobiographic and psychodynamic approaches in order to understand themes ingrained during adolescence, which continue to influence throughout the lifecycle. Dreams die hard, and pursuit of the dreams of glory formed during adolescence can drive a leader throughout his lifetime, having special force at the mid-life transition and during the later-years transition.

Because personality is stable over time, the longitudinal approach helps identify enduring patterns. Three important leader personality types – the Narcissist, the Obsessive-Compulsive, and the Paranoid – and their implications for political behavior have been described in order to illustrate this principle. Because these personality patterns are so deeply ingrained, they can be detected early in a political career, and can reliably be predicted to continue to affect leadership behavior throughout the political career, and become intensified with stress. When present, they permeate all aspects of political behavior, including crisis decision-making, strategic decision-making, negotiating behavior, worldview, and relationships with the leadership circle.

Having described these character types in detail, it is important to emphasize that most individuals, and most leaders, possess a broad array of characteristics that do not fit one pure type. Rather, it is the predominance of one style over another that affects outcomes. The healthy leader has personality characteristics that contribute to effective leadership, to sound decision-making, to accurately diagnosing of the environment, and to working effectively with a circle of advisors chosen for their expertise and wisdom, from whom the self-confident leader can learn and take wise counsel.

APPENDIX: FRAMEWORK FOR AN INTEGRATED POLITICAL PERSONALITY PROFILE

Part I: Psychobiography

1. Cultural and historical background – describe constraints of the political culture on the role of leader.
2. Family origins and early years

   a. Family constellation: grandparents, parents, siblings, relationships, politics of family
   b. Heroes and models.

3. Education and socialization

   a. Climate in country
   b. Student years, leadership.

4. Professional career

   a. Mentors
   b. Early career
   c. Successes and failures.

5. The subject as leader

   a. Key events
   b. Crises
   c. Key political relationships, influences.

6. Family and friends.

Part II: Personality study

1. General Personal Description

   a. Appearance and personal characteristics (lifestyle, work/personal balance, working hours, hobbies, recreation, etc.)
   b. Health (include energy level, drinking, drug use).

2. Intellectual capacity and style

   a. Intelligence
   b. Judgment
   c. Knowledge
   d. Cognitive complexity.

3. Emotional reactions

   a. Moods, mood variability
   b. Impulses and impulse control.

4. Drives and Character Structure

   a. Identify Personality Type (if possible)
   b. Psychodynamics

      i. Self-concept/self-esteem
      ii. Basic identification
      iii. Neurotic conflicts

   c. Reality (sense of/testing/adaptation to)
   d. Ego defense mechanisms
   e. Conscience and scruples
   f. Psychological drives, needs, motives (discriminate to degree possible among drive for power, drive for achievement, drive for affiliation)
   g. Motivation for seeking leadership role (to wield power, to occupy seat of power, to achieve place in history).

5. Interpersonal Relationships

   a. Identify key relationships and characterize nature of relationships

      i. Inner circle, including unofficial advisors, 'kitchen cabinet'
      ii. Superiors
      iii. Political subordinates
      iv. Political allies, domestic and international
      v. Political rivalries, international adversaries.

Part III: Worldview

1. Perceptions of political reality (include cultural influences/biases)
2. Core beliefs (include concept of leadership, power)
3. Political philosophy, ideology, goals, and policy views (domestic, foreign, and economic policy views; include discussion of which

issues most interest the leader, in which issue areas his experience lies, and which issues are particularly salient for his political psychology). Note that not all leaders have a core political philosophy or body of governing political ideas.

4. Nationalism and identification with country.

Part IV: Leadership style

1. General characteristics (include discussion of the role expectations, both general public and elite, placed on the individual emphasizing their political and cultural determinants and leader's skill in fulfilling them)

   a. How does subject define his role?
   b. Relationship with public
   c. Oratorical skill and rhetoric.

2. Strategy and tactics-goal directed behavior
3. Decision-making and decision-implementation style

   a. Strategic decision-making
   b. Crisis decision-making
   c. How does he use his staff/inner circle? Does he vet decisions or use them only for information? How collegial? Does he surround himself with sycophants or choose strong self-confident subordinates?
   d. Dealing with formal and informal negotiating style.

Part V: Outlook

1. Note particularly political behavior closely related to personality issues. Relate personality to key issues emphasizing in which direction the psychological factors point. Estimate drives, values, and characteristics that are the most influential.
2. Attempt to predict how the individual will interact with other political figures, including opposition leaders and other key foreign leaders.

10
Content Analysis

Margaret G. Hermann

Only movie stars, hit rock groups, and athletes leave more traces of their behavior in the public arena than politicians. Few of a US president's or a British prime minister's movements or statements, for example, escape the media's and archivists' notice. With 24/7 coverage and the Internet, what leaders from around the world discuss is often beamed into our televisions and put onto the Web. Through content analysis, such materials help us learn more about essentially unavailable public figures, because it does not require their cooperation. Computer-assisted software (such as Atlas.ti, Nudist, Profiler+) and the increase in Internet sources that record material from news services, television, elites' papers, and archives have improved the ease and reduced the time necessary for conducting such analysis.

Content analysis involves developing 'a set of procedures to make inferences from text' (Weber 1990: 19); it is a method 'capable of throwing light on the ways [people]... use or manipulate symbols and invest communication with meaning' (Moyser and Wagstaffe 1987: 20). A series of eight steps and a similar number of decisions need to be considered before beginning the analysis. (1) Does your research question involve extracting meaning from communications? (2) What kinds of materials are available and how accessible are they? (3) Does what you are interested in studying lend itself more to a qualitative or quantitative analysis? (4) Do you view the materials as representational or instrumental in understanding the subjects you are studying? (5) What is your unit of analysis, and what coding rules and procedures do you plan to use? (6) Can one contextualize to take into account situation, culture, and history? (7) Can others replicate your analysis? (8) Does the analysis capture what you are interested in learning about? To illustrate these types of decisions, I will show how content analysis can be used to determine leaders' responsiveness to political constraints.

Step 1: considering the research question

Does your research question involve extracting meaning from communication? I want to find out how much leaders discuss exerting control and influence over their environment and the constraints that the environment poses (as opposed to focusing on the need to be adaptable to the situation and the demands of various constituencies). For example, research shows that leaders who talk about challenging constraints are more intent on meeting a situation head-on, achieving quick resolution to an issue, being decisive, and dealing forcefully with the problem of the moment (Driver 1977; Hermann 1984; Tetlock 1991; Suedfeld 1992; Keller 2005). In effect, how political leaders talk about the constraints in their environments helps to shape their expectations, strategies, advisory systems, and the actions they urge on their governments (or other types of political units). Thus the research question involves extracting meaning from the communications of public figures. My response to the first question in contemplating doing a content analysis is 'yes.'

Step 2: selecting material

Consider the wide range of materials that are available for content analysis: books, films, pamphlets, party manifestoes, television programs, speeches, interviews, children's readers, newspapers, election commercials, blogs, diaries, letters, open-ended interviews, survey responses, cartoons. Anything that is intended to communicate a message is usable as material for content analysis. Moreover, the material does not need to involve words. Content analysis can also be used to examine nonverbal behavior (Hermann 1979; Hermann and Hermann 1990). The type(s) of relevant material generally depends on the research question.

Because of my interest in ascertaining how political leaders – in particular, heads of governments from around the world – interpret the constraints they perceive in their environments, I have focused my content analysis on their speeches, press conferences, and interviews. I have found the need to exercise some caution in using speeches since such materials often are written by speechwriters or staff members. In certain types of political systems, speeches may even be crafted by committee, reflecting the nature of the consensus that was achievable at that time.

Speeches are usually designed for particular audiences and occasions. Care and thought have generally gone into what is said and how it is said. During election periods, for example, the viewer can almost see candidates turning on their mental tape recorders as they move from place to place. In speeches, the leaders are presenting their public persona – how they would like to be perceived by the public. They are exhibiting what they believe will win votes, mobilize support for particular positions, and improve or maintain high approval ratings. Research suggests that such public statements reflect what the leader wants and is pledging to be (Winter and Stewart 1977; Winter *et al.* 1991; Winter 2005). This same research also suggests that there is a linkage between the motives expressed in speeches and how presidents engage in leadership during their time in office.

Press conferences and interviews, in contrast to speeches, are generally more spontaneous. Although there is often some prior preparation (such as consideration of what questions might be asked and, if asked, how they should be answered), leaders are on their own. During the give and take of a question and answer period, in particular, leaders must respond quickly without props or aid. What they are 'really' like can influence the nature of the response and how it is worded. The interview lets the analyst come closer to learning about the private persona of the leader – what the leader is like behind the scenes in the decision-making process. Of course, the most spontaneous interviews are those when the leader is caught in an impromptu setting, such as when leaving a meeting. Because I am interested in assessing leadership style and in learning as much as possible about the more personal side of the leader, interviews and the give-and-take in press conferences are my material of preference. (For research that explores the differences between speeches and interviews in the assessment of public figures, see Hermann 1986; Winter *et al.* 1991; Schafer 2000.)

Interviews, press conferences, and speeches of leaders are available in a wide variety of sources. Such materials for political figures located in governments outside the United States are collected in the *Foreign Broadcast Information Service Daily Report* and are reported by other governments' information agencies on their websites. Interviews with political elites who reside within the United States are often found in such newspapers as the *New York Times* and *Washington Post* as well as in weekly news magazines and on the websites for weekly television news programs. *Lexis-Nexus* provides such materials from a diverse number of news sources. Press conferences and other interviews with US presidents as well as their speeches can be found in each one's *Presidential Papers*.

Because I am interested in learning about what a political leader is like, it is particularly important in collecting speeches and interviews that I locate verbatim materials – the full text as spoken by the leader. At times, newspapers and magazines will overview or edit interviews with leaders – and even speeches – making it difficult to know how representative the material reported is. I am less interested in what the particular media outlet believes will sell newspapers or magazines than in how the leaders presented themselves. (Of course, other researchers may find that question worth pursuing, and checking what is left out and included by the media can turn into a research question amenable to content analysis.)

In the course of determining how responsive close to 200 national political leaders are to the constraints in their environments, it has become evident that the analyst can develop an adequate assessment based on 100 interview responses of 150 words or more. Any profile will suffer if it is based on less than 50 responses. (Confidence in one's profile, of course, increases with more interview responses.) To insure that responsiveness to political constraints is not context-specific, the interview responses that are analyzed should span the leader's tenure in office as well as have occurred in different types of settings and focus on a variety of topics. Collecting and categorizing interview responses by time, audience, and topic provides a means for assessing how stable what you are discovering is. Such data help the analyst know how relatively sensitive or insensitive to the context a particular leader is. With the advent of computer software (noted above) that can assist in the content analysis, it is feasible now to collect as wide a variety of machine-readable material as is available and to worry less about how much material is enough.

One question that is always raised about the use of speeches, press conference, and interviews in the study of leaders and leadership, particularly in countries outside the English-speaking world, concerns the effects of translation. Words mean different things in different languages and cultures. How can we assume that what I am considering an indication of the leader challenging constraints, for example, means the same in the United States and Uganda? One way of dealing with this issue has been to use material from such sources as the *Foreign Broadcast Information Service Daily Report* that involves native-born translators on site in the various countries whose media is being monitored. When these individuals do not know how to translate a word into English, they bracket the original word so that the reader knows the translator is unsure what the equivalent English word is.

Those of us interested in studying the characteristics of political leaders through content analysis have also run some tests having persons we have trained from other countries to do the content analysis in their original language while we do the same on the English translation. So far such tests have been conducted with documents in French, Swahili, Russian, and Mandarin Chinese. On average, the overlap in the results of the tests has been 87 per cent. Where there were differences, we have worked on considering why they were occurring, and where possible have developed rules to help minimize the so-called mistakes or added more words to our dictionaries in the case of the computer software.

Steps 3 and 4: deciding on the nature of the content analysis

After selecting the material to be analyzed, there are several decisions the researcher must make regarding what kind of content analysis to do. Does what you are interested in studying lend itself more to a qualitative or quantitative analysis? What kinds of assumptions are you making about the representational or instrumental nature of the material? The answers to these two questions are often interrelated, as I will illustrate.

Research about the degree to which leaders believe that they can influence what happens (or have a need for power) suggests whether they will challenge or respect the constraints that they perceive. Note that the focus is on 'the degree to which' leaders have 'more or less' of certain characteristics that would explain whether they are respecters or challengers of constraints. Therefore, doing a more quantitative analysis is appropriate. An assumption is made that the more frequent use by leaders of certain words and phrases in their interview responses indicates their belief that they can influence what happens (or have a need for power), the more salient such content is to them, and the more representative it is of what they are like. This answers both questions raised above. The analysis is going to be more quantitative in nature and representational in form. I presume that leaders' 'inner feelings are accurately reflected in what they say' (Holsti 1969: 32) and that frequency represents salience to the speaker.

Compare these responses to someone involved in propaganda analysis – say, examining the statements of a person like Osama bin Laden – and trying to ascertain when a particular action is likely to take place. Here the focus of attention is likely to be the 'presence or absence' of particular themes and targets. The analysis will be more qualitative in nature with an assumption being made that the interview responses or speeches being studied are instrumental in nature – that one cannot take the message at its face value but needs to examine 'what it conveys given its context and circumstances' (Holsti 1969: 32). In such an analysis, what is not said may be as important as what is said, particularly if a theme emphasized over a length of time all of a sudden disappears. Moreover, sometimes in this type of analysis, the conjunction of several themes or targets may become significant, such as when suddenly two ideas appear together that have been separated before.

Thus content analyses can range from being more qualitative to more quantitative, depending on whether the focus of attention is on the presence or absence of certain characteristics or on the degree to which the speaker exhibits the characteristics. It is, of course, possible to use numbers when a phenomenon is present versus absent but it is harder to judge the degree without the use of some quantification.

Most studies that use content analysis to assess what political leaders are like are representational in nature, because they are interested in inferring from what the leaders say something about what they are like, be it leadership style, beliefs, or motives. But the difference between considering speeches and interviews of leaders as representational versus instrumental reflects the ongoing consideration among those involved in such analysis of the distinction between public and private personas. After all, some might argue that everything a political leader says is instrumental – focused on persuading others. As Harry Truman is supposed to have said, 'I spend my day trying to persuade people to do things they should be doing anyway.' It is for this reason that I insist on examining interview responses that differ in degree of spontaneity and even in comparing the analysis of speeches to those of interviews. We know that speeches are often more planned and, thus, probably more reflective of what the leader wants others to perceive. The results from speeches can be used as a baseline against which to compare what one learns from analyzing the most spontaneous interviews, which are probably more representative of the person qua person. Analyses of things like Nixon's Watergate Tapes and Dag Hammarksjold's *Markings* (his poems written at the end of the day) suggest that the more spontaneous interview responses come close to matching the persona that is evident outside the public's view (see Schafer 2000).

Generally in the assessment of what political leaders are like, the focus is on doing a frequency analysis. The assumption is made that the more frequently leaders use certain words and phrases in their interview responses, the more salient such content is to them. There are, however, other types of content analysis that one can use, namely contingency analysis and evaluative assertion analysis.

Contingency analysis has as its focus exploring when words, phrases, or themes appear together – when one is contingent on the other. For example, in examining what types of reactions the political leaders involved in a transit strike were likely to exhibit when their stress levels were high, the author (Hermann 1977) studied the transcripts of interviews with these leaders for when indicators of stress were paired with defensive reactions suggesting denial or confrontation. Interest centered on the conjunction of the appearance of stress and what the leader did.

Evaluative assertion analysis focuses on the strength with which something is said. When a political leader talks about his administration, for instance, what kinds of adjectives does he use? His is a strong, coherent, effective administration or a problem-ridden, veto-prone, distracted administration. The adjectives can be scored according to the degree to which they are positive or negative, suggest cooperation versus conflict, indicate strength versus weakness. This type of analysis was used in the study of the leaders involved in the July 1914 crisis that led to the outbreak of World War I (Holsti 1972). Of interest was what the governments did when the leaders' perceptions of the hostility of the other parties increased.

Step 5: determining the unit of analysis and coding

Okay, decisions have been made regarding which way one wants to go on the qualitative–quantitative continuum, with reference to assumptions dealing with how representative versus instrumental the analysis will be, and about the type of content analysis. At issue next are the units of analysis one is going to use. What exactly are you going to code? In my case, I know the material will be a speech or interview, but what is it about the speech or interview that I plan to examine?

Units can range from words to phrases, sentences, paragraphs, themes, and whole documents. With an interest in discovering which political leaders challenge constraints as opposed to respect them, I want to learn when leaders take responsibility for an action – when they believe that they have some control over what happens and have a need to have influence. Thus, in examining interview responses, my focus is on verbs or action words. Assuming when leaders take responsibility for planning or initiating an action that they believe they have some control over what happens, of interest is actions proposed or taken by the leader or by a group with which the leader identifies. The content analysis therefore is centered on verbs whose subject is the leader or such a group. Do such verbs suggest that the leader is planning, initiating, or taking responsibility for an action? Or do they suggest that the leader is reacting to another's initiative, stating a fact or opinion, or commenting on what is happening? I am interested in the percentage of time the verbs in an interview response indicate that the speaker or group with whom the speaker identifies has taken responsibility for planning, initiating, or taking an action.

Consider some other ways of studying political leaders. David Winter (1992, 1995) wants to assess leaders' motivation and is interested in the stories that leaders tell in their speeches and in the kinds of themes represented in those stories. He codes for themes having to do with achievement, power, and relationships. Peter Suedfeld (1992; Suedfeld and Wallace 1995; also Young and Schafer 1998) studies how integratively complex political leaders are. He observes how leaders integrate ideas in the whole speech. Are they capable of integrating discrepant ideas in their speeches or do they tend to stop at differentiating among thoughts and objects? Suedfeld has developed a seven-point scale to rate speeches on the degree of integration of ideas that is present in what is discussed.

Note that in each of these examples, the researchers have done something to control for the length of the material; they have chosen a system of enumeration or unit of aggregation. Since speeches differ in the number of words they contain, and interviews in the number of questions asked, comparison becomes easier when these differences are taken into account. I use the percentage of time that an action verb meets the specified criteria among the number of such verbs in an interview response. That is, when the leader could have indicated a belief in being able to control events, how often did he or she? Winter determines the number of themes he finds in speeches per 1000 words. Suedfeld attaches a particular score on his seven-point integrative complexity scale to each speech.

Once the decisions are made regarding the units of analysis and enumeration, researchers are faced with designing the rules and procedures they are going to follow in drawing inferences from the materials. Let us elaborate on the example of differentiating between leaders who challenge and respect constraints.

As mentioned above, the belief that one can control what happens and a need for power seem to differentiate political leaders who challenge constraints from those who do not (McClelland 1975; Winter and Stewart 1977; Hermann 1980a; Walker 1983; Hermann and Preston

1998; Kaarbo and Hermann 1998; Keller 2005). Political leaders who are high in their belief that they can control what happens and in their need for power have been found to challenge the constraints in their environments; indeed, they generally try to push the limits of what is possible. Moreover, they are skillful both directly and behind the scenes in getting what they want. Leaders, however, who are low in these two traits appear to respect, or at the least accede to, the constraints they perceive in their environments and to work within such parameters toward their goals. Leaders who are moderate on both these traits have the ability of moving either toward challenging or toward respecting constraints, depending on the nature of the situation; they will be driven by their other characteristics, and what they believe is called for by the context.

What about a leader who is high on one trait and low to moderate on the other? Leaders who are high in the belief that they can control events but low in need for power are found to take charge of what happens and to challenge constraints, but they do not do as well in reading how to manipulate the people and setting behind the scenes to have the desired influence. Such leaders are not as successful in having an impact as those high in both the traits. They are too direct and open in their use of power, signaling others on how to react without really meaning to do so. And what about the leaders who are low in belief that they can control events but high in need for power? These individuals also challenge constraints but they feel more comfortable doing so behind the scenes, in an indirect fashion rather than out in the open. Such leaders are especially good in settings where they are the 'power behind the throne,' where they can pull the strings but are less accountable for the result.

In coding for the belief that one has some control over events, as was mentioned earlier, the focus is on verbs or action words. We assume that when leaders take responsibility for planning or initiating an action, they believe that they have some control over what happens. Consider the following response from a leader in an interview: 'I am sending our troops to the border to quell the uprising.' Compare this response to another: 'We are restrained by their actions.' In both cases, the leader or a group with whom he or she identifies is the actor, but in the first case the leader is initiating an action while in the second the leader is remarking about not being able to act. The first would be coded 'one' as indicative of a belief in being able to control what happens; the second does not reflect such a belief and would be coded 'zero.'

A score on this trait is determined by calculating the percentage of time the verbs in an interview response indicate that the speaker (or a group with whom the speaker identifies) has taken responsibility for planning or initiating an action. The overall score for any leader is the average of these percentages across the total number of interview responses being examined. This way of coding for belief in one's ability to control what happens was developed by examining the 'locus of control' measure constructed by Julian Rotter (1966; see also Lefcourt 1976) and is used extensively in the study of leadership in a variety of contexts (for a review, see Nahavandi 2003). Specifically, this set of coding rules emulates the items used by Rotter to assess an individual's internal locus of control that focused on taking the initiative and engaging in action. The items that evidenced a low internal locus of control were centered on the effects of fate, luck, chance, and the presence of constraints.

Need for power indicates a concern for establishing, maintaining, or restoring one's power or, in other words, the desire to control, influence, or have an impact on other persons or groups (Winter 1973). As with the previous trait, my coding focuses on verbs. Is the speaker proposing action that attempts to establish, maintain, or restore his or her power? Some of the conditions where need for power is scored are when the speaker (1) proposes or engages in a strong, forceful action such as an assault or attack, a verbal threat, an accusation, or a reprimand; (2) gives advice or assistance when it is not solicited; (3) attempts to regulate the behavior of another person or group; (4) tries to persuade, bribe, or argue with someone else so long as the concern is not to reach agreement or to avoid disagreement; (5) endeavors to impress or gain fame with an action; or (6) is concerned with his or her reputation or position. Once again the focus is on actions proposed or taken by the leader or a group with whom he or she identifies. A score on need for power is determined by calculating the percentage of time the verbs in an interview response indicate that the speaker or a group with whom the speaker identifies has engaged in one of these six behaviors. The overall score for any leader is the average of these percentages across the total number of interview responses coded.

Step 6: contextualizing the information

Having decided on a unit of analysis and developed a set of coding rules and procedures, it is time to consider how to contextualize the information you are collecting to account for the nuances and complexities that are part of any political phenomenon. Currently, I have information on close to 200 political leaders around the world (starting from 1945) including members of cabinets, revolutionary leaders, legislative leaders, leaders of opposition parties, and terrorist leaders in addition to heads of governments. Once a leader's interview responses have been coded and overall scores have been calculated across the interview responses, it is time for me to put the scores into perspective by comparing them with those of other leaders. Without doing such a comparison, there is little basis on which to judge if the particular leader's traits are unusually high or low or about average.

The issue is deciding what group of leaders to use as the comparison. A so-called norming group defines what is more usual – the norm – among a particular group of leaders (as opposed to more extreme or different). I am interested in whether or not a leader's scores are one standard deviation above or below the mean for the norming group, indicative of being higher or lower than the average leader in the comparison group. It is possible to break down these sets of leaders into particular regional, country, and cultural groups and compare the leader under study to a group that is close geographically and culturally.

For example, consider the scores on 'belief that one can control events' and 'need for power' for three Iranian leaders – the Ayatollah Khamenei, former President Khatami, and current President Ahmadinejad – when compared to a group of Middle Eastern leaders and one containing other Iranian leaders (Hermann 1999). Khamenei's scores (low in belief that he can control what happens and high in need for power) suggest that he will challenge constraints but do so in an indirect, behind the scenes manner. And, indeed, although Khamenei does have ultimate authority in the Iranian political system, he prefers to maintain control and maneuverability by not being 'out in front.' The former President Khatami's scores (low in belief that he can control events and low need for power) indicate a focus on respecting constraints and working within the system for change. In contrast, the current President Ahmadinejad's scores (high in belief that he can control what happens and low need for power) suggest that he challenges constraints but does so in an open and direct manner, often signaling where he is going and allowing others behind the scenes to out-maneuver him when it comes to actually wielding influence. Even though they are (or were in the case of Khatami) in positions of power in the same country, these leaders show different ways of responding to constraints that have implications for how policy will be made.

Research also suggests that while some leaders use contextual cues to determine what they do and, thus, may evidence changes in their trait scores depending on the nature of the situation, other leaders' styles are fairly stable across situations. By examining diverse material on a political leader, it is possible to determine how stable his or her leadership traits are. If there is variability in the scores, then we can determine if the differences give us insights into how political leaders adapt to the situations in which they find themselves. Selecting materials that cover a leader's tenure in office, and even before if such material is available, enables us to contextualize the profile of a leader. Computer software comes in handy, as it facilitates dividing the material in different ways and exploring how such differences affect leaders' characteristics. (In addition to Profiler + described in Young 2000, check out the Atlas.ti and Nudist programs described in Barry 1998.)

Another research question is whether leaders exhibit different styles when topics change; maybe they perceive themselves to be experts in some domains and not in others. Consider Jiang Zemin of the People's Republic of China. His scores regarding belief that one can control events differ by topic affecting, in turn, his willingness to challenge constraints. In considerations of regional politics, Jiang had a greater sense that he could control what happened than with regard to China's relations with the United States. He was willing to challenge constraints openly when the focus was on Chinese influence in the region but more likely to respect constraints when it came to dealings with the United States (Hermann 2000).

In order to examine if and how a leader's traits may differ by the substance being discussed, it is necessary to ascertain what topics are covered in the material under analysis. What the leader is talking about in each interview response that is being coded? It is generally possible to arrive at a set of categories by checking where the topics covered are similar and which topics are discussed the most. Topics that are covered only sporadically in the material are good candidates for combining into more generic categories. For instance, technological development might be collapsed into a category called economic issues. (Note the similarities with the discursive analysis in both Neumann and Dunn in this book.)

Interviews with political leaders are done in a variety of settings and, thus, are often targeted toward different audiences. Leaders often challenge constraints directly when facing their domestic public while challenging constraints more indirectly and behind the scenes when targeting leaders in other countries. Slobodan Milesovic is an interesting case (Hermann 1999). His scores suggest that as President of Serbia he generally challenged constraints domestically and regionally in an indirect manner, but when his focus was on the United States or Britain, he became more respecting of constraints and highly interested in interacting with the representatives of these countries to ascertain what would 'sell.'

To examine the effects of audience on a leader's scores, it becomes important to note who the interviewer is and where the interview is taking place. For example, in profiling a head of government, a researcher will want to record if the interview involves the domestic or international press. If the domestic press, is the interviewer closely affiliated with the particular leader, more affiliated with that leader's opposition, or neutral in orientation? If the international press, to whom is the interview likely to be reported – people in an adversary's country, an ally's country, a country whose government the leader would like to influence, or a fairly neutral source? Of interest is whether the leader's trait scores show a pattern of change across these various types of audiences.

It is also important to consider if there have been any events (such as negotiations, crises, scandals, or international agreements) that have occurred during the tenure of the leader under examination. By noting when these events happened and choosing interview responses that span these points in time, it is possible to explore whether or not the leader's scores are affected by specific types of situations. In demo-cratic societies, such an analysis might be conducted for periods before and after elections. For leaders with a long tenure in office, one might consider if there are any changes that have occurred across time with increased experience in the position or if the leader remains very much the same as when he or she began. Bill Clinton is an example (Hermann 2005; also Preston 2001; Preston and Hermann 2003).

If a researcher wants to assess mathematically whether changes in scores across time, topic, or audience are statistically significant, an analysis of variance will provide such data. Most statistical packages for personal computers have a one-way analysis of variance procedure, which can easily be applied to exploring this question. If the one-way analyses of variance (F-tests) are significant (have a probability value of 0.05 or less), then the leader's scores differ on that trait for that context factor (time, topic, audience); the leader is being adaptive in that type of situation.

Step 7: determining reliability of results

How easy is it to replicate the results of your content analysis? Can someone else using your coding rules and procedures end up with similar results to yours? There are two types of reliability that are often calculated, and in examining the leadership styles of political leaders, I have found it important to ascertain both. The first assesses how easy it is for those unfamiliar with the coding rules and procedures to learn and apply them to leaders' interview responses with the same skill as that of the author. The second examines the stability in leaders' scores. This reliability is another way of ascertaining how sensitive a leader is to the political context.

Across a number of studies (Hermann 1980a,b, 1984; Hermann and Hermann 1989), the intercoder agreement for the traits used as examples here – belief that one can control events and need for power – have ranged from 0.88 to 1.00 between a set of graduate student coders and me. Where there were disagreements, the discussions that followed with the coders led to refinements in the rules and procedures. Generally, a coder is not allowed to content analyze a leader's interview responses included in the larger norming data set until he or she achieves intercoder reliabilities with me that are 0.90 or higher. These figures suggest that the coder can do almost as well as the author of the coding system in applying the rules and procedures. With the automated coding system Profiler + now available, similar types of reliability coefficients are being calculated to determine how accurate the software is in reflecting the original intent of the author of the coding system.

By correlating a leader's scores on odd- versus even-numbered interview responses, the researcher can ascertain how stable the traits under study are across time and issues. This reliability indicates how driven the individual leader is by his or her leadership style as opposed to responding to the situation. In effect, this index provides another way of determining how open or closed the leader is to contextual information (Hermann 1980a,b, 1984).

Step 8: ascertaining validity

How well does your analysis do in helping you learn about what you are interested in studying? In other words, how valid is your content analysis? Although there are a number of ways of ascertaining validity, four types are of interest here: content, predictive, concurrent, and construct validity. Another name for content validity is face validity and it 'is usually established through the informed judgment of the investigator. Are the results plausible? Are they consistent with other information about the phenomenon being studied?' (Holsti 1969: 143). Predictive validity deals with the ability to use what has been learned from the content analytic technique to forecast or understand future events. Concurrent validity focuses on using the results. For instance, does what we learn via the content analysis about leadership style, say distinguishing between different types of leaders who exhibit particular styles, help us to differentiate among leaders whom historians and others have indicated challenged or respected constraints? Construct validity 'is concerned not only with validating the measure, but also the theory underlying the measure' (Holsti 1969: 148).

There appears to be a certain face validity to the at-a-distance assessment technique described above. It allows us to learn about what political leaders are like and to use somewhat similar procedures to those that are often employed to get at leadership style in the corporate world as well as in most counseling centers (see Nahavandi 2003). Moreover, it is possible to use what leaders say to infer certain characteristics that journalists, historians, biographers, psychologists, and political scientists have described as important to understanding political leadership. And political leaders appear to differ on these characteristics so that it is feasible to use the measures to compare and contrast the effects of leadership style not only on that person's behavior but on that of his or her government or other political unit.

A number of studies have been conducted to determine the predictive validity of the content analysis procedure described here. Generally the focus of this research has been to relate what we know about leadership style to what governments do. For example, one such study (Hermann and Hermann 1989) explored the behavior that leaders with different leadership styles urged on their governments. Among the findings were that those who challenged constraints were more likely to engage in conflictual and confrontational behavior, to take the initiative, and to commit the resources of their governments than those who respected constraints – results that were predicted from the literature exploring how leaders deal with constraints. Moreover, by comparing and contrasting the leadership styles of the various persons in positions of authority in Serbia during the Kosovo conflict, the analyst could understand why the crisis was being handled the way it was (Hermann 1999).

I have received numerous suggestions regarding how to assess the concurrent and construct validity of this methodology, ranging from running experiments with college students to participant observation in city councils. But it has always seemed important to find some means of comparing the results from the content analysis technique discussed in this chapter with the experiences of those who have interacted with heads of government and other prominent national leaders.

Thus, when given the opportunity to do such a project, I jumped at the chance to participate. In a series of studies, I developed profiles on 21 leaders from a variety of regions in the world following the rules and procedures described here and, based on these profiles, indicated on a set of rating scales the nature of the leadership behaviors the profile suggested that a particular political leader should exhibit (Hermann 1985, 1986, 1988). These ratings were compared with similar ratings made by people who had had the opportunity to observe or interact with these particular leaders.

At issue was how my results on leadership style could differentiate leaders recognized as different by journalists and former government personnel who had interacted with these leaders – concurrent validity. But it also tested the underlying logic and theory of the proposition that one could assess leadership style at-a-distance – construct validity. The correlations between the two sets of ratings averaged 0.84 across the set of 21 leaders, suggesting that the profiles derived from this at-a-distance measure furnished me with similar types of information on which to judge behavior as did the other raters' experiences with the actual figures.

Conclusion

The purpose of this chapter was to describe the steps and decisions involved in doing content analysis. I illustrated this method by using it to understand what political leaders are like. Content analysis provides us with a tool to gain some information about their beliefs, motives, and relationships with equals, subordinates, and constituents. It lets us take advantage of the fact that communication is an important part of what political leaders do. Indeed, archives are full of the speeches, press conferences, and writings of political leaders; the media seek to capture their interactions with political leaders on tape; and political leaders themselves often seek to preserve their legacies by building libraries around these materials or by donating them to universities and museums. By using materials from these various places, the technique described here is an unobtrusive measure of leadership style. And even though he or she may be shaping a communication for a specific audience or setting, we are able to take such intentions into account by varying the kinds of material we study.

Not only does content analysis make it feasible to construct a general profile of a particular leader or set of leaders but it is also makes possible placing such profiles into perspective by examining a number of contextual factors that indicate how stable the characteristics are with certain kinds of changes in the situation. We can ascertain what leaders are like in general and, then, what kinds of information they are likely to be responsive to in the political environment. Thus, the general profile indicates where a specific leader fits among his or her peers and in a broader discussion of leadership style; the contextualized profile suggests how that leader has individualized his or her responses to manifest more unique characteristics. With knowledge about both the general and the more individualized profiles, the researcher and analyst gain a more complete portrait of a leader. The person becomes not only representative of a particular type of leader, but we know when and to what degree he or she has modulated their behavior to take the context into account.

It is important to remember that in doing content analysis, one's research question should drive the choices that are made regarding how qualitative one is going to be in designing the rules and procedures to be followed during the analysis, whether or not the material will be viewed as representative or instrumental, the nature of the assumptions to be made, and the choice of units of analysis. But if exploring what leaders are like and their effect on what governments do is a part of that research question, there are a growing number of content analysis techniques available to the researcher. In addition to those discussed here, the reader should consult Jerrold Post's (2005) compendium of these techniques and consider the types of analysis that are available through the computer software program Profiler + (see socialscienceautomation.com).

11
Pragmatic Analysis

Gavan Duffy

Pragmatic analysis refers to a set of linguistic and logical tools with which analysts develop systematic accounts of discursive political interactions. They endeavor to identify the full range of inferences that a reader or a hearer would make when encountering the locutions of an author or a speaker, considered in context. Consequently, pragmatic analysis is suited to the practice of inquiry that Hall (1999: 210–16) terms 'specific history,' in which analysts reconstruct, through emplotment, historical episodes that were meaningful to historical actors before they became meaningful as objects of analysis. Analysts endeavor to recover this meaning in order to understand agents' actions and thereby to understand why events turned out the way they did rather than some other way.

The method is systematic, in the sense that any researcher may replicate the analysis of another. The method forces analysts to specify each inference explicitly. Critics who wish to dispute the substantive conclusions can point to the specific inferential steps that ostensibly misled them. This feature of pragmatic analysis focuses scholarly dispute on the source of intellectual disagreement, thereby promoting knowledge cumulation. Because it systematically examines meanings in the context of interaction, pragmatic analysis can be useful in empirically testing constructivist formulations, particularly those that theorize the role of agents in the creation of meanings, practices, structures, and institutions through their speech acts and communicative interactions.

Pragmatic analysis is a relatively new technique for analyzing political discourse. It arose from the Relatus Natural Language Understanding System, implemented by John Mallery and myself. Relatus is a collection of software tools that converts English text into a network representation in which nodes that represent concepts (or individuals) are related to other such nodes. Relatus arranges these networks in such a way that they support various inferential procedures. After parsing and representing a narrative, the model could respond to our queries in English about the narrative's context. Hurwitz (1989) applied Relatus in analysis of prisoners' dilemma game play. It was also used to induce general if-then production rules from Frank Sherman's interstate conflict event dataset, SherFACS (Unseld and Mallery 1991; Sherman *et al.* 1992; Mallery and Sherman 1993; Sherman 1994).

Despite these successes, we recognized a deficiency in Relatus that would sharply limit its social and political applicability: it could not handle figurative language. As political language is replete with metaphors and other tropes that convey meaning implicitly, beneath the surface of a text, we regarded this limitation as fundamental. We first sought guidance in the continental literature on hermeneutics, as it had long been associated with interpretive approaches to social science. We soon discovered that this literature, however suggestive, did not provide the operational guidance we needed. It speaks in vague metaphors about 'effective histories' and offers figurative language about 'the fusion of interpretive horizons' by which humans convey meanings to one another (Hurwitz *et al.* 1987). We required more specific, procedural guidance, which we found in the literature on linguistic pragmatics.

Because it concerns context-specific inferences, pragmatics does not lend itself immediately to computer automation. Conversely, because computer models lack the rich, contextual experience required for sensitive, nuanced interpretations, they do not lend themselves immediately to pragmatic analysis. Consequently, pragmatic analyses have been non-computational, pen-and-paper affairs, at least initially, and only relatively short texts have been analyzed (Duffy *et al.* 1998; Frederking 2000; Duffy and Goh 2007). Once we gain sufficient experience in making the implicit explicit, we hope to 'recomputationalize' the technique. This should allow us to analyze larger textual corpora. In the interim, however, non-computational applications are feasible, so long as texts under analysis remain manageably sized.

Below, I review step by step the procedures of pragmatic analysis. I first provide an overview of the operations of pragmatic analysis, describing each step in a typical analysis. Next, I identify the grounding of these components in linguistic and logical theory. Along the way, I will illustrate by reference to an existing analysis of a relatively brief interaction between Henry Kissinger, Mao Zedong, and Zhou En Lai (Duffy and Goh 2007). The chapter concludes with discussions of the present limits of pragmatic analysis and steps, computational and otherwise, that could be taken to extend them.

Operational overview

The flow chart in Figure 11.1 depicts the stream of operations in pragmatic analysis. I refer in the text to nodes in the figure by indicating

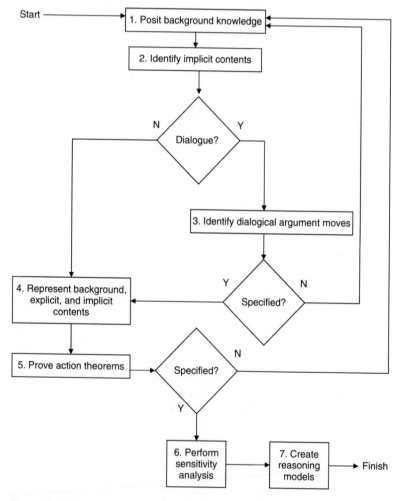

Figure 11.1 Flow chart of pragmatic analysis procedures.

the number of each within brackets. Space limitations prevent a full presentation here of the conversations between Kissinger, Mao, and Zhou, so examples will concentrate on just one utterance of Mao. Analyses of all the utterances in the conversation from which this line is drawn are available on-line at http://web.syr.edu/~gavan/pragmatic/testingsincerity-pragmatic-analysis.doc.

Pragmatic analysts first posit a set of background assumptions needed to interpret the text [1]. In hermeneutic terms, analysts specify a 'preunderstanding' necessary for interpreting the conversation. To avoid circularities in the analysis, these should be non-controversial. For instance, in modeling a conversation between Kissinger and Mao, it would be non-controversial to posit that Kissinger represents the United States and that Mao represents China, that China and the United States are states, and that states are sovereign. If the analytic interest were in modeling Kissinger's interpretation, then analysts might include propositions that are controversial, but non-controversial on (the analyst's understanding of) the mind-set of Kissinger. For example, analysts might non-controversially categorize Mao as a communist, but they might also add controversial propositions concerning the implications of communism, so long as evidence can be marshaled supporting the notion that Kissinger believed them, as we might glean from his writings.

Analysts next make their initial specification of the text's implicit contents [2]. They do so by explicitly drawing the inferences that make the text interpretable, given the background context. I should emphasize that these inferences, which I describe more fully in the section 'Linguistic Pragmatics' below, are entirely mundane. We are unused to stating them explicitly, but we all make them every time we read a text or hear someone speak. In our INF study (Duffy *et al.* 1998), for example, we made two inferences from the Soviet Union's offer during the INF negotiations to limit its missile deployment on condition that the United States cancel a planned deployment of its own: (a) that the Soviet Union wanted the United States to cancel its deployment and (b) that the Soviet Union believed that the United States wanted the Soviets to limit its deployment. In the preceding two sentences, I conveyed to you implicitly that these inferences would not prove difficult for you to draw were you to employ pragmatic analysis in your research.

If analyzing a debate or negotiation in which multiple parties are in conversation, one next conducts a dialogical argument analysis [3]. This step, described more fully in the 'Argument Analysis' section below, describes alternative moves and countermoves in the argument. Each such move or countermove is also a proposition stated explicitly in the text or inferred analytically in Step [2]. Analysts record as additional implicit contents any propositions that a party to the dialogue commits herself tacitly or is driven by her interlocutor to concede tacitly. Often, when preparing an argument analysis, the analyst discovers that additional background knowledge or additional inferences are needed in order to render the argument interpretable. In this case, the analysis returns back to Step [1].

Once the argument analysis is complete – or if there is no dialogical argument and thus no Step [3] – the analyst represents the background knowledge, the explicit contents, and the implicit contents in a semantic network representation [4]. This step, along with those that follow, we envision for computational analysis. With small corpora, we can perform these operations by hand.

Once these contents are represented, we posit an 'action theorem' – a proposition that expresses the outcome of the dialogue or the conclusion with which the author wants the reader to agree. In the INF negotiation, for instance, the action theorem was simply that the Soviets wanted to reach an agreement. Analysts then prove that theorem follows logically from the body of beliefs represented in the semantic network [5]. If unable to prove the action theorem, the analyst concludes that the model is underspecified and searches for the missing background knowledge [1] or implicit contents [2] that render the action theorem consistent with the represented beliefs.

By representing in semantic networks the background context, the explicit contents of the text, and implicit contents inferred pragmatically and in the argument analysis, we have created a model that makes explicit all the contents that had originally been implicit and left for others in the conversation to infer from the context of utterance. By making all this explicit, it becomes possible to use formal logic to derive the action theorems. Without the pragmatic analysis, I should emphasize, the logical inferencing machinery would be blind to any context-specific inferences, of which the participants were well aware, owing to the context-sensitivity of their inferences.

Once the action theorems are proven, a sensitivity analysis is performed [6]. Here, propositions are retracted sequentially from the semantic network. If the action theorem remains consistent with the body of beliefs so represented, that proposition is deemed inessential to the practical reasoning leading to the action theorem. Once the inessential propositions are eliminated the remaining propositions are used to construct a syllogism [7] that models the analyst's understanding of the reader's interpretation of the text.

Note that we do not claim to have modeled the actor's interpretation, but only our interpretation of the actor's interpretation. Others may disagree with us, claiming that one or more of our premises or inferences is incorrect. However, because we have by then explicitly identified every single analytical inference we have made – because our analysis is replicable – anyone who wishes to challenge our conclusions can point to the specific premises or inferences that putatively led us astray. In other words, pragmatic analysis is a qualitative tool that is analytically rigorous because it produces replicable models. Statistical models are rigorous in the same way. They force the analyst to specify every inference, so that criticism is focused on the source of analytical disagreement.

I will now redeem my promises to supply additional details on the identification of implicit contents [2] and the identification of argumentative moves [3].

Linguistic pragmatics

The Anglo-American tradition of linguistic pragmatics offers specific guidance concerning the inferences that readers make (and authors anticipate) as they confront a text (Gazdar 1979; Levinson 1983, 2000; Blakemore 1992; Mey 2001). Linguists generally conceive pragmatics as the level at which contextually conditional inferences are made. In other words, pragmatics concerns those aspects of meaning that context-free, truth-conditional semantics (formal logic) cannot capture. In one formulation, *pragmatics = meaning – truth conditions* (Gazdar 1979: 2). I offer here a brief account of pragmatic inference and its application.

The pragmatic facets of meaning consist of speakers' (or authors') intentions in context. Consider the utterance of a speaker (S): 'Do you know what time it is?' Two possible hearings are *reflected in*: (H1) 'Yes, I do,' and (H2) 'Yes, it is 1:30.' H1 only responds to the *narrow* meaning of the query, while H2 fully understands that S is asking for a report of the time of the day. This little example highlights the difference between sentence meaning and speaker meaning. Grice (1957) explained the distinction as a consequence of the intentionality of human communication.

Communication is intentional and is achieved by the hearer's reflexive recognition of the speaker's intention. It consists of a speaker causing a hearer to think or do something by motivating the hearer's recognition of the speaker's effort to cause that thought or action. For example, when I state that 'communication is intentional,' I seek to motivate you to recognize that I make the effort to state it because I believe it and I want you to believe it too. When earlier I promised to link pragmatic analysis to its linguistic foundations – which I am now endeavoring to do – I wanted you to recognize that I felt obligated to do so as a consequence of my promise.

Grice characterized speaker meaning as:

S meant *a* by uttering *U* if and only if:

  i. *S* intended *U* to cause some effect *a* in hearer *H*; and
 ii. *S* intended (i) to be achieved simply by *H* recognizing the intention (i).

As interaction unfolds, cooperative *speakers and hearers* convey to one another inferences about intentions that they draw from one another. By conveying and inferring intentions, these discourse partners progressively generate a body of 'mutual contextual beliefs' (Bach and Harnish 1979), a discourse context that conditions subsequent intentional conveyances and inferences. In this essay, I draw some examples from our pragmatic analysis of the February 1973 diplomatic interaction between Kissinger and Mao (with one contribution from Zhou) that appears in Table 11.1. Our analysis (Duffy and Goh 2007) teases out the intentions these discourse partners convey to and infer from one another in this conversation.

Grice's theory of meaning closely resembles Austin's (1962) and Searle's (1969) theory of speech acts, which holds that speakers intend their locutions to have illocutionary force on hearers. That is, in uttering an expression, the speaker intends to have some effect on the hearer. Assuming *uptake* (the hearer's successful recognition of the speaker's communicative intent), the utterance will have some (perlocutionary) effect on the hearer – usually but not always the effect the speaker intended. Austin and Searle each hold that, with a successful speech act, a hearer recognizes certain 'felicity conditions' of the speaker's utterances. These refer to the requisite thoughts, feelings, and intentions implicit in the speech act. A promise, for instance, carries with it an implicit claim of the speaker's sincerity. Promises are felicitous if the hearer believes the speaker's implicit sincerity claim.

Categorizations of performative verbs are useful because they group together verbs that evoke similar illocutionary and perlocutionary forces. Many have proposed categorizations. I find the Bach and Harnish (1979) taxonomy most appropriate, as it grounds itself in a plausible

Table 11.1 Interaction between Henry Kissinger (HAK), Mao Zedong (MAO), and Zhou En Lai (ZHOU) (February 1973, Beijing)

HAK:	We both face the same danger. We may have to use different methods sometimes, but for the same objectives.
MAO:	So long as the objective is the same, we would not harm you and you would not harm us. And we can work together to commonly deal with a bastard. In the West you always historically had a policy, for example, in both world wars you always began by pushing Germany to fight against Russia.
HAK:	But it is not our policy to push Russia to fight against China, because the danger to us of a war in China is as great as a war in Europe.
MAO:	***What I wanted to say is whether or not you are now pushing West Germany to make peace with Russia and then push Russia eastward.*** I suspect the whole of the West has such an idea, that is to push Russia eastward, mainly against us and also Japan. Also probably towards you, in the Pacific Ocean and the Indian Ocean.
HAK:	We did not favor this policy...
MAO:	The whole of Europe is thinking only of peace.
ZHOU:	The illusion of peace created by their leaders.
HAK:	Yes, but we will do our best to strengthen European defenses and keep our armies in Europe.
MAO:	That will be very good.
HAK:	We have no plan for any large reduction of our forces in Europe for the next 4 years.
MAO:	We should draw a horizontal line – The US-Japan-Pakistan-Iran-Turkey-and Europe.
HAK:	We have a very similar conception. There is a strong community of interest that is operating between us.
MAO:	What do you mean by community of interest? On Taiwan?
HAK:	In relation to other countries that may have intentions.
MAO:	You mean the Soviet Union?
HAK:	Yes, I mean the Soviet Union.

theoretical account of the inferential responses of hearers to speakers' utterances. Moreover, Bach and Harnish posit their taxonomy in the context of an account of speech acts that merges Grice's theory of meaning and his related theory of conversational implicature. Their most general categories are the following:

Constatives – The expression of a belief (such as assertions, denials, descriptions, attributions, suppositions).

Directives – The expression of an attitude regarding some prospective action of the hearer (such as requests, requirements, prohibitions, permissions).

Commissives – The expression of an obligation or a proposal to obligate oneself under certain conditions (such as promises, guarantees, invitations, offers).

Acknowledgements – The expression of (perfunctory or genuine) feelings toward the hearer (such as apologies, thanks, greetings, congratulations).

Bach and Harnish (1979: 53–5) include no account of felicity conditions, reflecting the then-emerging scholarly consensus that these can be subsumed wholly under Grice's (1957) theory of conversational implicature (Levinson 1983: 241). In uttering a constative, for instance, speakers express their own belief as well as their desire that the hearer form (or continue to hold) that belief.

Grice contends that speakers employ rational principles for the effective use of language in order to further their cooperative ends. This rationality allows hearers to infer contents implicit in utterances. Grice terms these inferences as 'conversational implicatures.' Hearers implicate implicit contents by relying on several maxims of conversation that jointly constitute the cooperative principle: *make your contribution such as is required, at the stage at which it occurs, by the accepted purpose of the talk exchange in which you are engaged* (Grice 1957: 47).

1. *The maxim of quality*

    i. Do not say what you believe to be false.
    ii. Do not say that for which you lack adequate evidence.

2. *The maxim of quantity*

    i. Make your contribution as informative as is required for the current purposes of the exchange.
    ii. Do not make your contribution more informative than is required.

3. *The maxim of relevance* – Make your contributions relevant.
4. *The maxim of manner*

    i. Avoid obscurity.
    ii. Avoid ambiguity.
    iii. Be brief.
    iv. Be orderly.

Conversational implicatures preserve the principle of cooperation because hearers assume that the maxims are being observed.

Speakers do sometimes fail to observe a maxim. But, unless acting irrationally, they do so with illocutionary intent. A flouted maxim signals to a reader/hearer that the speaker/author does not intend the literal meaning of the utterance. Comparing the utterance to the store of mutual contextual beliefs, the hearer tests whether the speaker intends sarcastic, ironic, metaphorical, or exaggerated meaning (Bach and Harnish 1979: 68–9). For instance, a prolix apology issued to someone who incorrectly believes herself the victim of a minor social slight, for instance, violates submaxim (iii) of the maxim of manner, to be brief. This violation allows the hearer to infer that the speaker is not apologizing at all. The discourse context usually contains sufficient clues as to the speaker's intent, because the speaker (being cooperative) expects to be understood by the hearer. In the unusual circumstance that the hearer does not hit upon the speaker's illocutionary intent, the speaker will notice (by the hearer's inappropriate response) the failure of uptake and take steps (perhaps by being more explicit) to repair the hearer's understanding of the speaker's intent.

In strategic political dialogues, participants sometimes say what they believe to be false. That is, they sometimes flout submaxim (i) of the maxim of quality for strategic purposes and not to signal non-literal communicative intent. Thus, in analyzing the talks between the United States and China, we view with some skepticism any implicatures that arise from this maxim, especially in the presence of other evidence that the participants are not communicating cooperatively. For instance, we consider Mao's statement, 'What I wanted to say is whether or not you are now pushing West Germany to make peace with Russia and then push Russia eastward,' to be an indirect speech act. We characterize it as formal locution (A) in Table 11.2. ('Formal locution' is our term for a restatement of the surface – or actually spoken – utterance to resolve pronoun antecedents and other indirect locutions.) Although it appears to be an expression of belief (constative) on the surface, Mao would have violated the maxim of relevance were he not indirectly asking Kissinger whether US policy toward West Germany was directed toward encouraging the Soviet Union's attention eastward. As an indirect question, Mao's proposition suggests reflexive intentions (C) and (D). Mao wants Kissinger to answer the question, stated explicitly in (B) and that he wants Kissinger to do so.

Implicature (G) helps to bring Mao into conformity with the maxim of relevance by noting that he asks this question because Kissinger's response to Mao's previous statement, 'But it is not our policy to push Russia to fight against China, because the danger to us of a war in China

Table 11.2   Analysis of italicized proposition in Table 11.1

What I wanted to say is whether or not you are now pushing West Germany to make peace with Russia and then push Russia eastward.

Formal locution

    A.   Is the US now pushing West Germany to make peace with the SU in order to push the SU eastward?

Indirect Speech Act: (Question, Directive)

Explicit Performative

    B.   Mao hereby asks (A).

Reflexive Intentions

    C.   Mao wants HAK to tell Mao whether the US is now pushing West Germany to make peace with the SU in order to push the SU eastward.

    D.   Mao wants HAK to tell Mao whether the US is now pushing West Germany to make peace with the SU in order to push the SU eastward at least partly because of Mao's desire (C).

Presuppositions

    E.   The US can push West Germany to make peace with the SU and then push the SU eastward.

    F.   If West Germany makes peace with the SU, the SU is free to turn its attention to its eastern front.

Implicatures

    G.   In (6), HAK failed to recognize Mao's intention in (5). *(5 and 6 refer to propositions earlier in the conversation)*

    H.   Mao believes that by pushing West Germany to make peace with the SU, the US indirectly pushes the SU eastward.

---

is as great as a war in Europe,' indicated a failure of uptake on Kissinger's part. Mao's locution, 'what I wanted to say...,' indicates that Mao found inappropriate Kissinger's response to Mao's reference to a putative Western policy in both world wars of pushing Germany eastward.

Implicature (H) concerns Mao's 'and then' locution. Ordinarily, this locution signifies a temporal interpretation. That is, a locution of the form 'x and then y' indicates that x temporally precedes y. In this case, however, in order to conform Mao's utterance to the maxim of relevance, the conjoined clauses represent a process – the United States pushes West Germany to make peace with the Soviets in order to push the Soviets eastward.

Our analysis of Mao's utterance also includes two presuppositions: (E) that the United States can perform the action about which Mao asks, and (F) that the Soviet Union can turn its attention to its eastern front. A presupposition of a statement is a proposition that must be true in order for that statement to have a truth-value. A speaker/author implicitly commits to the truth of the presuppositions simply by uttering the statement. For instance, consider Kissinger's assertion 'We did not favor this policy,' referring to Mao's contention that the United States sought to create trouble for China on its western front. Kissinger here presupposes that such a policy did exist (or was floated).

Presuppositions differ from entailments because they are constant under negation. If one negates Kissinger's statement so that it reads, 'We did favor this policy,' the inference remains. If this were an entailment, negating the statement would negate the inferred proposition. But it does not. Presuppositions are also non-cancelable without anomaly. Kissinger could not have said (without anomaly) 'We did not favor this policy, which did not exist.' If the prospective policy did not exist, then the question of whether to favor it would not have arisen. Implicatures, on the other hand, may be cancelled without anomaly (for instance, 'I promise to be truthful, but I'm insincere').

Many varieties of presupposition have been identified. Consider the factive verbs, such as 'regret': 'The Soviets regret shooting down KAL 007' presupposes that 'The Soviets shot down KAL 007.' Changes of state sometimes signal presuppositions. 'Germany ceased its bombardment' presupposes that it had been bombarding something. Levinson (1983: 179–85) reviews a number of 'presupposition triggers,' or linguistic forms that signal the presence of a presupposition. (Efforts to provide a semantic theory of presupposition have ultimately failed. The 'projection problem' presents an insurmountable obstacle to anyone interested in mechanizing presuppositional inferences and motivates a general linguistic preference for pragmatic over semantic accounts of presupposition. See Levinson 1983: 185–98.)

Although we do not use them in our example, scalar implicatures appear often enough to be mentioned here as a source of implicit content. These consist of inferences that hearers/readers make to bring speakers/authors into conformity with the maxim of quantity. There are a large variety of such scales, including <all, most, many, some, few>, <hot, warm>, <succeed in V-ing, try to V, want to V>, <n, ..., 5, 4, 3, 2, 1>, <love, like>, <always, often, sometimes>, and <necessarily p, p, possibly p>. For example, consider the scale <must, should, may>. As one replaces x with one of these modal operators in the proposition 'Iraq x withdraw from Kuwait,' then propositions with operators to the right of x are scalar implicatures of the proposition and thus count as implicit contents. So 'Iraq must withdraw from Kuwait' implicates 'Iraq should withdraw from Kuwait' and 'Iraq may withdraw from Kuwait.' Likewise, 'Iraq should withdraw from Kuwait' implicates 'Iraq may withdraw from Kuwait.' Note that we do not implicate in the other direction. 'Iraq may withdraw from Kuwait' implicates neither that it should nor that it must. It is important to remember that scalar implicatures, like all implicatures, are cancelable in context.

Deictic inferences concern the relative distances between objects in the text, as indicated by pronominal and other indexical expressions (such as here, there, now, then). Wilson (1990) analyzed deictic expressions in (the then) British Prime Minister Margaret Thatcher's speech. In addition, political actors can convey content by means of prosodic stress and intonation. If audio or video recordings are available, an analyst would be well advised to pay attention to verbal signals and gestures as additional sources of implicit content.

Argument analysis

We borrow and modify slightly Rescher's (1977) models of alternating and context-elaborating flow of argumentative dialogue. Patterned after the medieval procedures of thesis defense, Rescher has the proponent(s) of a thesis assert categorical or provisoed claims to the opponent(s), who skeptically issue(s) cautious or provisoed denials of these claims. He expresses provisos in the form P/Q, read as 'P ordinarily, if Q,' or 'if Q then, *ceteris paribus*, P.' In his notation, Rescher prefixes the categorical claims of the proponent with an exclamation point ($!$). He prefaces the cautious claims of the opponents with a dagger ($\dagger$). Table 11.3 presents a hypothetical illustration.

Table 11.3 Hypothetical illustration of Rescher's Formalism

Proposition		Proponent	Opponent
1.	P is the case.	$!P$	
2.	Please show P to be the case.		$\dagger \sim P$
3.	P is ordinarily the case when Q and I assert Q.	P/Q & $!Q$	
4.	P ordinarily isn't the case when Q and R and, for all you've shown, Q and R could be the case.		$\sim P/(Q$ & $R)$ & $\dagger(Q$ & $R)$
5.	R is ordinarily not the case when T, and I assert T.	$\sim R/T$ & $!T$	
6.	P is ordinarily not the case when U, however, and for all you've shown, U could be the case.		$\sim P/U$ & $\dagger U$

In the process of the argument, proponents accumulate commitments to particular propositions and opponents concede particular propositions. By Move 6, for instance, our hypothetical proponent is committed to propositions P, Q, $\sim R$, and T. The opponent, meanwhile, tacitly concedes Q by responding in Move 4 with $P/(Q\ \&\ R)\ \&\ \dagger(Q\ \&\ R)$ instead of $\dagger\sim Q$. Of course, the opponent may subsequently retract this concession by denying (with or without proviso) Q in later moves. As these commitments and concessions accrue, they become implicit beliefs of the proponent or opponent.

In applying Rescher's formalism to Thucydides' Melian dialogue, Alker (1988) showed it to be capable of modeling political argument. Nevertheless, some modifications of Rescher's formalism are needed. In particular, our use requires that we enable the discourse partners to shift to one another the burden of proof. In the thesis defense scenario, the proponent always bears the argumentative burden. However, because burden-shifting is a pervasive argumentative strategy in modern discourse (Gaskins 1992), we expect the burden to shift frequently across participants, especially in strategic settings. For this reason, we modify Rescher's formalism to allow either side to advance new propositions and to deny propositions advanced by their adversaries.

The argument analysis of the Kissinger – Mao conversation appears in Table 11.4. Associated with each proposition is a cognate from the speech act analysis of the dialogue (found on the webpage referenced above). In Proposition 3, Mao issues a provisoed denial ($\sim S/F\ \&\ !F$) of Kissinger's contention (S) that China and the United States share objectives on the grounds that the United States is encouraging the Soviets to attack China (F). This encouragement, Mao further contends in Proposition 4, means that China and the United States cannot maintain peaceful relations. Kissinger responds in Proposition 5 with a provisoed denial of F ($\sim F/D\ \&\ !D$). The United States would not encourage a Soviet attack on China because a Sino-Soviet war would endanger the United States.

Mao responds in Proposition 6 (the example sentence analyzed in Table 11.2) with a provisoed assertion ($F/W\ \&\ \dagger W$) that the United States is encouraging the Soviets to attack China indirectly, by pushing West Germany to make peace with the Soviets. Kissinger first responds in Proposition 7 by categorically denying ($!\sim W$) that this is US policy. He immediately supports this denial in Proposition 8, by promising (E) that the United States will maintain its forces in Europe. We interpret this as a provisoed assertion ($\sim W/E\ \&\ !E$). Note that in Proposition 9, Mao accepts this promise ('That will be very good,' he says), which we interpret as his acceptance of the provisoed assertion. Kissinger reinforces $\sim W$ in

Table 11.4 Argument analysis of the Kissinger–Mao interaction

| Kissinger | | Mao | |
Proposition	Cognate	Proposition	Cognate
1. *!S*	2g		
		2. $\sim P/\sim S$ & $\dagger \sim S$	3k
		3. $\sim S/F$ & *!F*	5g
		4. $\sim P/F$ & *!F*	3h, 5g
5. $\sim F/D$ & *!D*	6a		
		6. F/W & $\dagger W$	7h
7. *!* $\sim W$	10a		
8. $\sim W/E$ & *!E*	14k		
		9. $\sim W/E$ & *!E*	15e
10. $\sim W/M$ & *!M*	16f		
11. *!S*	19a		

S: The US and China share objectives; *P*: China can maintain peaceful relations with the US; *F*: The US is encouraging the SU to attack China; *D*: A Sino-Soviet war would be dangerous to the US; *W*: The US is pushing West Germany to make peace with the SU and push the SU eastward; *E*: The US will strengthen its European defenses and keep its armies in Europe; *M*: The US does not plan any large reduction of its forces in Europe for the next 4 years.

Proposition 10 with another provisoed assertion, ($\sim W/M$ & *!M*), which conveys that the United States plans no near-term force reductions in Europe. Then Kissinger restates in Proposition 11 the assertion with which he opened the interaction, that the United States and China share a common interest (*!S*). In the remainder of the interaction, unanalyzed here, Kissinger and Mao go on to clarify that this common interest extends only to relations with the Soviet Union, and not to the issue of Taiwan.

Due to the relative brevity of the Kissinger–Mao–Zhou interaction, we need not create computational models, derive action theorems, and perform sensitivity analyses in order to generate a practical reasoning model. We can do this by hand, as Mao's argument is relatively straightforward and simple. The propositional logic model in Table 11.5 succinctly expresses our understanding of Mao's reasoning. It supports the action theorem we posit, which denies the sincerity of Kissinger's claim that the United States and China share objectives ($\sim S$). In Step 4, from his belief that the United States is pushing West Germany to make peace with the Soviets (*W*), Mao infers that the United States (indirectly at least) is encouraging a Soviet attack on China (*A*). From this, Mao infers in Step 5 that Kissinger's overture is insincere.

Table 11.5 Model of Mao's reasoning

1.	W	premise
2.	$W \supset A$	premise
3.	$A \supset \sim S$	premise
4.	A	1,2 MP
5.	$\sim S$	3.4 MP

W: US is pushing W. Germany to make peace with the Soviet Union; A: The US is encouraging the Soviet Union to attack China; S: HAK, when claiming that the US and China share objectives, is sincere.

On this analysis, Kissinger can establish sincerity only by dissuading Mao of the validity of these inferences. He does this, first, by observing that a Sino-Soviet war would pose dangers for the United States. Shortly thereafter, he reinforces this by promising to maintain and even bolster European defenses. These steps effectively deprive Mao of the premise $W \supset A$, and thus Mao can no longer infer $\sim S$, that Kissinger's overture to the Chinese leaders is insincere. Duffy and Goh (2007) rely on this demonstration to show that these leaders in this real-world context of strategic interaction test the sincerity of other actors' utterances by assessing their consistency with those actors' interests – just as has been suggested for pragmatic analysis (Duffy *et al.* 1998) and for game analyses that integrate verbal interaction with game models.

We analyze the Mao–Zhou–Kissinger conversations in order to discover how Kissinger's plan to engineer a tripartite equilibrium between the United States, China, and the Soviet Union eventuated in what amounted to a secret alliance between the United States and China. Our analysis of this early conversation cannot address this question, but it does provide some insights into the specific history of the interaction. These raise questions that could inform our subsequent analyses of later conversations. Most importantly, did Chinese skepticism of Kissinger motivate Kissinger to offer China what amounted to a secret alliance – intelligence on Soviet troop movements, establishment of a hotline to inform China of US early warning information, and other forms of material and technical military assistance?

The scope of pragmatic analysis

Every analytic technique has a scope – a range of questions over which it can and cannot find application. Pragmatic analysis is no exception.

It is inappropriate for the practice of inquiry that Hall (1999) terms 'analytical generalization,' and should not be judged on those terms. Pragmatic analysts do not test hypotheses derived from general theoretical propositions by examining the associations of operational variables to see whether they associate as theory predicts. Neither do they conduct experiments or quasi-experiments in which they examine how different treatments (or lack of treatment) affect experimental subjects, be they individuals or polities. However widely read their views on qualitative method may be, King, Keohane, and Verba (1994) would inappropriately restrict the range of inferences appropriate for political analysis.

Although pragmatic analysis appears just as constructivism is rapidly advancing in international studies, it cannot readily receive application to all questions in the constructivist vein. As Crawford (2002) discovered, the method is simply impractical for addressing questions of world-historical scope. This limitation notwithstanding, pragmatic analysis nonetheless has utility for constructivist research projects. '[T]he minimum we should expect of any effort to test constructivist claims,' writes a prominent liberal institutionalist critic of constructivism, 'is not just the derivation of fine-grain empirical predictions...but also the utilization of methods capable of distinguishing between spurious and valid attributions of ideational causality' (Moravcsik 1999: 675). Although I prefer to speak of 'intentionality' over the clumsy 'ideational causality,' pragmatic analysis – by reconstructing the intentions of political agents – is a method capable of making such distinctions.

In the Netherlands, van Eemeren and Grootendorst (2004; van Eemeren *et al.* 1993) have developed argument analysis techniques that share some features with the method described here. Their 'pragma-dialectical approach' draws upon speech act theory to analyze argument moves and countermoves. The philosophical and theoretical underpinnings of their approach broadly cohere with those of pragmatic analysis. There are several important differences, however. For instance, van Eemeren and Grootendorst do not analyze argument commitments and concessions as in Rescher's formalism. Neither do they conduct sensitivity analyses to produce the core of arguments expressed in logical notation. Owing to their practical interest in improving the reasonableness of argumentation across a wide range of venues, van Eemeren and Grootendorst posit a normative model of reasonable argumentation and show how particular arguments have deviated from that norm. Pragmatic analysis has thus far been deployed to study the arguments of political elites. Because political elites tend to be highly educated (or at least surrounded by highly educated advisers), their arguments (with each other, at least) tend to conform to the norms of reasonable argumentation. These differences aside, anyone interested in conducting a pragmatic analysis would be well advised to examine the work of van Eemeren and his associates, as their numerous insights into argument modeling can usefully inform any such project. Close attention to this work is warranted should one wish to analyze the arguments of non-elites.

In the development of any new technique, it makes a great deal of sense to begin with relatively small, more tractable problems. Once they gain experience using the technique, developers can then scale it up to address larger problems. Pragmatic analysis can be scaled up, to some extent at least, by automating steps in the technique. The theorem-proving tasks – proving the action theorems and conducting sensitivity analyses – can readily be automated, as they are context-independent operations. Techniques for theorem proving are well known and a proto-type has already been implemented in a Relatus-like knowledge network.

Because their operations are context dependent, it will not be feasible to automate fully earlier steps in the analysis. The argument analysis step, for instance, cannot in principle be automated, as decisions regarding the propositions to select for each argumentative move depend entirely upon interpretations of the context that only humans can perform. I suppose one day these operations might be automated, but mechanizing them presumes a solution to the Artificial Intelligence problem – the provision of an artificial intelligence indistinguishable from human intelligence. Until we get there, we should stick with human intelligence.

Prospects for automation are rosier where speech act analyses are concerned. Levinson's (1983) discussion of presupposition, for instance, reviews a dispute that raged between linguists who advocated a prag-matic account of presupposition and linguists who advocated a semantic account. The semantic account proposed a context-independent theory of presupposition that was modified each time an advocate of the pragmatic account found some new context-dependent anomaly the semantic theory could not handle. In the end, Levinson casts his lot with the pragmatic account, as context-dependent counter-examples kept cropping up, no matter how many complexifications semantic advoc-ates added to their theory. However much it may have failed to offer a context-independent theory of presupposition, the semantic theory offers crucial guidance for the design of a program that would *suggest* potential presuppositions to a pragmatic analyst.

Likewise, straightforward programs could be written that would suggest speech act categories and reflexive intentions to an analyst, who could accept them or – if a speech act were indirect or if the main verb were used in an unusual sense – override them. The crucial point here is this: although the context-dependent operations of pragmatic analysis cannot in principle be fully automated, they could usefully be partially automated as a toolkit that analysts could use as they 'code' or interpret an interaction. Pragmatic analysis may never satisfy Crawford's (2002) desire for a method capable of analyzing world-historical trends over several centuries. But it is not difficult to envision scaling the method up to support analyses of larger corpora than the relatively brief exchanges we have thus far analyzed.

Conclusion

I close with a plea. Whether or not pragmatic analysis is appropriate for analyzing the substantive problems that interest you, the pragmatic theory on which it relies should interest anyone pursuing familiarity with qualitative methods. Most of these, if not all of them, involve the examination of meanings that people produce in social contexts. Pragmatic theory is our best theory of meaning in social context. As such, pragmatic theory serves for qualitative methods the same found-ational role that probability theory serves for quantitative methods. We can get along fairly well without awareness of this relationship, as pragmatic theory concerns inferences that we all make routinely as we exchange meaning-contents with others in our everyday lives. However, reflection on the nature of exchanges of meaning-contents can make us better qualitative analysts. Studying and understanding pragmatic theory – even if not explicitly practicing pragmatic analysis – yields that reflection.

12
Agent-based Modeling

Matthew J. Hoffmann

This book on qualitative methods fills a significant gap in the international relations methods literature by avoiding the attempt to create or reify orthodoxy around a particular set of methodological tools. The book also addresses a second problem with the methods literature: the lack of serious discussion of the multiple methods of qualitative analysis, including a comparison of their kind of scholarship or knowledge production. Of course, given the goals and title of this book, one has to ask, Who let in the formal modeler?

This chapter discusses a relatively peculiar method for inclusion in a book on qualitative methods: agent-based modeling (ABM). While a number of applications fall under the ABM umbrella, the unifying goal of this method is to simulate and understand processes through which macro- or social patterns emerge from the actions and interactions of agents (and their context). While well known in other social sciences (Parker *et al.* 2003; Macy and Willer 2002), ABM has only recently made inroads in international relations (Harrison 2006; Johnson 1999; Rousseau and van der Veen 2005; Majeski 2004, 2005; Simon and Starr 2000). Robert Axelrod (1984, 1997) introduced it with his prisoner dilemma tournaments; he has also simulated the growth of empires and tribute systems. Lars Erik Cederman (1997, 2001, 2003) has produced an impressive array of models that capture the emergence of nations and the distribution of wars over time. Ian Lustick (2000) and his collaborators (Lustick *et al.* 2004) have worked with cultural transmission and political identity. Recently I modeled the emergence and evolution of social norms in environmental politics (Hoffmann 2005a).

The inclusion of ABM in this book is potentially curious because most of those who use the tool would likely **not**, at first thought, consider it to be a qualitative method. Yet, its inclusion here is entirely appropriate if only because it allows us to problematize the perceived distinction between formal and qualitative methods. Yes, ABM is a formal method. It involves writing computer programs (formal algorithms) to simulate social/political behavior. Yes, ABM could technically be considered a quantitative method in that numbers are used to represent political concepts. However, beyond these surface observations we can note characteristics of ABM that confound easy classification. While the method does begin with formal algorithms, it does not deductively prove theorems or reach closed form analytic solutions, as do the more familiar formal methods like game theory. In addition, while ABM is numerical in important senses, it does not operationalize political concepts into numerical variables in order to test statistical hypotheses like econometrics.

Instead, ABM is more of a social laboratory and, depending on the model written, shares more in common with rich process tracing case studies or metaphorical analysis than it does with game theory or econometrics. If we consider that qualitative analysis aims at understanding the qualities and meanings of political relationships (while quantitative analysis aims at hypothesizing about the implications of varying quantities of political variables), then ABM is indeed a qualitative method, despite its formal and numerical characteristics.

The rest of this chapter defends the claim that ABM belongs in this book and in the toolkit of international relations. My main purpose is to introduce the general idea of ABM, along with a set of guidelines to enable someone to answer the question: Should I learn to model? I begin by providing the basic philosophy and practical steps for constructing ABM simulations. With an example from my model of social norm dynamics, I then show the method used to approach social facts usually dealt with by constructivist case study analysis. I follow this with a discussion of what kind of knowledge is produced in ABM exercises and its epistemological and practical implications (both good and bad). While the chapter does make a case for ABM as an appropriate tool for studying world politics, I do not advocate modeling in the absence of additional empirical methods.

Methodology: what is simulation modeling?

In principle, the logic of ABM is very simple. The construction of a simulation model is encompassed in four steps (see Epstein and Axtell 1996; Conte *et al.* 1997; Johnson 1999; Page 1999). The essence of ABM lies in the creation of artificial agents. These can be envisioned as individuals, organizations, or even states depending on the research question. 'Creating' an agent consists of endowing computer objects with: (a) characteristics, like age, identity, and behavioral rules, that can change from simulation to simulation; (b) the ability to perceive the environment, such as reception of information about their surroundings and/or fellow agents; and (c) a decision-making apparatus, providing the ability to take actions.

Second, the modeler defines the artificial environment within which the agents interact. This environment can be wholly social, consisting only of interaction rules that govern how agents relate to one another. The environment can also have spatial and physical (though still artificial) characteristics. Agents can be placed on grids, with each having a set location or the ability to move (Lustick 2000). Alternatively, they can be placed in a soup with no set location and random interactions with each other (Axelrod 1997; Hoffmann 2005a). Agents can be placed on a representation of an actual landscape, for instance, marrying geographic information systems (GIS) with ABM. The environment itself can be merely a place for agent interactions, or it can have characteristics of its own like resources and growth dynamics (Epstein and Axtell 1996; Hoffmann *et al.* 2002; Janssen 2002; Parker *et al.* 2003).

The third step is simulating histories in this artificial world. The modeler initializes the agents and environment with a set of conditions and then lets the agents (or agents and environment) interact for a specified amount of time. These simulations are usually calculated in rounds of actions taken by the agents or time-steps that may or may not be analogous to real-world time steps. As the simulation history progresses, data are gathered.

Finally, the modeler analyzes the history through visual (graphic) or statistical means. This analysis is done to ascertain what happened in the simulation, that is, how the initial micro-parameters correspond with the emergent macro-parameters, and/or how the simulation history matches empirical observations. In this stage there are significant concerns with validation, both internal and external. (For more on this much debated topic, see Oreskes *et al.* 1994; Casti 1997; Parker *et al.* 2003.)

The key to ABM is its flexibility. It is possible to endow the agents and environment with almost any kind of attributes, decision-making rules, and interactions imaginable. For instance, agents can be heterogeneous and adaptive, rather than homogeneous and rational. (ABM can accommodate game theoretic and rational choice analysis, making game theory a special case of ABM, where closed form solutions are possible.)

No longer does a commitment to non-rational behavioral models or process-oriented theorizing require eschewing formal analysis. ABM's adaptive agents are often designed with limited computational ability, and its artificial environments are worlds of less than complete information (in the rational choice sense of completeness), which many theorists claim is a more accurate representation of reality than calculating the optimal course of action based on (often) full information of all alternatives. These adaptive agents 'rely on heuristics or rules of thumb' that are learned over time, through experience (Kollman *et al.* 1997: 465). In addition, they 'inhabit a world that they must cognitively interpret – one that is complicated by the presence and actions of other agents and that is ever changing'; they 'generally do not optimize in the standard sense...because the very concept of an optimal course of action often cannot be defined' (Arthur *et al.* 1997: 5).

This type of analysis defies easy classification. The deductive or formal aspect is the *a priori* designation of what actors look like and how they behave. The modeler creates agents as well as a context of interaction. As the goal is to understand some macro- or social phenomenon, the initial designation of characteristics or rules is essentially a hypothesis or conjecture about how micro-characteristics are related to macro-phenomena through a specified process. I consider the initialization as akin to 'cutting-in' to a dynamic process at a specific point to begin analysis with process tracing case studies.

Yet ABM is not solely a deductive approach. Once the rules and characteristics are initialized, the modeler simulates histories of the population of agents and their interactions, varying parameters of interest. Analyzing the results entails an inductive assessment of the simulated histories. Axelrod (1997) calls it a third way of doing science that is both deductive and inductive. Epstein and Axtell view the simulations as '*laboratories*, where we attempt to "grow" certain social structures in the computer – or *in silico* – the aim being to discover fundamental local or micro mechanisms that are sufficient to *generate* the macroscopic social structures and collective behaviors of interest' (1996: 4).

ABM's flexibility opens up possibilities for formalizing approaches to social life that have heretofore distanced themselves from rational choice. Applied to theories that highlight the importance of ideas, language, and interpretation, ABM can bring together classic qualitative approaches, like those represented in this book, with formal theory. To demonstrate this potential, I briefly discuss my application of ABM to social norms, which draws on the constructivist IR literature (Hoffmann 2005a,b).

A modeling example – the norm life cycle

Finnemore and Sikkink's (1998) norm life cycle provides a set of conjectures about norms in a society, including how they constitute agents, and how they emerge and evolve. Their framework essentially comprises a verbal model of norm dynamics. I model this more formally by (Step 1) endowing artificial agents with behavioral characteristics and (Step 2) setting up interaction rules, along the lines suggested by ideas of mutual constitution. I then (Step 3) let the agents interact creating simulated histories of norm dynamics, under varying conditions, and (Step 4) analyze the results to see what emerges. As I will discuss in greater detail below, this is a heuristic model designed to apprehend some generic features of the emergence and evolution of norms.

Agents in some constructivist theorizing are conceived of as striving to behave appropriately. Appropriateness is defined by the agents' social context. This context, in turn, is constructed by the behaviors and interactions of the agents. Norms are ideas about appropriate behavior that are intersubjectively held within a population. According the Finnemore and Sikkink (1998), this norm life cycle encompasses four stages. First, a norm entrepreneur makes a suggestion to a population about a new way to conceive of appropriate behavior. When a 'critical mass' of actors have accepted the new idea, we can say a norm has emerged. In the third stage, there is a cascade of acceptance as the norm spreads from the critical mass to the whole population. Finally, after use and reification, the norm is internalized and becomes taken for granted.

I constructed a model to formalize this norm life cycle. It simulates 10 agents, an arbitrary but manageable number. Each are driven by the desire to match their individual behavior to that of the group, that is, to act appropriately. Their behavior is very simple. In each round of the simulation, agents pick a number between 0 and 100, an arbitrary range that provides significant room for variation in behavior. Their goal is to match this pick with the group outcome, which I have defined to be the average (arithmetic mean) of the choices from the entire group.

Many constructivists envision actors to be rule-driven agents, so my agents make their predictions with a universe of seven (very) simple rules. The rules drive the agents to pick numbers from bounded sets of numbers. The actual choice of number is drawn from a uniform distribution of integers within the specified boundaries: Rule 1, 0–10; Rule 2, 15–25; Rule 3, 30–40; Rule 4, 45–55; Rule 5, 60–70; Rule 6, 75–85; Rule 7, 90–100. In essence, the rule provides a broad sense of what an agent thinks is an appropriate behavior (or number, in the simulation), and the agent picks a specific number from within that broad sense.

Initially each agent is randomly assigned three of these prediction rules (without repeats) in order to insure diversity in the population of agents. These initial conditions can be considered in two ways. One could begin in a state-of-nature, with a few hardwired rules with which agents approach social interaction. I prefer to view the initial rule assignments as akin to 'cutting in' to a dynamic process at a specific point in time, when the rule distribution looks as it does. Because I am not attempting to simulate a specific political situation or norm, the initial distribution of agent attributes is less significant than it is for empirical analysis, when it is necessary to understand how actors came to be socialized as they are when you begin to study them (the importance of which is highlighted in both the Leander and Checkel contributions to this book).

In line with at least some constructivist thought, these are reflective agents – they do not blindly follow the social context but actively consider what behavior is appropriate. Each agent uses one of its three rules – the public rule – to make the prediction that is sent to the entire group, while privately making predictions with the other two rules. The public rule generates the prediction to which the whole group of agents has access. Each agent determines which rule is public by keeping track of scores for the rules in its repertoire. Starting with a baseline of 100, each score rises and falls depending on how close its predictions have been to the group outcome. The rule with the highest current score is the public rule.

In order to judge satisfaction with their rules, the agents evaluate the behavior produced by the public rule as well as the potential behavior of their other two private rules. Once the group outcome is known, agents compare their three predictions (one public, two private) with that outcome. They reward or penalize their rules depending on the closeness of the prediction. In this model, 'close enough' is governed by a parameter called precision, set (in most runs) at 5 per cent. This means that rules which predict the group outcome within +/− 5 are rewarded (+1) and others are punished (−1). A private rule becomes public when its score exceeds that of the current public rule. To facilitate adaptation and change over time, each agent discards a poorly performing rule at set intervals (10–20 rounds) and is randomly assigned a new rule from the universe of rules. The new rule starts with a fresh score of 100. Such shuffling of rules could be conceived of as domestic change within a state or shift within an international organization.

The agents' social context is limited in this simple model; they only perceive the group outcome. This characteristic is designed to mimic the limited sociality of world politics. It should be noted that the model does not explicitly simulate how agents obtain an understanding of their social environment (such as through communication and other social activities). Instead, it focuses exclusively on what happens once agents have a picture of their social environment. This choice allows me to concentrate on how an entrepreneur can catalyze norm emergence and change, the major mechanism in the norm life cycle.

The catch is that while the true outcome is exactly the average of the predictions from the population, the outcome that each agent perceives is obscured by noise (a random draw from a uniform distribution bounded by zero and the specified maximum noise level). Noise can be thought of in two ways. First, it could be simulating a lack of information or uncertainty. Second, it could be conceived as representing the complexity of the social environment – the higher the noise levels, the less clear agents are on what the appropriate group outcome should be.

An additional aspect of the social context is the existence of a natural attractor or natural norm in this system. Rule 4, which produces predictions between 45 and 55, is a pre-ordained focal point or natural norm. (Some constructivists have argued that intrinsic characteristics of certain ideas make them more likely to become norms.) Averaging random numbers between 0 and 100 will produce a mean of around 50 in the long run, and thus agents should be drawn to this rule because of its intrinsic characteristics. The baseline model explores the conditions under which the agents can find this natural attractor through uncoordinated, adaptive behavior.

The real test of the logic of the norm life cycle begins as entrepreneurs are introduced into the model. (My model could easily be modified to examine other aspects of norm dynamics.) Norm entrepreneurs suggest a rule to the agents at specified intervals (every 50 rounds). Each agent replaces its currently worst performing rule with the norm entrepreneur's suggestion, and the suggested rule starts with a fresh score of 100. In the base version of the model, the entrepreneur is able to reach all agents simultaneously, and automatically convinces all the agents in the simulation to add the suggestion to their repertoire of rules. Crucially, the agents will only use the suggested rule if their other rules have been weakened through past punishments – just because a new idea about appropriate behavior is presented does not mean it will automatically influence behavior. From this baseline, I then also test the effects of limited reach – how entrepreneurship works when entrepreneurs can only reach a portion of the population.

With the artificial agents and their environment created, simulations can be run to analyze how different parameter values influence norm dynamics. The model of the norm life cycle enables me to 'experiment' with various conditions that influence norm dynamics, such as the existence of a norm entrepreneur, the ability of the norm entrepreneur to make suggestions to the population, the levels of social complexity, or the sizes of populations, to name just a few possibilities. One advantage to this method, then, is the ability to fully control the parameters of interest in the artificial world and to create as many simulated histories as desired. Data creation is very simple when you can create 50 or 100 simulated histories that last 10,000 time steps in a matter of seconds. There is creativity involved here. Because one can create an infinite number of simulated histories, it is necessary to think carefully about which parameters are of most interest to test and setting up a protocol for producing simulations is crucial. The notion of knowing when to stop gathering data is analogous to the conundrum raised by Checkel, Dunn, and Leander (in this book) but is especially acute because the simulations can create as much or as little data as the researcher desires.

I used graphical analysis to picture how the group outcome changed over time. I used simple descriptive statistics to determine when norms emerged and how long they remained in existence. At a more sophisticated level, I also analyzed the data for the existence of statistical distributions called power laws, which reveal important features about the kind of process that facilitates norm emergence and change (Hoffmann 2003, 2005b). While space constraints limit a full reporting on the results of the simulation here, Appendix A presents some of the key modeling outcomes in visual form.

Beyond modeling norm dynamics

Modeling the norm life cycle is but one of an infinite number of possibilities for using ABM, because modelers have flexibility both to endow agents with decision-making procedures and to place them within an environment. ABM can accommodate *any* decision-making logic that can be formalized into algorithms. Agents can be almost entirely autonomous (following Post's emphasis on psychology in this book), mostly calculated (along the lines of Checkel in this book) or significantly constrained by discourse and social context (consistent with most of the contributors in this book). For example, I have worked with a land-use model that uses modified expected utility procedures and a spatially explicit, dynamic landscape (Hoffmann *et al.* 2002). Axelrod (1997) has worked with a model where the agents are essentially rational actors playing the prisoner's dilemma in a repeated fashion, in a soup. Lustick (2000) confines his agents to a grid and their decision logic is based on the local distribution of cultural expressions (represented by different colored agents). Cederman (1997), in his national emergence model, even allows agent boundaries to change as some agents subsume smaller agents. The *Journal of Artificial Societies and Social Simulation* provides a sense of the diversity of applications. The modeler's creativity and skill with programming are the only limits.

This flexible modeling of agency is what sets ABM apart from other computer-assisted approaches to social science that could be considered qualitative. For instance, systems dynamics models tend to neglect agency – there are no actors, as those models simulate stocks and flows of a system. The dialogic content analysis presented by Duffy (in this book) also uses algorithmic formalisms to study social life, but his analysis looks for patterns in empirical statements. Agency is represented by the content of speech acts, whereas ABM seeks to recreate agency artificially to simulate actors' behavior under a variety of conditions.

This discussion of the logic of ABM and a description of a particular model are more an introduction to the method than a defense of it. Although ABM has a number of advantages, there are a number of challenges that must be addressed, if not overcome. In the next section, I address these through the broader epistemological question which I frequently hear: Why on earth would you model constructivist IR thought?

Epistemology: why model?

It is entirely appropriate to ask modelers what one learns from their research. (Pepinsky 2005 asks this question explicitly.) ABM is *not* an empirical method, so the question is even more apt. The way I have described at least one type of ABM is that you start with an abstraction of reality (a verbal model like the norm life cycle), abstract it further to put it on the computer, and then simulate the second-order abstracted world. What kind of knowledge can such an exercise produce?

The ABM rubric can be considered a continuum between two ideal points. The first is what I call abstract heuristic modeling. With this approach, the models are kept very simple and no attempt is made to capture empirical detail. In other words, neither the agents nor the artificial world are meant to represent specific real-world actors or situations. These models are used primarily as a way to explore fundamental logics. I wrote my norm life cycle model from this perspective (see also Axtell and Epstein 1994; Axelrod 1997; Cederman 2003). The other end of the spectrum is what I call flight simulator models. These are explicitly designed to capture important empirical features of actual histories and to create realistic future scenarios. For example, artificial agents can 'live' on GIS-informed landscapes (see Brown *et al.* 2005; Parker 2005). Given this range of possible models and approaches, I discuss three epistemological distinctions and a set of challenges associated with pursuing ABM in social research.

Heuristic/empiric distinction

ABM analysis provides a means for assessing the logic of verbal frameworks. We all approach empirical analysis with some abstract way of organizing information that tells a story about the world – a model. Most qualitative researchers use verbal models. For instance, the norm life cycle is a verbal model about how social norms emerge, diffuse, and evolve in a population. I used ABM as a way to assess its logic. Putting the essential elements of a verbal model into the computer helps to ascertain whether its conjectures are plausible and consistent, as parameters change in the simulations. This allows us to test a range of verbal models in a way that was heretofore unavailable.

Since ABM is not really an empirical research method, I envision its simulations as heuristic devices that provide insight into fundamental social processes. By simulating the norm life cycle, I am not learning about the emergence or evolution of any particular norm. Rather, I am learning things about the dynamics of norm emergence and evolution in general. ABM is perhaps best suited to testing explanations or verbal models in order to find 'candidate explanations' (Epstein 1999) for social phenomena. Such knowledge is crucial for empirical investigation. In this sense, ABM exercises can act as a plausibility probe or a pseudo-existence proof for our verbal models (Axelrod 1997; also see Klotz, in this book, on the role of plausibility probes in case selection). Also, ABM seems ideally suited to examining alternative processes, similar to the use of counter-factuals (as Checkel suggests, in this book). However, no matter how detailed the model, always remember that simulations are heuristics rather true mirrors of reality.

Model/reality distinction

Despite the heuristic nature of the knowledge produced by ABM simulations, most modelers have a desire to learn something about the empirical world through this type of modeling. In other words, how do I know that I have a decent heuristic if not by comparing the model results from the artificial world to the empirical world? At some level, this implies at least some commitment to truth through correspondence with observation. ABM fits well within the tradition of scientific realism (Wendt 1999; Checkel in this book). But rather than just positing unobservable mechanisms, the modeling tool allows for a simulation of the unobservable mechanisms.

Axtell and Epstein (1994) have considered how to assess model results vis-à-vis the empirical world by thinking about how we can judge the worth of a candidate explanation. They offer four levels of model performance in relation to empirical observations:

Level 0: Model generates agents whose behavior qualitatively matches 'real' agents being studied;
Level 1: Model generates macro-patterns that qualitatively match empirical patterns;
Level 2: Model generates macro-patterns that quantitatively match empirical patterns;
Level 3: Model generates micro-patterns that quantitatively match empirical patterns.

Because I explicitly put a behavioral model onto the computer that has some basis in theorists' observations of empirical agents, this model reached Level 0 by definition.

My model results demonstrate Level 1 performance. The fact that emerging and evolving social norms are evident in the results gives us reason to be optimistic that the verbal model captures some important empirical dynamics. Note that this qualitative match means that the model produces results consistent with general empirical patterns, not specific empirical instances. To reiterate, the simulation exercises are not empirical tests. Rather, the question here is whether the model results track empirical patterns in any meaningful way. If the simulation model of the norm life cycle had not produced emerging and evolving social norms, this would have told us something important about the underlying verbal model (that perhaps it was not plausible).

I am not convinced that we can or should go beyond Level 1 for work with social phenomena. There are two pitfalls in trying to achieve quantitative correspondence with empirical events. First, it gives a false sense that you have gone beyond heuristics. The model is not reality and therefore the simulation will always be different from the empirical world, no matter how much detail is included. Attempting to 'tune' a model to empirical details is fraught with peril. The best we may be able to do is something akin to Cederman's (2003) analysis of the distribution of wars in his model and in the real world. He did not recreate World War II, but instead, his model produced a distribution of wars that corresponds with the distribution of wars in the historical record (size of war, not necessarily the sequencing of wars). The match of the distributions lends plausibility to his explanation for the dynamics of conflict.

Second, the more detail that is included, the harder it is to follow the dynamics of the model. It becomes more difficult to decipher which factors are driving the results as more parameters are added. Thus, I follow Axelrod's (1997) KISS principle: Keep It Simple, Stupid. Simpler, generic models capture fundamental dynamics. Deciding whether or not the dynamics observed in the model are 'real' or evident or plausible in actual social systems can only be done through empirical work. Any number of empirical methods discussed in this book (especially process tracing, ethnography, or pragmatic analysis), depending on the research question and phenomenon being simulated, can be used to ascertain this correspondence.

Indeed, the correspondence between a model and reality beyond Level 1 may not be an important question. The non-empirical nature of ABM for those doing heuristic (rather than flight simulator) modeling is not necessarily a problem. ABM provides a series of conjectures drawn from an artificial world that was constructed from a theoretical framework – an exercise in testing logical consistency and a search for fundamental dynamics. Given the absolute control that modelers have over the (initial) parameters of any model, it is possible to create multiple histories and to 'push' the logic of a verbal model in a variety of ways. This provides the social laboratory generally denied to social scientists (outside the narrow confines of some experimental economics).

This social laboratory can be enormously useful. By experimenting widely with the model parameters, it is possible to discover boundary conditions and novel empirical hypotheses that may be unavailable upon inspection of the verbal model. In the norm life cycle, for example, I can push the framework to find out how it works under different conditions. I attempted to ascertain under what conditions entrepreneurs are necessary to catalyze norm emergence and change. The results of these simulation experiments can then be probed empirically.

Subject/object distinction

ABM confounds some of the normal lines of epistemological debate, notably the subject/object or researcher/researched distinction. The researcher in ABM simulations is god. In the models, I define everything about the artificial world. The outcomes may not be known in advance, but it is indisputable that they flow directly from the design of the artificial world. I very explicitly influence my subjects. There is no question or argument about whether the observer influences the observed – I created the observed. Yet there is a radical separation of researcher/researched, because my *observation* of this created world (as opposed to my initialization of the model) does not influence the outcomes. The artificial reality is objective in the sense that the model exists on the computer, where it is a closed system. During the course of most simulations, the researcher merely waits for the agents to run through their history. (It is possible to design models that are more interactive.) The agents I create do not respond to me as people or organizations being researched do.

This control is what makes flight simulator modeling attractive, if problematic. If one could capture essential elements of an actual social system, it would make testing policy scenarios relatively quick and easy. Applications have been developed for human-model interaction as well as scenario testing in a number of settings, giving one the sense of capturing reality. But given that the model can never capture reality in entirety (the simplest model of the world is the world), control of simulations can lead to hubris. Thus ABM is not a panacea for the methodological quandaries that face international relations scholars, nor is it suitable as a stand-alone method for all (or even most) research questions.

Potential limitations

A number of pitfalls with ABM must be at least considered. These range from the theoretical to the practical and professional. I will focus first on the potential reification of agents, then turn to the start up costs and the sociology of the discipline.

There are serious concerns about agent reification when representing social reality through ABM. Indeed, the focus of ABM is the decision-making of individual, *autonomous* agents, and Jeffrey Checkel and

Stefano Guzzini, among others, warn constructivists against implementing their insights through individualist behavioral models. Guzzini
(2000: 150) cautions against 'mixing an intersubjective theory of knowledge with an individualist theory of action,' while Checkel laments
that 'all too many constructivists rely' on behavioral models that 'are
decidedly individualist in nature' (2001: 561). At first blush, these
concerns seem to be damning for ABM. Its social structure is often a
very simple aggregation of agent actions, something Guzzini blames for
'individualist reductionism' (2000: 164).

Yet ABM does not necessarily reify agents. They often change their
preferences and behavior throughout a simulated history, and they can
even change into other 'kinds' of agents. And while social aggregation
is usually explicitly modeled in a simple fashion, it does not have to be.
The simplicity of its representation of structure is, in some ways, less
important than the fact that social structures are explicitly emergent;
agency constitutes social structure. When agents' attributes are tied to
the social context, simulation allows researchers to get at mutual constitution without bracketing. Neither the agents nor the structures are held
constant.

In addition, focusing on internal decision rules does not necessarily
equal an individualist ontology. Constructivists and others interested
in language and meaning have struggled with how to characterize individual agency and the logic of appropriateness. Rationalist thinkers
rely on methodological individualism, but when agents are socially
constituted through intersubjective reality, the task becomes more difficult. Yet, these ontological differences may have been overstated. Even
Kenneth Arrow claims that '...individual behavior is always mediated
by social relations' (1994: 5). One change in the verb – from 'mediated' to 'constituted' – would make it amenable to constructivists. As
Checkel concedes, 'where to draw the line between individual and social
ontologies is no easy task' (2001: 559).

Beyond such theoretical concerns, it is imperative to get enough experience with modeling to pursue interesting tests of verbal models and to
avoid 'programming in' the results. As it stands now, there is no way
to begin ABM analysis without learning both a computer language and
principles of programming agent-based models in at least a rudimentary
way. Just like learning any language, one needs to grasp the vocabulary,
grammar, and syntax of computer languages and learn how to make
coherent statements (or algorithms). Unquestionably, this is a barrier to
the widespread adoption of ABM; it requires a commitment similar to
that of area specialists who must become at least functional in a foreign

language and immerse themselves in the life of their research area. (On investments in cultural competence, see Neumann in this book.)

Fortunately, the barrier is not insurmountable. All computer science departments offer basic courses, the ABM platforms are widely available as freeware on the web, and texts for all skill levels can be found in any major bookstore. Many of us who use the method do have prior engineering or natural science backgrounds. For instance, I earned a degree in environmental engineering. For those without programming experience, the time investment will likely be more than a year to get up and running.

In terms of the technical specifics, most ABM scholars use an object-oriented programming language like Visual Basic, C++, or JAVA. The object-oriented aspect is crucial because it allows the programming of varied, individual agents. Recently, a number of ABM programming platforms have proliferated (ASCAPE, SWARM, REPAST, MASON), allowing researchers to choose between building a model from scratch or taking advantage of infrastructure developed by others. The advantage of using such a platform is that many functions are already programmed; for instance, it is not necessary to create agents from scratch. The disadvantage is that the modeler loses some control over the design of the artificial world. I built my simulation of norms from scratch, using visual C++. To get a sense of what this language looks like, see Appendix B for a piece of my norm life cycle model code.

Finally, there are disciplinary challenges. The sociology of the discipline of international relations has created a series of (false) methodological dichotomies that have real consequences for researchers. ABM challenges these dichotomies and therefore offers a useful corrective. However, challenging the status quo is not always the safest course of action. While ABM has the potential to be a bridge between different methodological and theoretical inclinations, it can also be eyed with suspicion by both sides.

Conclusion

ABM is a technique that provides a rigorous alternative formal method for exploring theoretical insights. I find invaluable insights that I could not obtain by going directly from verbal models to empirical research. However, it is not a tool to be taken up lightly – I will not counsel that everyone learn to program computers. The objections to this type of modeling are not baseless and the modeling endeavor should be modest, but I find that the potential benefits of using ABM exceed the pitfalls.

Because ABM on its own is heuristic, it forces researchers who want to do empirical work to be methodologically diverse. I do not really see alternatives to modeling as much as I see complementary approaches. Empirical work is necessary in both the design and the analysis of the simulation models. Numerous methods can be used in conjunction with ABM simulations; the choice is a matter of research question. Indeed, the choice of tool should *always* be subordinated to the research question. For my work with social norm dynamics, process tracing is the natural complement. Tracing the norm life cycle empirically – picking a case or two and tracing what the verbal framework and modeling results say could/should happen – allows me to directly address the empirical research questions that drove the modeling in the first place.

This provides a recursive process. The modeling gives me a series of hypotheses or boundary conditions about generic norm dynamics to explore, and the case studies provide an empirical test of them. In turn, the empirical work provides new insights for further modeling experiments. Thus, we should not be thinking either formal analysis or case studies. Instead, the formal analysis enhances the empirical analysis, and in turn the empirical analysis should inform further modeling efforts. Combining the insights garnered with both methods provides the best analysis.

Acknowledgment

I thank Alice Ba, Owen Temby, Paul Hartzog, the editors, and members of Audie Klotz's 2005 graduate methods seminar for their insightful comments on earlier versions of this chapter.

APPENDIX A: MODELING RESULTS

Life without norm entrepreneurs

When norm entrepreneurs are absent from the system, two types of macro-patterns emerge in the simulations. Depending upon the noise levels in the system, the simulation exhibits a strict dichotomy between stability and volatility in the system. Figures A.1 and A.2 are typical runs without norm entrepreneurs. As the noise in the system increases, the simulation switches from stable to volatile. Each figure reports the average predictions (group outcome) made in each round by the agent population over 1000 rounds. Each of these simulations was run with 10 agents and a precision level of 5 per cent. The only variable altered

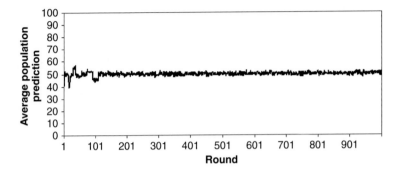

Figure A.1 Population predictions – low noise, no entrepreneur 10 agents, 6% noise.

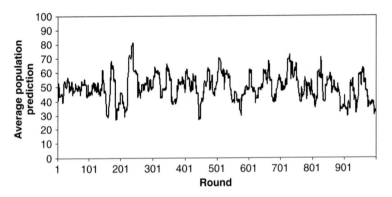

Figure A.2 Population predictions – high noise, no entrepreneur 10 agents, 10% noise.

from run to run was the level of noise added to the average prediction. In Figure A.1, the predictions reach a stable level relatively quickly as the agents arrive at the same rule. As the noise increases in Figure A.2, however, the agents are unable to come to agreement and thus the average predictions fluctuate wildly.

These figures demonstrate that when the noise level is low enough, the agents hit upon the dominant rule (often very quickly) in the system, rule 4. As the noise increases (as the agents are less able to see the true outcome and are thus are less certain about its appropriateness), the agents are unable to come to agreement on any rule and the average prediction reflects this uncertainty. The agents are unable to find a rule that can be intersubjectively agreed upon and thus the agents continually cycle through rules.

Without norm entrepreneurs the agents' actions produce either a volatile or a incredibly stable macro-pattern with a strict break-point between the two types of patterns. The macro-patterns, in turn, alter/reinforce agent behavior and identity (constituting agents) leading to cycling in rule use or the domination of a single rule. The dynamism of the system is either out of control (volatility) or disappears (stability). We see the natural norm emerge or no norm at all. However, this simple set of outcomes does have interesting implications. The model suggests that there are situations where norm entrepreneurs are entirely *unnecessary* for norm emergence. When an idea is intrinsically attractive and the social complexity is low enough such that all the agents can appreciate the attractiveness of the idea, the idea can become a norm without any entrepreneurial effort.

Life with norm entrepreneurs

In contrast to the dichotomous patterns exhibited when the system lacks norm entrepreneurs, their presence creates different patterns. First, norm entrepreneurs are able to influence which rule rises to dominant status when the noise/precision levels would otherwise lead to stability around the dominant rule. See Figure A.3 for a demonstration of this effect. The simulation depicted in Figure A.3 is similarly configured to the simulation run in Figure A.2, except that a norm entrepreneur is now present.

The impact of the norm entrepreneur was significant. The agents still 'crystallized' around a single rule for the majority of the simulation, but

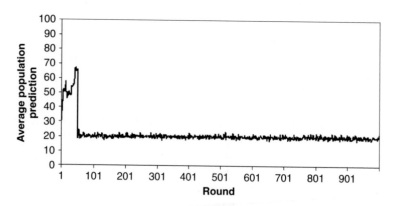

Figure A.3 Population predictions – low noise, no entrepreneur present 10 agents, 6% noise.

instead of the dominant rule 4, the agents crystallized around rule 2 (which returns a prediction between 15 and 25) after the suggestion of the norm entrepreneur. The norm entrepreneur was able to alter the manner in which the agent population crystallized around a single rule – a rule that generates a prediction different from the otherwise dominant prediction that hovers around 50. Repeated trials demonstrated that *any* of the rules can rise to normative status under these conditions.

Lock-in is not the only effect that norm entrepreneurs can have on the system. At higher levels of noise, entrepreneurs catalyze metastable patterns in contrast to a strict breakpoint between volatility and stability. Norm entrepreneurs allow the system to walk the line between volatility and stability and they create patterns of rising and falling norms over time. Metastable patterns occur when pockets of stability arise but do not last – there is stability in the system but it is not robust. In these simulations, the agents can coalesce around any of the rules and we see the rise and demise of intersubjective agreement among the agents. In essence, the norm entrepreneurs are able to catalyze intersubjective agreement, but the agreement does not 'dampen' the dynamism of the system. Instead, the agreement (or norm) lasts for a while before eroding via agent choices and new norm entrepreneur suggestions. The stability erodes because the system is too noisy to support long-term stability and norm entrepreneurs periodically prod the system with new suggestions. Norm entrepreneurs are thus able to catalyze both norm change and norm evolution.

Figure A.4 demonstrates the impact of norm entrepreneurs on a simulation similar to the one run in Figure A.2. Here a metastable pattern of

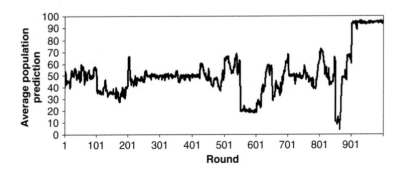

Figure A.4 Population predictions – high noise, no entrepreneur present 10 agents, 10% noise.

emerging and dissolving norms is evident instead of cycling, a pattern that results from the norm entrepreneur's suggestions at a level of noise high enough to cause volatile outcomes in systems lacking an entrepreneur. The norm entrepreneurs catalyze periods of intersubjective agreement among the agents – they make it possible for agents to crystallize around a rule for relatively short periods in an environment that would otherwise lead to volatile patterns.

APPENDIX B: NORM LIFE CYCLE MODEL CODE

This part of the code enables the agents to decide whether to take the entrepreneur's suggestion. The agent is given the suggestion and determines whether it will take the suggestion by comparing its current susceptibility to suggestions against its attribute for baseline susceptibility. If it takes the suggestion, the agent determines which rule to change. This is one of the functions of the agents and each agent runs through this function, though with different outcomes due to agents having different attributes. The entire code consists of about 500 lines (a relatively short model).

```
void agent::alter_rules(int suggestion)
{
        int change = 0;
        int choice;
        int susceptible;
        susceptible = rand()%100;

        if (susceptible<=susceptibility){
        if ((score[0]<score[1]) && (score[0]<score[2])){
                rules[0] = suggestion;
                score[0] = 100;
                change = 1;
        }
        if (change == 0){
        if ((score[1]<score[0]) && (score[1]<score[2])){
                rules[1] = suggestion;
                score[1] = 100;
                change = 1;
        }
```

(Continued)

```
        }
    if (change == 0) {
    if ((score[2]<score[0]) && (score[2]<score[1])){
            rules[2] = suggestion;
            score[2] = 100;
            change = 1;
    }
    }
    if (change == 0) {
    if ((score[2] == score[1]) && (score[1] == score[0])){
            choice = rand()%rules_avail;
            rules[choice] = suggestion;
            score[choice] = 100;
            change = 1;
    }
    }
    if (change == 0){
            if (score[0] == score[1]){
                    choice = rand()%2;
                    rules[choice] = suggestion;
                    score[choice] = 100;
                    change = 1;
            }
    }
    if (change == 0){
            if (score[1] == score[2]){
                    choice = 1 + rand()%2;
                    rules[choice] = suggestion;
                    score[choice] = 100;
                    change = 1;
            }
    }
    if (change == 0){
            if (score[0] == score[2]){
                    choice = rand()%2;
                    if (choice ==0){
                    rules[0] = suggestion;
                    score[0] = 100;
                    change = 1;}
```

```
                              if (choice ==1){
                                     rules[1] = suggestion;
                                     score[1] = 100;
                                     change = 1;}
                    }
              }
              change = 0;
              }
      }
```

Part IV: Implications

13
'Qualitative' Methods?

Samuel Barkin

In this chapter, I neither present a method nor draw conclusions about the methods presented in the substantive chapters of this book. Rather, I reflect on the category around which this book is organized. The term 'qualitative' evokes a narrative or analytical richness, a method that brings out more detail and nuance from a case than can be found by reducing it to quantitative measures. But in practice, the term is generally used simply to mean 'not quantitative,' as Matthew Hoffmann notes in his discussion of agent-based modeling. Qualitative methods are, in this sense, a default category.

At first glance this categorization seems benign. What harm is there in a default category for methods that are not covered in the quantitative methods classes that so many graduate programs in political science require of their students? But the categorization is problematic, for two sets of reasons. The first of these is that to speak of qualitative methods is pedagogically counterproductive. It misleads students, and to the extent that we internalize the categorical distinction, it misleads researchers as well. The second set of reasons is that the phrase is politically fraught. To speak of qualitative methods is to stake a claim in the methodological disputes that divide the field of political science. Discussion of 'qualitative methods' becomes a proxy for claims about what does or does not constitute legitimate political science, because any method that fails to fit even into the default category cannot really be legitimate. To speak of some methods under the heading of qualitative implicitly but clearly stigmatizes others.

I should stress at this point that the argument here is about categorization – it is not about the legitimacy or utility of any particular method. Of course, a claim that discussion of 'qualitative methods' as a category inherently makes claims about what constitutes legitimate political science by its own logic must make a claim about what constitutes legitimate political science. The perspective underlying this discussion is one of methodological pluralism, but at the same time of a need for methodological specificity. The conclusion will return to the idea of methodological specificity, making the argument that real pluralism is incompatible with the dichotomization implied by a quantitative/qualitative divide.

Pedagogy and qualitative methods

The use of the phrase 'qualitative methods' is often found in the context of pedagogy, of teaching people how to use method(s). And that is the primary point of this book. Therefore, an important step in assessing the effects of having this category (as opposed to whatever particular methods we may put in it) is to ask what the pedagogical effects are. Not only does this particular categorization not help in the teaching of international relations methods, but it can be actively misleading, for three general reasons. First, it implies that these methods have some core feature in common. This has the effect of highlighting similarities and obscuring differences. Second, it confuses the difference between analysis and research design. This has the effect of highlighting differences and obscuring similarities among methods that cross the quantitative/qualitative divide. (I'll comment below on the place of formal methods.) Third, it fetishizes method, which both contributes to the reification of particular methodological divides and privileges empirical analysis over theory.

There's no core

What does one teach in a qualitative methods course? Much the same as one puts in a book on qualitative methods – some of everything, except for quantitative methods. The range in this book goes from discourse analysis to personality profiling, from feminism to agent-based modeling. It is, after all, a default category. Let us leave for now the question of what gets left out of the course (or book) – I will return to that in the next section, on the politics of qualitative methods in international relations. Many approaches to the pedagogy of qualitative methods are self-consciously pluralist, and as such aim to include as broad a range of specific methods in the course (or book) as possible. (For an assortment of syllabi, see the website of the Consortium on Qualitative Research Methods at http://www.asu.edu/clas/polisci/cqrm/syllabi.html.)

Such inclusiveness, however, leaves one in a pedagogical quandary. One cannot cover all qualitative methodologies, if for no other reason than there is no discrete set of methodologies that one can claim to have covered comprehensively. At the same time, the more one strives for inclusiveness, the less one can do justice to most, if not all, of them, due to lack of time or expertise. That leaves a hodge podge that does not build on the sort of common core found in introductory quantitative methods classes. It implies, for example, that small-n inferential analysis bears more categorical similarity to Foucauldian genealogy than to statistical analysis.

The lessons are twofold. First, one is suggesting that there is a discrete number of qualitative methods that can sensibly be reviewed in the absence of a research question/focus. While it is true that courses in quantitative method also cover a variety of specific techniques, these build from a core that is taught at the beginning. Second, there is an implication that an understanding of individual qualitative methods takes only a week or two, unlike an understanding of quantitative methods, which takes a sequence of courses. So there cannot be as much to them.

The goal of a course on quantitative methods is clear: to teach a discrete set of techniques useful in analyzing certain types of data (those that have been quantified) once these data have been gathered. This raises the question of the analog for qualitative methods. There are no clear guidelines about how to interpret when using interpretive methods. Chapters in this book, ranging from Leander, Neumann, and Dunn to Checkel, ultimately rely on the good sense of the researcher, rather than clear replicable rules for deciding on issues of evidence and interpretation (although Duffy seeks to remedy this problem).

There are writing skills that are perhaps analogous to the statistical skills taught in data analysis classes. Learning how to write better may serve many of our students well, but that is not what we generally teach in qualitative methods classes. Or we might teach things like epistemology and research design that are not directly analogous to the quantitative techniques. For example, the categorical distinction between positivism and post-positivism would make much more sense if one went beyond a general survey. But questions of epistemology and research design are not best divided along quantitative–qualitative lines.

Analysis and research design

Since courses intended as qualitative equivalents of quantitative methods courses are, in a sense, inherently hollow, they tend to be filled with things other than analytical technique. These range from data-gathering techniques, such as elite interviewing and content analysis, to discussions of epistemology and the philosophy of the social sciences. What these things have in common is that they are not inherent to the category of qualitative methods.

Teaching (and thinking about) them in the context of discussions of qualitative method, understood in categorical terms as the contradistinction to quantitative method, has the effect of confusing issues of analytic technique with broader issues of research design. Few issues of research design are specific to quantitative analysis, understood as the use of statistics, other than the need to find data that are quantifiable. If one understands quantitative analysis more broadly as international-relations-with-numbers (or more precisely with mathematical symbols), there are no issues of research design that are specific to it.

This confusion artificially delimits the flexibility of specific data-gathering techniques, in a relatively straightforward way. Few specific data-gathering techniques are suited only to statistical analysis. Typically, any information-gathering techniques can be used to generate either quantitative or qualitative data. Compare, for example, Hermann on content analysis and Duffy on pragmatic analysis (in this book). To use techniques only to generate quantifiable data would be to lose much, if not most, of the meaning and nuance in the information. Assigning the discussion of data-gathering techniques to courses on qualitative and/or quantitative analysis is either redundant (if done in both) or misleading (if done in one but not the other).

A second effect of the confusion of analytical techniques with research design is that it obscures distinctions in research design that do not correlate with a quantitative/qualitative distinction. As King, Keohane, and Verba argue in *Designing Social Inquiry* (1994), the requirements of research design necessary to substantiate inferential claims is the same whether or not the cases will be subjected to statistical tests. The need for care in the specification of variables, case selection, and data validity are the same either way. Checkel makes a similar case (in this book) on causal process tracing, although he notes differences between causal and correlational analysis that King, Keohane, and Verba fail to address. This is not to suggest that we should be focusing on research that makes inferential claims, only that many scholars of international relations do make such claims, and the requirements of research design to do so cross the quantitative/qualitative boundary.

Similarly, critical theory research looks not at 'objective' data, but at the discourses through which we understand the political; see, for example, Neumann and Dunn (in this book). This sort of distinction also does not correlate with a quantitative/qualitative divide. Critical approaches are more reasonably introduced in general epistemology courses (and expanded upon in methods courses that focus specifically on the discursive), rather than lumped in qualitative methods courses along with small-*n* inferential studies with which they are epistemologically incompatible. In a discipline in which (particularly in the United States) quantitative methods courses are often required of graduate students but qualitative methods courses are not (Schwartz-Shea 2005), to discuss critical approaches primarily in the context of a course on qualitative methods is to allow students who focus on quantitative methods to avoid learning about it altogether.

The upshot of these observations is that there is an argument to be made for teaching epistemology and research design issues comparatively, rather than separately through distinct qualitative and quantitative methods courses. This still leaves scope for teaching particular techniques or approaches, be they analytical techniques such as statistics, data-gathering techniques such as surveys, or philosophical approaches such as critical theory. The common theme in all three of these examples is that they are organized around a core of ideas.

Fetishizing method

These three examples are not fully analogous, however. Statistics are a method of data analysis. Surveys are a method of data gathering. Critical theory, however, is not necessarily best understood as method. While it does involve method (which both Neumann and Dunn discuss in a gratifyingly accessible way), understanding critical theory also requires thinking about epistemology in a way that thinking about quantitative methods does not.

Statistical analysis can be approached from a mutually incompatible array of epistemologies, from logical positivism to philosophical realism, and a quantitative methods course can do a perfectly good job of training students in statistical techniques without addressing these epistemological distinctions. A course in critical theory cannot. This makes discussion of critical theory in a 'methods' course incomplete in a way that is not true of discussion of statistical techniques. A response to a prevalence of quantitative methods courses and literatures that focuses on qualitative methods as a category thus risks fetishizing method at the expense of broader issues of epistemology, methodology, and theory.

This is not to suggest that getting method right, and doing it well, is not important. But too great a focus on method can distract from other key parts of the research process. For example, studying technique in the absence of a broader epistemological context can lead to a commitment to technique without a clear grasp of its uses and limits. Another part is theory and theory-building. Too great a focus on method biases our work toward empirical analysis and away from theory. More broadly, fetishizing method risks distracting us from the study of politics. One often sees statistically elegant studies of politically banal questions. Accepting the quantitative focus on method and mapping it onto non-quantitative approaches risks importing a norm that how you study international politics is more important than what you study. Beyond fetishizing method generally, the creation of 'qualitative methods' as a category in response to the prevalence of quantitative methods courses reifies that divide as the predominant feature of international relations pedagogy. This is problematic both because it is misleading, thereby leading to muddled thinking about epistemology and method, and because it is prone to becoming a focus of debate in the field, distracting from the actual study of international politics.

While the problems with qualitative methods as a category have been discussed above, quantitative methods as a category may seem more straightforward. Quantitative analysis is analysis of numerical (or quantified) data using statistical techniques. But this category is often used to refer to any approach that uses mathematical symbols. For example, game theory is often lumped in with statistical techniques, because both seem to be mathematically intensive, and practitioners of both are prone to claiming the mantle of science for their approach alone. This lumping is sometimes done on the qualitative side of the divide. Witness the absence of game theory in most qualitative methods courses (although not all – witness the inclusion of the Hoffmann chapter in this book). It is also done on the quantitative side. See, for example, the National Science Foundation funded Empirical Implications of Theoretical Models project, which is premised on the idea that good political science requires bridging the gap between formal modeling and statistical modeling, without addressing any of the epistemological issues raised by this premise (NSF 2002).

Other than a common use of mathematical symbols, these two approaches have little in common and are in important ways epistemologically mutually incompatible (MacDonald 2003). Lumping them together may make social and sociological sense, given the construction of the academic field of international relations in the United States at this point in time, but it makes neither methodological nor epistemological sense. The fetishization of method obscures these differences.

A reification of a quantitative/qualitative divide also leaves a number of approaches in a categorizational limbo (and missing from this book's attempt at inclusiveness). If we consider complex game theory to be a quantitative method, what do we do with narrative game theory? Is a discussion of the prisoners' dilemma quantitative or qualitative? And what about network analysis? At one level it should not matter at all – if one wants to do agent-based modeling, one should read Hoffmann's chapter, learn the requisite computer skills, and then just do it. But at another level, if we reify a methodological divide in the sociology of the field, fitting into neither category means not fitting into the field's map at all (as Hoffmann discusses).

This last observation leads to my second general point, and the next section. The categorization of methods is not just a pedagogical act. It is also a political act. It is not just about what gets put where, but about who gets put in which side of a dichotomy, and who gets excluded altogether. And these inclusions and exclusions affect who gets research resources, and who gets published.

Power and qualitative methods

Whatever the pedagogical effects of the creation of qualitative methods as a category, it is both a result and a cause of the politics of exclusion in the discipline of international relations. The creation of the category and its ancillary courses, books, and organizations is a response to the perceived privileged position of quantitative methods in various journals, academic departments, and funding organizations. It is also a cause of these politics, because discussion of what gets included in the category is in effect discussion of what constitutes real social science.

The Perestroika movement in Political Science is a case in point – it is a forum dedicated to the reform of the American Political Science Association, but at the same time it functions as a forum for the promotion of methodological pluralism against the dominance of quantitative methods in the discipline (Monroe 2005). The issue of reform suggests that the creation of the category of qualitative methods is, in part at least, a political attempt by those who do not use quantitative methods to improve their access to the professional resources of the discipline. (I discuss the question of pluralism below.)

To the extent that it is a political attempt, one can reasonably ask whether or not it is likely to be successful. The answer is unlikely to be an unqualified yes. Committing to a disciplinary politics of quantitative/qualitative divide has the effect of reifying a dichotomy between scholars who use mathematic symbols in their research, and scholars who do not. As an exercise in political coalition-building, this is questionable. It puts all of those perceived to have privileged access to resources in one camp, thereby presumably reinforcing their incentive to cooperate among themselves to protect this privilege. It also cedes to them the mechanism for doing so, the mantle of 'science.' In a discipline in which claims to science are based on the sorts of symbols used, those same statisticians and game theorists are in a much better position to access the resources linked to the claim to science (the Empirical Implications of Theoretical Methods project comes to mind here). Helping to create this disciplinary geography is not necessarily an effective political move by scholars who do not use those symbols.

The reification of qualitative methods as a category not only helps to cement existing in-group/out-group dynamics within the discipline, it also creates tension within the out-group. It does this by defining the boundaries of the out-group. If a method for the study of international relations is neither quantitative nor qualitative, then by implication it is not really a legitimate social science method at all. As such, any attempt to define what constitutes qualitative methods is by implication an attempt to define away the legitimacy of any method not included. Since there is no core element to 'qualitative methods' as a category, discussions of the category need to enumerate methods. Inevitably some are left out. The process of enumeration thereby becomes a political process of defining the legitimate methodological boundaries of the discipline.

This process of exclusion is sometimes undertaken self-consciously. For example, in *Designing Social Inquiry*, King, Keohane, and Verba clearly claim that inferential logic is the only logic appropriate to the empirical study of political science, implying that non-inferential approaches are illegitimate. Similarly, works that associate 'qualitative methods' with interpretation (including, to a certain extent, this book) are in effect attempts to legitimate interpretive methods. But the process of exclusion can also operate by default, even when not intended. For example, a discussion of qualitative methods as a 'toolkit' of inductive research techniques has the effect of implying that theory-driven research, such as critical theory, does not involve actual method, and is therefore not really social science. The exclusion may be unintentional, but it has disciplinary political effects nonetheless.

The answer to this politics of exclusion is a politics of pluralism. Methodological pluralism is in a way the qualitative camp's response to the quantitative camp's claim of science. Yet it is ultimately a political claim more than a methodological claim. Underlying a call for method-ological pluralism is the idea that we should all have the freedom to do our research as we see fit, rather than the claim that the research that we do is all equally valid. Many of the methodological perspectives repres-ented in the qualitative camp, broadly defined, are not themselves plur-alist. Critical theory is no more sympathetic to behavioralist research, for example, than behavioralism is to critical theory. For that matter, even within the qualitative camp, critical and inferential methods are not mutually compatible in an epistemological sense (despite Klotz's attempt to reconcile them in the case selection chapter in this book).

In other words, the politics of pluralism in qualitative method is belied by the epistemology of pluralism in qualitative method. If one believes, following Robert Cox (1981), that social theory should be crit-ical rather than problem-solving, the political call to pluralism generated by qualitative methods as category is selling the study of politics short in exchange for disciplinary gain. The benefits of methodological plur-alism become an unexamined assumption rather than a question to be asked.

If not 'Qualitative,' then what?

My argument is not in favor or against any particular method or methodology. Nor is it in any way a critique of any of the chapters in this book. Method should be done well, and the contributors provide excellent guidance. My point is about categories. We should be cautious about investing too much in 'qualitative methods' as a category, because it can be pedagogically counterproductive, and it reinforces a discip-linary political divide that its adherents should be questioning rather than reifying.

But if not qualitative methods, then what? If I argue against the category, what is it that I favor? My answer lies in categories that are both broader and narrower. The broader ones are general '-ological' categories that do not assume particular divisions. And the narrower ones survey specific sets of analytic and research tools that have core foci upon which they build, rather than reviewing disparate tools that have little in common.

Our thinking about how to think about method should begin with principles of epistemology, methodology, and research design (some-what like Part I in this book). In terms of epistemology, the major issues need to be thought about equally by scholars on both sides of the qualitative/quantitative divide. Similarly, many of the research design issues apply across a variety of approaches and are equally applicable to research that uses qualitative or quantitative methods. Feminist scholars and quantitative scholars, for example, may use different terminology to discuss the need to make sure that information gathered is appropriate to arguments made, but there are similar research design issues either way. Thinking about and teaching these common themes helps scholars to communicate across the divide and to think about their work in a way that de-emphasizes the fetishization of technique.

Of course, some techniques do require much specific instruction. This includes statistics techniques and formal modeling, as well as interviews, participant observation, and reading documents in Chinese. And it includes critical theory. Furthermore, it includes some approaches that do not fit neatly into categories, like agent-based modeling. But there is no analytical equivalence among most of these techniques – they do not provide skills that are useful at equivalent stages of research. The narrow categories, then, should involve courses designed around specific techniques. Individual departments will not be able to provide courses in the whole array, but categorizing techniques as 'qualitative' or 'quantitative' will not change that. And losing the category of 'qualitative methods' need not eliminate comparative method, because that should be taught in the general '–ology' courses.

That the category of 'qualitative methods' makes some sense in a disciplinary sociology, as a response to a perception that 'quantitative methods' hold a privileged place, does not make it a good idea. Categorizations have implications, and the implications of this one are worth discussing before we reify it in our teaching as well as our research.

14
Practicing Pluralism

Deepa Prakash

The authors in this book have offered a variety of 'tools' for qualitative research. In this chapter, I offer ways to keep those tools sharpened. While my chapter, like the others, is informed by personal experience, I write as a 'learner' and as a representative of my peers. It is based on two integral elements of the process of writing this book: the qualitative methods course that was the testing ground for the manuscript and the students who took part in it.

Each chapter in this book was originally assigned in draft form in Audie Klotz's qualitative methods course. The authors received feedback from not just one or two but nearly 40 graduate students. In turn, students used the chapters to probe their research questions. In both iterations of the course, they also had the opportunity to interact with practitioners of the various methods; in Fall 2005, this meant a chance to meet with the authors themselves. The entire process reflected the book's emphasis on dispensing user-friendly advice. The 'student voice' was part of the book project from the outset, and it is only fitting that it is represented in the final book.

A note on the 'methodology' used for this chapter is pertinent here. I gathered my data (student responses to the course, the chapters and the category of 'qualitative methods') through a mix of methods. I first sent out an emailed questionnaire to all the participants of the course, followed by interviews with the people who responded to further probe their responses to the questionnaire. Finally, I held a focus group with 12 people to get in-depth feedback and to have a wider discussion about qualitative methods. The various illustrations and responses are presented anonymously throughout this chapter.

Let me also preface with some words about the representativeness of the group of students and their responses. The Political Science

Department at Syracuse leans toward the pluralism emphasized in this book and therefore is atypical of the discipline. The introductory qualitative methods course is required along with quantitative courses, and students are actively encouraged to take methods classes in other departments. However, in most other respects, the students 'testing' these chapters are broadly representative. They did not necessarily specialize in International Relations; there were Americanists and public policy specialists as well as students from other disciplines altogether. They were also at different stages of their graduate careers. Some had just entered graduate school and others were in the midst of writing dissertations. Most had never taken a qualitative methods class, while some had taken those offered by anthropology and sociology departments. Thus the teaching tools in this chapter are informed and inspired by the views of students encompassing a wide range of interests, experience and expertise.

In the first part of this chapter, I offer practical tools for learning and teaching qualitative methods, for students and teachers alike. These ideas are primarily based on the homework assigned in Klotz's course and the innovative ways that students applied them. I outline the assignments and pedagogical strategies that proved most helpful to students as well the frustrations they continue to face. In the second part, I engage in a wider discussion about the category of qualitative methods from the perspective of students. Responding to the concerns Samuel Barkin raises, I assess to what extent and in what ways the debates surrounding the quantitative–qualitative divide resonate with students.

Learning tools

Teaching and learning do not occur in the classroom alone and do not always come under the guidance of professors. As many authors in this book suggest, there is an inherent self-pedagogy. Few would say that they have learnt all they need about their respective methods, and many imply that learning methods is a lifelong process. In this sense, my initial foray into qualitative methods was auspicious.

The first time I explicitly thought about methods was as a first-year doctoral student getting ready to write a summer research proposal. I had a fair idea of the question I wanted to explore and the theoretical literature I wanted to engage, but 'methods' was a different problem altogether. I could summarize my method in one line: 'Read things, analyze them, talk about what they might mean.' I realized with dismay that this would not do. So I did what most grad students do when confronted with academic dilemmas: I talked to my peers, scoured the Internet, and skimmed through primers on the subject.

Quickly I learned that I was going to do 'discourse analysis,' that there were various ways to do this, and that all of these involved a lot more Foucault than I knew! Three years later, with a qualitative methods course under my belt and having read more deeply, I am able to think about the methods in my research with some degree of clarity. But I remember how daunting it felt to go off and teach myself methods 'on the job' of writing a major research paper.

As I talked to my peers in preparation for this chapter, it became apparent that my experience was far from unique. Many of us begin our methods training in this *ad hoc* fashion, often while working on a large project, sometimes the dissertation itself. Like the authors in this book, we do (usually) manage to figure it out (more or less), but there *is* a better way. The following six 'learning tools' encompass our suggestions.

Start early

Taking an introductory class on specific methods – as part of thinking about research methodology generally – has obvious benefits. So the first lesson underscored by my peers is that it pays to think about methods early. Starting early gives you time to get the training necessary to do methods well. Just like learning a language, waiting until the third or fourth year places too much pressure on students. This is particularly true for the more 'cutting edge' methods such as ABM (Hoffmann), profiling (Post), content analysis (Hermann) and pragmatic analysis (Duffy), but applies to all methods.

While there is no cut off for learning methods, an early exposure to the basic terrain of qualitative methods enables students to make informed choices. In particular, it helps to dispel constraining preconceptions. For instance, studying the discourse of foreign policy elites about topic X by doing discourse analysis can be unduly limiting. One student had gone into the course convinced of discourse analysis as the appropriate method for his research but discovered that pragmatic analysis helped him clarify that he was essentially interested in the *dissemination* of discourse and language. Probing a research question from a variety of methodological approaches illuminates new facets of questions that would have otherwise remained unexplored.

Starting early is not as simple as it sounds. Many programs require students to take a set of quantitative methods classes as part of the course work, but do not have such requirements for courses on qualitative methods. Thus, students may take qualitative methods when they are finally *able* to, making the decision to use a mix of methods less considered. So it may be worth it for students to lobby to have qualitative methods courses offered regularly and for these to be accorded equal status in programs.

Of course, the question of *how* early one should take methods courses is also important. Taking a methods course steeped heavily in epistemological debates may be intimidating and even counter-productive without knowledge of the basic vocabulary of the discipline. But as I shall argue below, a practice-oriented approach to teaching methods surmounts this problem to some extent.

Start small

Another tip from students is not to bite off more than you can chew. Hopefully, reading this book has enabled you get a sense of what QM entails and the range of techniques it contains. Maybe your interest has been piqued by one or more methods or maybe it has enabled you to rule out others altogether. However, you might not be ready to commit to any particular method yet, and maybe you are not sure how to proceed in the stage between learning methods and what to use in a dissertation. What do you do next?

One way is to apply these tools to a small project or a sliver of your larger project. Exposing your research question to the gamut of methodological approaches can be overwhelming if you are learning methods for the express purpose of writing a major research project, with a lot of complex data or a huge fieldwork component. This is where a homework-based approach may be useful. As students taking the Syracuse qualitative methods course reiterated, focused assignments were a way to get a taste of doing 'real' research within manageable parameters. The assignments in Klotz's class (see the section on 'Teaching Tools') typically required students to do a small piece of research, analyze or make inferences from it, and then reflect on the limitations of the method for their research. The emphasis was on bite-sized pieces of research, making use of the resources and opportunities immediately available.

Another way to keep the proportions manageable is to rely initially on a few major guidelines for the method, rather than plunging into its entire history and philosophical underpinnings. For readers using this book outside a formal course, it may be useful to look up a few QM syllabi and identify one or two important texts that are typically assigned in such courses to read in addition to the method-specific chapters in this book.

Look around you

As Ackerly's example of how she 'teaches' curb cutting illustrates, with a little imagination, our every day environment can provide resources in learn new skills. Campuses are a great place to practice interviewing, discourse analysis or ethnography in arenas that approximate your research focus. For instance, one creative student interested in fair trade movements spent a few caffeine-infused days at the local university coffee shop talking to people about fair trade coffee, embodying a mini-version of the 'deep hanging out' Gusterson advocates.

For another student examining the discursive formations from conflict situations involving extremist groups, a sports bar became an interesting site in which to conduct his 'fieldwork' for the homework on ethnography. Since he could not feasibly hang out with a militant group, he 'thought of other situations in which people develop negative attitudes toward strangers based on certain qualities found in those strangers.' Luckily, the baseball playoffs were going on at the time, and the Yankees and Red Sox happened to be playing one night. As baseball fans will attest, it was an apt choice for his research!

Similarly, since flying to Washington DC to hang out for a day at the Department of State or studying the plethora of speeches, official documents and treaties that make up US foreign policy was not feasible, a student interested in the discourse of US foreign policy used the environs of the Maxwell School as an intriguing substitute. Simply listening more closely to the 'discourse' on International Relations and Foreign Policy in his various classes for a week enabled him to 'scrutinize the power structures and implicit norms' underlying it. So the third tip in teaching yourself methods is to practice and to use the resources around you, enabling you to save travel and funding for your large project.

Assess yourself

For students who have a less concrete idea about the intricacies of their interest areas, using resources around campus in small but innovative ways is a useful way to practice tools without investing too much time learning about substantive issues. Those who already had a good idea of the data they would be working with approached the assignments in more traditional ways. Here too, doing exercises proved revealing.

For those who already had some training in qualitative methods (say, through a sociology or education course), the exercises were a way to hone their skills and try out new tools. As one student who was working on his dissertation proposal put it, 'The innovative element was trying to weave one large project across the homeworks enabling me to see my topic in new ways.' For others, the assignments opened up tantalizing avenues for research. One student was excited by the potential that agent-based modeling offered to analyze the patterns and effects of state interactions. Learning more about its techniques also exposed him to new theoretical literatures. Yet another student found *all* the exercises extremely frustrating, forcing her to reframe her research topic in a more accessible manner and to contend with nagging questions about the feasibility of her entire project.

Doing actual research is very different from thinking about it in your head. As the students found out, what looked simple or difficult in their heads was not necessarily so in practice. You may find out that you are not very good at something you thought would be easy to do. Maybe 'deep hanging out' with people you are normatively opposed to is harder than you may have thought when contemplating research abstractly, or it might prove transformative, as Gusterson found with nuclear scientists. If you are interested in Political Personality Profiling but discover that you are not good at reading people or lack the 'psychological mindedness' that Post notes is required, you may want to supplement with – or shift completely to – other tools.

The point is that the exercises can go either way; they can lead you to reject certain methods in answering some questions or they can prove to be successful from the very start. In all three cases, students learnt something about the limitations of their topic and of themselves that they would not have known without actively trying their hand. Exercises can give you valuable lessons about what your innate strengths and weaknesses are.

Read exemplars

Most of the students told me that the chapters in this book provided a road map for research, to be augmented by other works and illustrations. Once you get a sense of the basics and you decide to explore one or more of the techniques, a good next step is to read other works by the chapter's author, to get a sense of what such work looks like in detail. Another step is to read the works the authors cite as good examples of the use of their methods.

If you continue to find the method useful and want to learn more, it is then helpful to read some of the philosophical underpinnings of the works and to immerse yourself in, say, Foucault or Bourdieu. Even without taking a QM class, one can be attentive to methods in the books and articles that get assigned in topics courses. Read appendices and methodological sections of works you find persuasive. These are simple ways to adopt tools that appeal to you and to look out for pitfalls.

Triangulate advice

Although most students identify certain 'go to' persons (such as advisors or methods experts in the department) to talk to about methods, there are other sources they can and should consult. Looking for additional resources and opportunities also benefits researchers by putting them in contact with peers wrestling with similar questions and, especially useful for graduate students, creating networks with established experts in their fields.

Like my experience with 'teaching myself' discourse analysis revealed, a vital source of advice comes from peers. For example, while talking with the focus group for this book, one student asked us where she should take someone she was going to interview for a research paper. Since the interviewee was a refugee and they would be talking about sensitive issues, she was worried about meeting with him in a crowded or intimidating place. A range of opinions and ideas offered by peers helped her figure out her concerns and how to address them.

Particularly for those of you intrigued by the 'boundary crossing' techniques, such as agent-based modeling or pragmatic analysis, get in touch with the scholars working with such methods. Typically, these are small, growing communities whose researchers are, as some of the students I spoke to found out, particularly willing to help students interested in their tools and to suggest future avenues.

Since most departments realistically cannot offer a full array of methods courses, many students I spoke with also recommended taking methods courses in departments such as Sociology, Anthropology, Women's Studies and Education. Thus if you were interested in Ackerly's chapter, for instance, find whether another department offers a course specifically on feminist epistemology or methods (if yours does not). In this way, researchers meet each other, enabling them to form working groups with people well versed with qualitative techniques of various kinds. Such inter-disciplinary study groups have proven to be invaluable to students for both the fresh perspective they provide and the exposure to new works with methodological insights. Interdisciplinary perspectives are particularly useful given the complex nature of the international relations.

The growing number of methods workshops at major conferences is another source of advice. Forums such as the 'methods café' at the International Studies Association and the American Political Science

Association's Qualitative Methods working group, along with a growing number of similar workshops at regional conferences, are great places to meet practitioners of particular methods and network with people that are working in similar areas.

And as others in this book have already highlighted, the Institute for Qualitative and Multi-Method Research located at the Maxwell School, Syracuse University, is a venue for students to receive focused feedback on their projects and to network. Its website provides even more resources, including syllabi (with other ideas for homework and other exemplars from additional literatures). It is useful to ask whether your department is a member of the consortium and even to lobby for this if it is not, as this guarantees the departments some spaces at the annual training workshop.

Teaching tools

As the above section has shown, there are a number of ways to keep your methods tool kit sharpened. However, much training does happen in classrooms. So it is not surprising that students also have strong opinions on the kind of pedagogical strategies that work. In this section, I will outline the aspects of the course we took that students benefited from and identify continuing challenges, in order to help others designing their own courses. The bottom line: have more practice and less epistemological debate. This translates not just to the course content but also to the sorts of assignments that students do.

Syllabi

The vast majority of qualitative methods courses (at least in Political Science and IR) follow a certain pattern: a significant amount of time is devoted to the enduring debates about the philosophy of science. Students typically learn about these debates by reading secondary literature and exemplars of the methods. As Barkin points out, courses also tend to treat research design as the main goal of learning qualitative methods. Finally, most syllabi stick to what are presented here as the 'classical techniques,' thus reinforcing the qualitative–quantitative divide. Barkin's point that few courses teach students concrete skills or techniques, analogous to quantitative methods courses, is also borne out. (I base these claims on a perusal of syllabi on the CQRM website, http://www.maxwell.syr.edu/moynihan/programs/cqrm/syllabi.html.)

But this is not necessarily inevitable or desirable. There are ways to ensure that students learn how to 'do' qualitative methods, rather than just think about them, and from my conversations with students, it appears that students would prefer this latter equation. Achieving the balance between epistemological debates and practicing tools is difficult and will be somewhat specific to each department. To some extent, the ability to practice reflects the structure of our department at Syracuse, because there is a separate foundational philosophy of social science course where students first encounter the broader epistemological debates. However, most departments have such a course. For those that do not, the qualitative methods course can become the default primary venue for these discussions.

It is important to note that the students I talked to were divided about how much of each they wanted. What is clear, though, is that they definitely want opportunities to try out the techniques. Their responses suggested that students probe the epistemological implications of the methods, even in a course that is practice oriented. This reflection comes as a natural part of the process of doing research. As one student put it,

> Perhaps the biggest gain for me was an increased ability to think self-consciously and reflexively about the epistemological implications of these methodologies. How do I conceptualize language and communication? What are the tradeoffs involved in adopting a more positivist versus a more interpretivist research perspective? What kinds of textual elements – if any – can be 'counted' in a meaningful way?

Assignments

Qualitative methods courses typically make students undertake three types of exercises and assignments: book reviews and critiques with a focus on methods and research design; practice-oriented exercises; and a final research design paper. Students I talked to uniformly found the practice-oriented assignments most useful. As one student put it, it gave her the 'first taste of field work' and allowed her to *be* a researcher instead of acting like one. I should note that the course we took did not ask us to do a book review or critique, so I cannot comment on whether students might also find that useful. (Note, however, the advice above to look at exemplars.)

In Klotz's course, the homeworks changed between the two iterations of the class, reflecting an increasing emphasis on practice. While the first iteration of the course more closely incorporated the epistemological debates typical of qualitative methods courses, the second iteration was more practice oriented. The emphasis in the short assignments was on describing what was actually done, how students conceptualized certain terms, who they talked to, what inferences were made – the focus was on the details.

For example, the assignment for ethnography in Fall 2005 asked students to answer, first, 'Which aspects of their projects initially seem suited to the tools of analysis generally associated with ethnography? Are other aspects less suited? Why – on what basis are you making these initial assessments?' Second, the students had to 'apply one technique in ethnography in some way that is relevant to their research.' Students had to follow the guidelines from the readings to perform this exercise and write up 'what they did, whether it worked well or not, and how they might expand and/or modify your application of the technique for your research project.'

The final section of the assignment then asked an epistemological question: 'Ethnography is often associated with an epistemological position that rejects the notion that social phenomena, especially meanings, are stable enough to be categorized as variables. Based on your reading and your preliminary foray into the application of this "interpretive" method, what is your initial position on this debate?' By the second iteration in Fall 2006, this third part had been pared down almost entirely and the emphasis was on how to do a small slice of ethnography:

> For most of you, doing a little bit of participant-observation in an appropriate field-setting will not be possible for the purposes of this assignment. Instead, simply practice in an alternative setting: go to an organization's meeting, hang out in Eggers café or the TA bays, or talk with your housemates. Try to find a setting that might enable you to probe a question similar to one that you might have in your research. Tell me what you did, what you hoped to learn, whether it worked well or not, and how you might expand and/or modify your application of the technique for your research project. Alternatively, you might conclude that ethnography doesn't look like a viable technique for your research project; if so, tell me why.

Doing these small applications of ethnography meant that straight away we realized some of its strengths and limits for our research. For instance, for a few of us working on extremist groups and political violence, ethnography had clear limitations. Who could one interview and 'hang out' with when studying the discourse of Al-Qaeda? Should we rule out participant observation altogether? It forced us to make choices about how far we were willing to go and anticipate issues for any larger project.

The exercises also prepared us for one of the most memorable aspects for students: the chance to meet with practitioners of the various methods. In the Fall 2005 class, students met most of the book's contributors themselves, getting even more of a personal insight into the life of a researcher than they got from the remarkably candid chapters. In Fall 2006, the experts came from around the various departments in the Maxwell School. Drawing local expertise is a rich resource that most courses can easily capitalize on, yet few appear to do so (from what I saw in posted syllabi).

Such interactions with experienced scholars humanize and demystify the process of research. Instead of seeing a perfect finished product such as a book, students learn how seasoned researchers cope with problems and often make arbitrary decisions. Homework assignments, furthermore, were timed so that students had already attempted to apply a particular tool *before* the expert's presence in the classroom. This allowed for more sophisticated discussion and more precise questions.

As a pedagogical tool, this one seems like something that is relatively simple to do and that goes a long way in fostering the kind of dialogue on methodological pluralism envisioned in this book. It also helped us think about some of the issues involved in turning an initial small slice of research into a full project, as we were then asked to do in our final assignment, the Research Design Paper.

The standard final paper in qualitative methods classes often takes an 'as if' approach. The brief is, Pretend *as if* you have resources, funding, language capability, the ability to travel and enough time. How then would you design your research? While this has its uses, it can mean that students write idealized designs based more on reviews of exemplars than their own knowledge of the feasibility of their methods.

In contrast, the final assignment in Klotz's course focused on methods rather than a comprehensive proposal. Students were asked to write a terse grant proposal but only write up the methods section of it, selecting two of the techniques surveyed in the course. Students at various stages in their graduate career found this useful because they did not have to spend too much time on doing an exhaustive literature review or developing theoretical sections, which can be particularly difficult for students just beginning to think about their research topics. For teachers, such an approach ensures that they are able to give feedback on methods, rather than contending with a wide variety of substantive issues about which they have varying degrees of expertise.

However, there are also some limitations that result from this narrow focus on methods. Barkin raises the point that qualitative methods

courses are ill equipped to teach analysis or inference in the same way
that quantitative methods classes can. The experience of my peers reit-
erates this concern. Reacting to the chapters as well as the QM course,
students consistently brought up the problem of not knowing what to
do with data after they had collected it. Their feedback was that while
they learnt how to conceptualize and collect data, they were less certain
about the analysis part. Are there rules for analysis that correspond to
the way statistical data can be read? How does one standardize analysis
of qualitative data? Is this even possible or desirable?

Most qualitative methods classes do not focus on these questions in
a general manner because they remain (understandably) geared to each
student's research interest. Assignments ask students to apply methods
like historiography or process tracing to 'some aspect relevant' to the
students own research. For the most part this approach is necessary
because students need the methods for their own work and are unlikely
to be motivated by working on some general data set or to encounter the
questions pertinent to their own topics in generic data. However, this
means that students cannot see whether the frustrations they experience
in analyzing and understanding data through a particular method are
unique or general problems.

One solution is to have more of a mixture of assignments, whether
in class or as homework, with most geared toward the student's own
research but one or two uniform to the entire class. Possible assignments could be for all students to read through the same textual sources
with the aim of producing a short analysis or to work in groups on
one of their peer's research topics. Exercises such as coming up with a
few words to make a dictionary from a commonly assigned text as part
of the content analysis section shows to what degree methods can be
replicable or not. Such exercises demonstrate the inherent variability
of interpretation and analysis as well as opening a discussion on how
to assess the validity and persuasiveness of interpretation, and whether
this is possible at all. These collective exercises can also be done in
class, achieving the balance between individual and group assignments.
Another more commonly used strategy is to have students critique
methodological sections of already published works. Assigning one book
review from a choice of three or four books gets at the question of
assessing method and its analysis.

Finally, it is possible simply to address the 'what do I do with this data'
question explicitly in class. Perhaps the rules of analysis or inference do
not directly translate from statistical methods. If so, what are the ways
that students can assess the validity of their interpretations? What are

the uncertainties inherent in this approach and how have scholars dealt with them? A discussion on this topic would go a long way in addressing this concern of students and allaying their fears that there is a correct way to analyze data.

Such a discussion may actually lead to the answer that it is not necessarily bad to come away with questions about how to analyze data. These are precisely the sorts of questions that can be probed with advisors, in topics courses, and as you read further into the literatures relevant to you. It is misleading to think that one course or one phase in graduate school can tell you all you need to know about analysis. Instead, conceiving of research as a multi-stage process alleviates some of these anxieties.

Advanced courses

Teaching qualitative methods is difficult, as Barkin points out. How does one do justice to methods as rich and varied as discourse analysis or ethnography in one semester? Yet it was resoundingly clear that students want courses on qualitative methods, even if they do tackle ethnography in one week. They also want more than just a basic course and are acutely aware of the need for more training, thus echoing Barkin's concern that courses become a 'hodge podge' of rushed sessions. These concerns may be addressed by offering *advanced* qualitative methods courses. A couple of syllabi are available on the CQRM website, but for the most part these seem rare and mainly focused on comparative case studies.

Students I spoke with had some ideas for what an advanced qualitative methods course could look like. It might involve a semester long course focused on an individual method, such as discourse analysis or ethnography. Given the constrained resources of most departments and the unlikely scenario of having resident experts in all techniques, one option may be to team-teach courses structured in month-long modules for each method. (Professors and departments would have to make arrangements for teaching credit.) Another option would be to divide students into groups by methods and give readings and assignments to these groups within the class, along with some common topics that the class can do together.

'Qualitative' methods as category: 'the view from below'

Students are acutely aware of the power stakes in qualitative and quantitative methods. My peers recognize that being seen as 'qualitative researchers' puts us in a minority in American academia (though perhaps less so elsewhere), with disadvantages on the job market and for being published in many mainstream journals. And we agree with Barkin that categorization is a political act.

But this does not mean that we are unhappy with the category. It helps us compete and cope with the demands of the profession. And it helps us avoid working in an isolated bubble. Students I talked with saw the category as giving them a voice and a vocabulary in academia. Many expressed a sense of relief at being able to find language that allows them to justify their choices to an outside audience.

In concrete terms, training in 'qualitative methods' gives us the vocabulary to do things like apply for grants (and perhaps attend a major annual workshop). A student from the history department told me that he received more grants than his colleagues, who receive little methods training, after being able to explicate what he was doing. This training also helps us to get proposals passed by committee members who may question the legitimacy of discourse analysis or to give job talks confidently to a potentially critical audience. Having a category that is intelligible to the mainstream, no matter how nebulous or flawed it may be, is better than a situation where quantitative and formal methods are juxtaposed with 'the rest' (especially given the artificial nature of these boundaries, as Hoffmann argues).

So while we are aware of the pedagogical and political implications of categorization, it has its advantages. But this is not the only reason for our support of the qualitative methods category. We recognize that exposure to different tools genuinely allows us to explore our questions and illuminates new ones. Students I spoke with unanimously believe that qualitative methods should be a required course in the same way as quantitative courses are, because both types of methods make us better scholars. And that means we believe that students who identify themselves as quantitative researchers would also benefit from exploring their questions with different tools.

Barkin's point that qualitative methods courses give the impression that one can understand individual qualitative methods in only a week or two is indeed troubling. One of the more awkward silences during the focus group was when I asked my peers whether they thought they could do qualitative research before they had taken a course. Quite a few of us agreed that we came in with the sense that you can do qualitative methods to some extent without training. Only after we took a course did we realize that we were wrong; you are not doing qualitative methods if you can read a book and interpret it. Barkin should be reassured to know that as students, the introductory course demonstrated how much more training we need. It did not give us the (false) impression that we were now well versed as qualitative researchers.

Nevertheless, I was struck by a tension in how my peers do view qualitative methods as a residual category. Particularly for those of us who identified ourselves as users of qualitative methods, there was a measure of defensiveness coupled with a sense of superiority. Students can be quick to decry quantitative work as being shallow and 'easy' but powerful and 'legitimate,' while they see qualitative work as more esoteric and deep, but undervalued. The politics of categorization is not benign, and it will not allow students to truly embrace pluralism until the power disparities are reduced. Thus the lack of conversations between researchers vested in particular methods noted in the Introduction and by Barkin is perpetuated by students too, making the challenge to overcome these barriers and embrace genuine methodological pluralism even harder.

I remain more optimistic than Barkin, however, because most students enter graduate school with few preconceived notions or rigidly held beliefs about methods. It strikes me as ironic when students are told to be open to mixed methods, not to be too dogmatic, and not to fetishize. In the student view, these are hallmarks of the academic environment into which we are slowly socialized. Few of us come in with firm positions on epistemological debates; instead the politics of categorization and the necessity of picking a camp happen as we seek a place in the profession. As students, we are the most open to pluralism as we enter graduate school. If pluralism is the goal, our initial training needs to reinforce dialogue across methodologies.

Conclusion

In keeping with the candid and self-reflective tone of this book, let me conclude by recounting my own story of the methods I employed for this chapter, in a far messier manner than the contributors to this book would prescribe. As Leander might have predicted, my plan was ambitious. I was optimistic about the responses I would be able to collect as I sent out an initial questionnaire to all the students who took the class in the two years it was offered. And I had mental plans to expand my research to other universities. My initial optimism was dampened when less than half the people who received the questionnaire wrote back, despite several pleas.

Here is where my 'cultural competence' started to come into play; fortunately, I had learned a trick or two from Neumann and Gusterson.

As a grad student I knew that expecting people to send detailed responses to my questions toward the end of the semester was unreasonable. Interviews with people during their breaks were one way to address the problem. Finally, I decided that a focus group approach might be the optimal strategy, given the constraints of all the participants, as well as my own goal of getting a range of feedback on teaching tools.

By now, my expectations for people's participation were much more realistic, reflecting an adaptation based on my preliminary experiences in my 'field' (graduate students). I resorted to a combination of cajoling, nagging and offering material incentives (donuts and coffee, the grad student's ultimate weakness). Finally, a dozen people sat down with me and talked about their experiences. Despite my best attempts to survey a wide range of opinions, my 'sample' or focus group really consisted of my loyal friends.

With more funding and resources, I may have been able to garner more participation, perhaps from graduate students from other universities or even countries. I was constrained by money, time and my other commitments. Yet, the focus group session produced a free-wheeling discussion about the adequacies of qualitative methods as a category, what worked in the course, the use of the homework assignments, and the other comments I have provided in this chapter. The insights gained through this 'triangulation' of methods – questionnaire, interviews and focus group – were pivotal, confirming one of Checkel's main points. All in all, my partial survey was infinitely better than no survey at all!

With this illustration in mind, let me offer two final thoughts that are easy to forget in the concern with achieving rigor in methodology. My first point may seem strangely placed at the end of a book on (qualitative) methods: We must remind ourselves not to get too obsessed with methods. Students are aware of arguments, such as Barkin's, pointing to the dangers of method driven research. Often this argument is associated with quantitative research, but the same argument also applies to 'qualitative' methods. What initially excites us as researchers and makes us pursue grad school are questions that bedevil or anger us, regions that fascinate us, and puzzles that remain unresolved. Treat methods as tools to put the pieces together, not as the puzzle itself.

Second, it is worth keeping in mind that no matter how explicit the recommendations of the authors in this book and other works are, these are recommendations and not blue prints or formulas. They will work differently for you. As one student found while conducting a survey for the World Values database, 'cultural competence' means knowing when to break the rules. Conducting surveys in her native Turkey, she found, was nothing like the formal protocol handed to volunteers, which forbade surveyors to enter participants' homes or to engage in prolonged conversations with them. Instead, she found herself participating in ladies afternoon gossip sessions and drinking tea in various homes, all the while learning much more than the survey could have ever revealed. Apart from leaving her skeptical about the 'objectivity' of surveys, her experience reinforced the lesson that research requires flexibility, humor, persistence and a little bit of a *laissez faire* attitude.

Acknowledgment

I thank all my peers who helped me write this in many different ways, particularly my focus group: Hannah Allerdice, Angela Fitzpatrick, Seth Fischer, Matt Guardino, Mike Makara, Ryan McKean, George Mitchell, Paloma Raggo, Eric Rittinger, Braden Smith and Matthew Smith. Special thanks to Asli Ilgit and to Audie Klotz for invaluable suggestions, ideas and chats.

Bibliography

Ackerly, B. (2000). *Political Theory and Feminist Social Criticism*. Cambridge: Cambridge University Press.

Ackerly, B. (2001). 'Women's Human Rights Activists as Cross-Cultural Theorists.' *International Feminist Journal of Politics* 3: 311–46.

Ackerly, B. (2007a). 'How Does Change Happen? Deliberation and Difficulty.' *Hypatia* 22: 46–63.

Ackerly, B. (2007b). 'Sustainable Networking: Collaboration for Women's Human Rights Activists, Scholars, and Donors.' In *Sustainable Feminisms: Enacting Theories, Envisioning Action*, ed. S. Sarker. Oxford: Advances in Gender Research, Elsevier.

Ackerly, B. (forthcoming 2008). *Universal Human Rights in a World of Difference*. Cambridge: Cambridge University Press.

Ackerly, B. and J. True (2006). 'Studying the Struggles and Wishes of the Age: Feminist Theoretical Methodology and Feminist Theoretical Methods.' In *Feminist Methodologies for International Relations*, eds B. Ackerly, M. Stern and J. True. Cambridge: Cambridge University Press.

Ackerly, B. and J. True (forthcoming). *Doing Feminist Research in Social and Political Science*. Basingstoke: Palgrave.

Ackerly, B., M. Stern, and J. True, eds (2006). *Feminist Methodologies for International Relations*. Cambridge: Cambridge University Press.

Adcock, R. and D. Collier (2001). 'Measurement Validity: A Shared Standard for Qualitative and Quantitative Research.' *American Political Science Review* 95: 529–46.

Adler, E. (1997). 'Seizing the Middle Ground: Constructivism in World Politics.' *European Journal of International Relations* 3: 319–63.

Adler, E. (2002). 'Constructivism and International Relations.' In *Handbook of International Relations*, eds W. Carlsnaes, T. Risse, and B. Simmons. London: Sage.

Agathangelou, A. (2004). *The Global Political Economy of Sex: Desire, Violence, and Insecurity in Mediterranean Nation States*. New York: Palgrave Macmillan.

Alderson, K. (2001). 'Making Sense of State Socialization.' *Review of International Studies* 27: 415–33.

Alker, H. (1988). 'The Dialectical Logic of Thucydides' Melian Dialogue.' *American Political Science Review* 82: 805–20.

Arrow, K. (1994). 'Methodological Individualism and Social Knowledge.' *American Economic Review* 84: 1–9.

Arthur, B., S. Durlauf, and D. Lane (1997). *The Economy as an Evolving Complex System II*. New York: Addison Wesley Longman.

Ashley, R. (1989). 'Imposing International Purpose: Notes on a Problematique of Governance.' In *Global Changes and Theoretical Challenges: Approaches to World Politics for the 1990s*, eds E. Czempiel and J. Rosenau. Lexington, MA: Lexington.

Austin, J. (1962). *How To Do Things With Words*. Oxford: Clarendon.

Axelrod, R. (1984). *The Evolution of Cooperation*. New York: Basic Books.

Axelrod, R. (1997). *The Complexity of Cooperation: Agent Based Models of Competition and Collaboration*. Princeton: Princeton University Press.

Axtell, R. and Epstein, J. (1994). 'Agent based Modeling: Understanding Our Creations.' *Bulletin of the Santa Fe Institute* 9: 28–32.

Bach, K. and R. Harnish (1979). *Linguistic Communication and Speech Acts.* Cambridge: MIT Press.

Barry, C. A. (1998). 'Choosing Qualitative Data Analysis Software: Atlas/ti and Nudist Compared.' *Sociological Research Online* 3, http://www.socresonline.org.uk/socresonline/3/3/4.html (accessed 25 October 2006).

Barthes, R. (1981). 'The Discourse of History.' *Comparative Criticism* 3: 7–20.

Bates, R., A. Greif, M. Levi, J.-L. Rosenthal, and B. Weingast (1998). *Analytic Narratives.* Princeton: Princeton University Press.

Bauman, Z. (1992). *Postmodern Ethics.* Oxford: Blackwell.

Bell, V. and J. Butler (1999). 'On Speech, Race and Melancholia: An Interview with Judith Butler.' *Theory, Culture and Society* 16: 163–74.

Bennett, A. and C. Elman (2007). 'Case Study Methods in the International Relations Subfield.' *Comparative Political Studies* 40: 170–95.

Berreman, G. (1974). 'Bringing It All Back Home: Malaise in Anthropology.' In *Reinventing Anthropology*, ed. D. Hymes. New York: Vintage.

Berreman, G. (1980). 'Are Human Rights Merely a Politicized Luxury in the World Today?' *Anthropology and Humanism Quarterly* 5: 2–13.

Beyers, J. (2005). 'Multiple Embeddedness and Socialization in Europe: The Case of Council Officials.' *International Organization* 59: 899–936.

Bigo, D. (2005). 'La Mondialisation de l' (in)sécurité? Réflexion sur le champ des professionels de la géstion des inquiétudes et analytique de la transnationalisation des processus de l' (in)sécuritisation'. *Cultures & Conflits* 58: 53–100.

Blakemore, D. (1992). *Understanding Utterances.* Oxford: Blackwell.

Borofsky, R. (2005). *Yanomami: The Fierce Controversy and What We Can Learn From It.* Berkeley: University of California Press.

Bourdieu, P. (1984). *Distinction: A Social Critique of Judgement of Taste.* Cambridge: Harvard University Press.

Bourdieu, P. (1985). *In Other Words: Essays Toward a Reflexive Sociology.* Cambridge: Polity.

Bourdieu, P. (1990). *The Logic of Practice.* Cambridge: Polity.

Bourdieu, P. (1992). *Language and Symbolic Power.* Cambridge: Polity.

Bourdieu, P. (1993). *The Field of Cultural Production: Essays on Art and Literature.* Cambridge: Polity.

Bourdieu, P. (1995). *Outline of a Theory of Practice.* Cambridge: Cambridge University Press.

Bourdieu, P. (1996a). *The Political Ontology of Martin Heidegger.* Cambridge: Polity.

Bourdieu, P. (1996b). *The Rules of Art: Genesis and Structure of the Literary Field.* Cambridge: Polity.

Bourdieu, P. (1998). *State Nobility: Elite Schools in the Field of Power.* Cambridge: Polity.

Bourdieu, P. (1999). *The Weight of the World: Social Suffering in Contemporary Society.* Cambridge: Polity.

Bourdieu, P. (2000a). *Pascalian Meditations.* Cambridge: Polity.

Bourdieu, P. (2000b). *Homo Academicus.* Stanford: Stanford University Press.

Bourdieu, P. (2002). *Practical Reason: On the Theory of Action.* Stanford: Stanford University Press.

Bourdieu, P. (2004). *Science of Science and Reflexivity.* Chicago: University of Chicago Press.

Bourdieu, P. (2005). *The Social Structures of the Economy*. Cambridge: Polity.

Bourgois, P. (1995). *In Search of Respect: Selling Crack in El Barrio*. New York: Cambridge University Press.

Brady, H. and D. Collier, eds (2004). *Rethinking Social Inquiry: Diverse Tools, Shared Standards*. Lanham: Rowman and Littlefield.

Brody, R., D. Mutz and P. Sniderman, eds (1996). *Political Persuasion and Attitude Change*. Ann Arbor: University of Michigan Press.

Brown, C. (2005). *Postmodernism for Historians*. London: Pearson Longman.

Brown, D. G., R. Riolo, D. T. Robinson, M. North, and W. Rand (2005). 'Spatial Process and Data Models: Toward Integration of Agent-Based Models and GIS'. *Journal of Geographical Systems* 7(1): 25–47.

Brown, W. (1995) *States of Injury: Power and Freedom in Late Modernity*. Princeton: Princeton University Press.

Campbell, D. (1993). *Politics Without Principles: Sovereignty, Ethics, and the Narratives of the Gulf War*. Boulder: Lynne Rienner.

Caporaso, J., J. Checkel, and J. Jupille, eds (2003a). 'Integrating Institutions: Rationalism, Constructivism and the Study of the European Union.' Special Issue of *Comparative Political Studies* 36: 5–231.

Caporaso, J., J. Checkel, and J. Jupille, eds (2003b). 'Introduction – Integrating Institutions: Rationalism, Constructivism and the Study of the European Union.' *Comparative Political Studies* 36: 7–41.

Casti, J. (1997). 'Can You Trust It? On the Reliability of Computer Simulation and the Validity of Models.' *Complexity* 2: 8–11.

Cederman, L. (1997). *Emergent Actors in World Politics*. Princeton: Princeton University Press.

Cederman, L. (2001). 'Modeling the Democratic Peace as a Kantian Selection Process.' *Journal of Conflict Resolution* 45: 470–502.

Cederman, L. (2003). 'Modeling the Size of Wars: From Billiard Balls to Sandpiles.' *American Political Science Review* 97: 135–50.

Checkel, J. (2001). 'Why Comply? Social Learning and European Identity Change. '*International Organization* 55: 553–88.

Checkel, J. (2003). 'Going Native' in Europe? Theorizing Social Interaction in European Institutions. '*Comparative Political Studies* 36: 209–31.

Checkel, J. (2005a). 'International Institutions and Socialization in Europe: Introduction and Framework.' *International Organization* 59: 801–26.

Checkel, J. ed. (2005b). 'International Institutions and Socialization in Europe.' *International Organization* 59 (Special Issue).

Checkel, J. (2006). 'Constructivism and EU Politics.' In *Handbook of European Union Politics*, eds K. E. Jørgensen, M. Pollack, and B. Rosamond. London: Sage.

Chernoff, F. (2002). 'Scientific Realism as a Meta-Theory of International Politics.' *International Studies Quarterly* 46: 189–207.

Chernoff, F. (2005). *The Power of International Theory: Reforging the Link to Foreign Policy-Making through Scientific Enquiry*. New York: Routledge.

Clark, C., E. Sprenger, L. Vaneklasen, and L. Alpízar Durán (2006). *Where Is the Money for Women's Rights?* Washington, DC: Just Associates.

Clifford, J. (1997). *Routes: Travel and Translation in the Late Twentieth Century*. Cambridge: Harvard University Press.

Clifford, J. and G. E. Marcus, eds (1986). *Writing Culture: The Poetics and Politics of Ethnography*. Berkeley: University of California Press.

Cochran, M. (2002). 'Deweyan Pragmatism and Post-Positivist Social Science in IR.' *Millennium* 31: 525–48.

Collier, D. and J. E. Mahon, Jr (1993). 'Conceptual "Stretching" Revisited: Adapting Categories in Comparative Analysis.' *American Political Science Review* 87: 845–55.

Collins, P. H. (1991). *Black Feminist Thought: Knowledge, Consciousness, and the Politics of Empowerment*. Boston: Unwin Hyman.

Comaroff, J. and J. Comaroff (1991). *Of Revelation and Revolution: Christianity, Colonialism, and Consciouness in South Africa*. Chicago: University of Chicago Press.

Congressional Record, 12 August 1960: 16281; 17 August 1960: 16641; and 16 February 1961: A955.

Conte, R., R. Hegselmann, and P. Terna, eds (1997). *Simulating Social Phenomena*. New York: Springer-Verlag.

Council of Europe (1997). *European Convention on Nationality and Explanatory Report*. Strasbourg: Document DIR/JUR (97) 6 (14 May).

Council of Europe (2000). *1st European Conference on Nationality: Trends and Developments in National and International Law on Nationality*. Strasbourg, 18–19 October 1999. Strasbourg: CONF/NAT (99) PRO 1 (3 February).

Cox, R. (1981). 'Social Forces, States, and World Orders: Beyond International Relations Theory.' *Millennium* 10: 126–55.

Crawford, N. (2002). *Argument and Change in World Politics: Ethics, Decolonization, and Humanitarian Intervention*. Cambridge: Cambridge University Press.

D'Costa, B. (2006). 'Marginalized Identity: New Frontiers of Research for IR?' In *Feminist Methodologies for International Relations*, eds B. Ackerly, M. Stern, and J. True. Cambridge: Cambridge University Press.

Derlugian, G. (2005). *Bourdieu's Secret Admirer in the Caucasus: A World System Biography*. Chicago: Chicago University Press.

Dever, C. (2004). *Skeptical Feminism: Activist Theory, Activist Practice*. Minneapolis: University of Minnesota Press.

Doty, R. (1996). *Imperial Encounters*. Minneapolis: University of Minnesota Press.

Drezner, D. (2006). 'Notes from a Generalist.' *Qualitative Methods: Newsletter of the American Political Science Association Organized Section on Qualitative Methods* 4 (Spring): 34–7.

Driver, M. (1977). 'Individual Differences as Determinants of Aggression in the Inter-Nation Simulation.' In *A Psychological Examination of Political Leaders*, ed. M. G. Hermann. New York: Free Press.

Duffy, G. and E. Goh (2007). 'Testing Sincerity: Kissinger's Opening Encounter with the Chinese Leadership.' *Journal of Language and Politics*. In press.

Duffy, G., B. Frederking, and S. Tucker (1998). 'Language Games: Dialogical Analysis of INF Negotiations.' *International Studies Quarterly* 42: 271–94.

Dunn, K. (2003). *Imagining the Congo*. New York: Palgrave Macmillan.

Economist (2002). 'The Brussels Consensus.' 7 December.

Economist (2003). 'Cracks in the College.' 13 September.

van Eemeren, F. and R. Grootendorst (2004). *A Systematic Theory of Argumentation: The Pragma-dialectical Approach*. Cambridge: Cambridge University Press.

van Eemeren, F., R. Grootendorst, S. Jackson, and S. Jacobs (1993). *Reconstructing Argumentative Discourse*. Tuscaloosa: University of Alabama Press.

Ehrenreich, B. (2002). *Nickel and Dimed: On (Not) Getting By in America*. New York: Owl Books.

Elman, C. and M. F. Elman (2001). *Bridges and Boundaries: Historians, Political Scientists, and the Study of International Relations*. Cambridge: MIT Press.

Elster, J. (1998). 'A Plea for Mechanisms.' In *Social Mechanisms: An Analytical Approach to Social Theory*, eds P. Hedstroem and R. Swedberg. Cambridge: Cambridge University Press.

Enloe, C. (1993). *The Morning After: Sexual Politics at the End of the Cold War*. Berkeley: University of California Press.

Enloe, C. (2000). *Maneuvers: The International Politics of Militarizing Women's Lives*. Berkeley: University of California Press.

Enloe, C. (2004). *The Curious Feminist: Searching for Women in a New Age of Empire*. Berkeley: University of California Press.

Epstein, J. (1999). 'Agent-based Models and Generative Social Science.' *Complexity* 4: 1–60.

Epstein, J. and R. Axtell (1996). *Growing Artificial Societies: Social Science from the Ground Up*. Washington, DC: Brookings Institution.

Erikson, E. (1963). *Childhood and Society*. New York: Norton.

Fearon, J. (1991). 'Counterfactuals and Hypothesis Testing in Political Science.' *World Politics* 43: 169–95.

Fearon, J. and A. Wendt (2002). 'Rationalism v. Constructivism: A Skeptical View.' In *Handbook of International Relations*, eds W. Carlsnaes, T. Risse, and B. Simmons. London: Sage.

Fernea, E. (1969). *Guests of the Sheikh: An Ethnography of an Iraqi Village*. New York: Anchor Books.

Finnemore, M. (1996). *National Interests in International Society*. Ithaca: Cornell University Press.

Finnemore, M. and K. Sikkink (1998). 'International Norm Dynamics and Political Change.' *International Organization* 52: 887–918.

Fluehr-Lobban, C. (1998). 'Ethics.' In *Handbook of Methods in Cultural Anthropology*, ed. H. Bernard. Walnut Creek, CA: Altamira Press.

Fluehr-Lobban, C. (2003). *Ethics and the Profession of Anthropology: A Dialogue for Ethically Conscious Practice*. Walnut Creek, CA: Altamira Press.

Forum (2005). 'Responses to Rosato, "The Flawed Logic of the Democratic Peace Theory."' *American Political Science Review* 99: 453–72.

Fraser, A. (1999). 'Becoming Human: The Origins and Development of Women's Human Rights. '*Human Rights Quarterly* 21: 853–906.

Fraser, N. (1997). *Justice Interruptus: Critical Reflections on The 'Postsocialist' Condition*. New York: Routledge.

Frederking, B. (2000). *Resolving Security Dilemmas: A Constructivist Explanation of the INF Treaty*. Aldershot, UK: Ashgate.

Fujimura, J. (1996). *Crafting Science: A Sociohistory of the Quest for the Genetics of Cancer*. Cambridge: Harvard University Press.

Gaskins, R. (1992). *Burdens of Proof in Modern Discourse*. New Haven: Yale University Press.

Gazdar, G. (1979). *Pragmatics: Implicature, Presupposition, and Logical Form*. New York: Academic Press.

Geertz, C. (1968). *Islam Observed: Religious Development in Morocco and Indonesia*. New Haven: Yale University Press.

Geertz, C. (1973). *The Interpretation of Cultures*. New York: Basic Books.

George, A. (1979). 'Case Studies and Theory Development: The Method of Structured, Focused Comparison.' In *Diplomacy: New Approaches in History, Theory, and Policy*, ed. Paul Gordon Lauren. New York: Free Press.

George, A. and A. Bennett (2005). *Case Studies and Theory Development in the Social Sciences*. Cambridge: MIT Press.

Gerring, J. (2007). *Case Study Research: Principles and Practices*. New York: Cambridge University Press.

Gheciu, A. (2005a). 'Security Institutions as Agents of Socialization? NATO and Post-Cold War Central and Eastern Europe.' *International Organization* 59: 973–1012.

Gheciu, A. (2005b). *NATO in the 'New Europe': The Politics of International Socialization After the Cold War*. Stanford: Stanford University Press.

Ginsburg, F. (1989). *Contested Lives: The Abortion Debate in an American Community*. Berkeley: University of California Press.

Gluck, S. B. and D. Patai, eds (1991). *Women's Words: The Feminist Practice of Oral History*. New York: Routledge.

Goertz, G. (2006). *Social Science Concepts: A User's Guide*. Princeton: Princeton University Press.

Goodenough, W. (1981). *Culture, Language and Society* . Reading, MA: Addison-Wesley.

Grice, H. P. (1957). 'Meaning.' *Philosophical Review*. 67. Reprinted in *Philosophical Logic*, ed. P. F. Strawson. Oxford: Oxford University Press, 1971.

Gusterson, H. (1995a). 'Becoming a Weapons Scientist.' In *Technoscientific Imaginaries: Conversations, Profiles, and Memoirs*, ed. G. Marcus. Chicago: University of Chicago Press.

Gusterson, H. (1995b). 'Short Circuit: Watching Television with a Nuclear Weapons Scientist.' In *The Cyborg Handbook*, ed. C. Gray. New York: Routledge.

Gusterson, H. (1996). *Nuclear Rites: A Weapons Laboratory at the End of the Cold War*. Berkeley: University of California Press.

Gusterson, H. (2003). 'Anthropology and the Military – 1968, 2003, and Beyond?' *Anthropology Today* 19 (3): 25–6.

Gusterson, H. (2004). *People of the Bomb: Portraits of America's Nuclear Complex*. Minneapolis: University of Minnesota Press.

Gusterson, H. (2005). 'The Ethics of Spying.' *Anthropology Today* 21 (4): 25.

Guzzini, S. (2000). 'A Reconstruction of Constructivism in International Relations.' *European Journal of International Relations* 6: 147–82.

Haas, P., ed. (1992). 'Knowledge, Power and International Policy Coordination.' *International Organization* 46 (Special Issue).

Hacking, I. (1999). *The Social Construction of What?* Cambridge: Harvard University Press.

Hall, J. R. (1999). *Cultures of Inquiry: From Epistemology to Discourse in Sociohistorical Research*. Cambridge: Cambridge University Press.

Hall, P. (2003). 'Aligning Ontology and Methodology in Comparative Research.' In *Comparative Historical Analysis in the Social Sciences*, eds J. Mahoney and D. Rueschemeyer. New York: Cambridge University Press.

Hamberg, S. (2005). 'From Causal Effects to Causal Mechanisms: Improving the Democratic Peace Propositions.' Unpublished manuscript, Department of Political Science, University of Oslo.

Hansen, L. (1997). *Western Villains or Balkan Barbarism? Representations and Responsibility in the Debate over Bosnia.* PhD dissertation, Institut for Statskundskab, University of Copenhagen.

Haraway, D. (1988). 'Situated Knowledges: The Science Question in Feminism and the Privilege of Partial Perspective.' *Feminist Studies* 14: 575–99.

Harrell, M. (2003). 'Gender and Class-Based Role Expectations for Army Spouses.' In *Anthropology and the United States Military: Coming of Age in the Twenty-First Century*, eds P. R. Frese and M. C. Harrell. New York: Palgrave Macmillan.

Harrison, N., ed. (2006). *Complexity in World Politics: Concepts and Methods of a New Paradigm.* Albany: SUNY Press.

Hedstroem, P. and R. Swedberg, eds (1998). *Social Mechanisms: An Analytical Approach to Social Theory.* Cambridge: Cambridge University Press.

Hermann, M. (1977). 'Verbal Behavior of Negotiators in Periods of High and Low Stress: The 1965–66 New York City Transit Negotiations.' In *A Psychological Examination of Political Leaders*, ed. M. Hermann. New York: Free Press.

Hermann, M. (1979). 'Indicators of Stress in Policy Makers during Foreign Policy Crises.' *Political Psychology* 1: 27–46.

Hermann, M. (1980a). 'Explaining Foreign Policy Behavior Using Personal Characteristics of Political Leaders.' *International Studies Quarterly* 24: 7–46.

Hermann, M. (1980b). 'Assessing the Personalities of Members of the Soviet Politburo.' *Personality and Social Psychology Bulletin* 6: 332–52.

Hermann, M. (1984). 'Personality and Foreign Policy Decision Making: A Study of 53 Heads of Government.' In *Foreign Policy Decision Making: Perceptions, Cognition, and Artificial Intelligence*, eds D. Sylvan and S. Chan. New York: Praeger.

Hermann, M. (1985). 'Validating a Technique for Assessing Personalities of Political Leaders at a Distance: A Test Focusing on Heads of Government.' Report prepared for Defense Systems, Inc. (Washington, DC).

Hermann, M. (1986). 'Effects of Speech and Interview Materials on Profiles of Leaders at a Distance: A Validation Exercise.' Report prepared for Defense Systems, Inc. (Washington, DC).

Hermann, M. (1988). 'Validating a Technique for Assessing Personalities of Political Leaders at a Distance: Profiles of 12 Leaders from the Same Culture.' Report prepared for Defense Systems, Inc. (Washington, DC).

Hermann, M. (1999). 'Leadership Profile of Slobodan Milosevic.' *Social Science Automation.* Columbus: Ohio.

Hermann, M. (2000). 'Leadership Profile of Jiang Zemin.' *Social Science Automation.* Columbus: Ohio.

Hermann, M. (2005). 'William Jefferson Clinton's Leadership Style.' In *The Psychological Assessment of Political Leaders*, ed. J. Post. Ann Arbor: University of Michigan Press.

Hermann, M. and C. Hermann (1989). 'Who Makes Foreign Policy and How: An Empirical Inquiry.' *International Studies Quarterly* 33: 361–87.

Hermann, M. and C. Hermann (1990). 'Hostage-Taking, Stress, and the Presidency.' In *The Origins of Terrorism: Psychologies, Ideologies, Theologies, and States of Mind*, ed. W. Reich. Cambridge: Cambridge University Press.

Hermann, M. and T. Preston (1998). 'Presidents, Leadership Style, and the Advisory Process.' In *Domestic Sources of American Foreign Policy*, eds J. McCormick and E. Wittkopf. New York: Rowman and Littlefield.

Hirschmann, N. (2003). *The Subject of Liberty: Toward a Feminist Theory of Freedom.* Princeton: Princeton University Press.

Hoffmann, M. (2003). 'Self-Organized Criticality and Norm Avalanches.' Paper presented at the annual meeting of the North American Association of Computational Social and Organizational Science, Pittsburgh, PA, June.

Hoffmann, M. (2005a). *Ozone Depletion and Climate Change: Constructing a Global Response*. Albany: SUNY Press.

Hoffmann, M. (2005b). 'Self-Organized Criticality and Norm Avalanches.' *Proceedings of the Symposium on Normative Multi-Agent Systems* AISB: 117–25.

Hoffmann, M., H. Kelley, and T. Evans (2002). 'Simulating Land-Cover Change in South-Central Indiana: An Agent-Based Model of Deforestation and Afforestation.' In *Complexity and Ecosystem Management*, ed. M. Janssen. Cheltenham, UK: Edward Elgar.

Holsti, O. R. (1969). *Content Analysis for the Social Sciences and the Humanities*. Reading, MA: Addison Wesley.

Holsti, O. R. (1972). *Crisis, Escalation, War*. Montreal: McGill-Queens University Press.

Hooghe, L. (2005). 'Several Roads Lead To International Norms, But Few via International Socialization: A Case Study of the European Commission.' *International Organization* 59: 861–98.

Hopf, T. (2002). *Social Construction of International Politics: Identities and Foreign Policies, Moscow, 1955 and 1999*. Ithaca: Cornell University Press.

Hopf, T. (2007). 'The Limits of Interpreting Evidence.' In *Theory and Evidence in Comparative Politics and International Relations*, eds R. N. Lebow and M. Lichbach. New York: Palgrave Macmillan.

Hovi, J. (2004). 'Causal Mechanisms and the Study of International Environmental Regimes.' In *Regime Consequences: Methodological Challenges and Research Strategies*, eds A. Underdal and O. Young. Boston: Kluwer Academic Publishers.

Hug, S. and T. Koenig (2000). 'Ratifying Maastricht: Parliamentary Votes on International Treaties and Theoretical Solution Concepts.' *European Union Politics* 1: 93–124.

Hug, S. and T. Koenig (2002). 'In View of Ratification: Governmental Preferences and Domestic Constraints at the Amsterdam Intergovernmental Conference.' *International Organization* 56: 447–76.

Hurwitz, R. (1989). 'Strategic and Social Fictions in the Prisoner's Dilemma.' In *International/Intertextual Relations*, eds J. Der Derian and M. Shapiro. Lexington, MA: Lexington Books.

Hurwitz, R., J. C. Mallery, and G. Duffy (1987). 'Hermeneutics.' In *The Encyclopedia of Artificial Intelligence*, ed. S. Shapiro. New York: John Wiley and Sons.

Hutchinson, S. (1996). *Nuer Dilemmas: Coping with Money, War and the State*. Berkeley: University of California Press.

Jacoby, T. (2006). 'From the Trenches: Dilemmas of Feminist IR Fieldwork.' In *Feminist Methodologies for International Relations*, eds B. Ackerly, M. Stern, and J. True. Cambridge: Cambridge University Press.

Janssen, M., ed. (2002). *Complexity and Ecosystem Management*. Cheltenham, UK: Edward Elgar.

Johnson, J. (2002). 'How Conceptual Problems Migrate: Rational Choice, Interpretation and the Hazards of Pluralism.' *Annual Review of Political Science* 5: 223–48.

Johnson, P. (1999). 'Simulation Modeling in Political Science.' *American Behavioral Scientist* 42: 1509–30.

Johnson, P. (2006). 'Consequences of Positivism: A Pragmatist Assessment.' *Comparative Political Studies* 39: 224–52.

Johnston, A. (2001). 'Treating International Institutions as Social Environments.' *International Studies Quarterly* 45: 487–515.

Johnston, A. (2005). 'Conclusions and Extensions – Toward Mid-Range Theorizing and Beyond Europe.' *International Organization* 59: 1013–44.

Johnston, A. (2007). *Social States: China in International Institutions*. Princeton: Princeton University Press.

Kaarbo, J. and M. Hermann (1998). 'Leadership Styles of Prime Ministers: How Individual Differences Affect the Foreign Policymaking Process.' *Leadership Quarterly* 9: 9243–63.

Kane, S. (1998). *AIDS Alibis: Sex, Drugs and Crime in the Americas*. Philadelphia: Temple University Press.

Katzenstein, P., ed. (1996). *The Culture of National Security: Norms and Identity in World Politics*. New York: Columbia University Press.

Katzenstein, P. and R. Sil (2005). 'What is Analytic Eclecticism and Why Do We Need It? A Pragmatist Perspective on Problems and Mechanisms in the Study of World Politics.' Paper presented at the Annual Convention of the American Political Science Association (www.apsanet.org).

Keller, J. (2005). 'Constraint Challengers, Constraint Respecters, and Foreign Policy.' *Political Psychology* 26: 835–67.

Kelley, J. (2004). *Ethnic Politics in Europe: The Power of Norms and Incentives*. Princeton: Princeton University Press.

Keohane, R. (2001). 'Governance in a Partially Globalized World.' *American Political Science Review* 95: 1–13.

King, G., R. Keohane, and S. Verba (1994). *Designing Social Inquiry: Scientific Inference in Qualitative Research*. Princeton: Princeton University Press.

Klotz, A. (1995). *Norms in International Relations: The Struggle against Apartheid*. Ithaca: Cornell University Press.

Klotz, A. (2002). 'Transnational Activism and Global Transformations: The Anti-Apartheid and Abolitionist Experiences.' *European Journal of International Relations* 8: 49–76.

Klotz, A. and C. Lynch (2006). 'Translating Terminologies,' *International Studies Review* 8: 356–62.

Klotz, A. and C. Lynch (2007). *Strategies for Research in Constructivist International Relations*. Armonk, NY: M. E. Sharpe.

Klotz, I. (1986). *Diamond Dealers and Feather Merchants: Tales from the Sciences*. Boston: Birkhaüser.

Knorr Cetina, K. (1999). *Epistemic Cultures: How the Sciences Make Knowledge*. Cambridge: Harvard University Press.

Kollman, K., J. Miller, and S. Page (1997). 'Computational Political Economy.' In *The Economy as an Evolving Complex System II*, eds B. Arthur, S. Durlauf, and D. Lane. Reading, MA: Addison Wesley.

Koselleck, R. (1988). *Critique and Crisis: Enlightenment and the Pathogenesis of Modern Society*. Cambridge: MIT Press.

Kratochwil, F. and J. G. Ruggie (1986). 'International Organization: A State of the Art on An Art of the State.' *International Organization* 40: 753–75.

Laclau, E. and C. Mouffe (1985). *Hegemony and Socialist Strategy: Towards a Radical Democratic Politics*. London: Verso.

Laffan, B. (1998). 'The European Union: A Distinctive Model of Internationaliz-ation.' *Journal of European Public Policy* 5: 235–53.

Lahire, B., ed. (1999). *Le travail sociologique de Pierre Bourdieu. Dettes et critiques.* Paris: La Découverte.

Lane, R. (1996). 'Positivism, Scientific Realism and Political Science: Recent Developments in the Philosophy of Science.' *Journal of Theoretical Politics* 8(3): 361–82.

Lasswell, H. (1936). *Politics: Who Gets What, When, How.* New York: McGraw-Hill.

Latour, B. and S. Woolgar (1986). *Laboratory Life: The Construction of Scientific Facts.* Princeton: Princeton University Press.

Lazreq, M. (2002). 'Development: Feminist Theory's Cul-De-Sac.' In *Feminist Post-Development Thought: Rethinking Modernity, Postcolonialism & Representation,* ed. K. Saunders. London: Zed.

Leander, A. (2001). 'Pierre Bourdieu on Economics. '*Review of International Political Economy* 8: 344–53.

Leander, A. (2002). 'Do we really need reflexivity in IPE? Bourdieu's two reasons for answering affirmatively (contribution to a colloquium on Pierre Bourdieu). '*Review of International Political Economy* 9: 601–9.

Lebow, R. N. and M. Lichbach, eds (2007). *Theory and Evidence in Comparative Politics and International Relations.* New York: Palgrave Macmillan.

Lee, J. (1986). 'Steven Mosher vs. Stanford.' *The Monthly,* April: 33–40.

Lefcourt, H. (1976). *Locus of Control: Current Trends in Theory and Research.* New York: Halstead.

Lévi-Strauss, C. (1963). *Structural Anthropology.* New York: Basic Books.

Levinson, D. (1978). *The Seasons of a Man's Life.* New York: Ballantine.

Levinson, S. (1983). *Pragmatics.* Cambridge: Cambridge University Press.

Levinson, S. (2000). *Presumptive Meanings: The Theory of Generalized Conversational Implicature.* Cambridge: MIT Press.

Lewis, J. (2005). 'The Janus Face of Brussels: Socialization and Everyday Decision-Making in the European Union.' *International Organization* 59: 937–71.

Ling, L. H. M. (2002). *Postcolonial International Relations: Conquest and Desire between Asia and the West.* New York: Palgrave.

Little, D. (1991). *Varieties of Social Explanation: An Introduction to the Philosophy of Social Science.* Boulder: Westview.

Luhrmann, T. (2001). *Of Two Minds: An Anthropologist Looks at American Psychiatry.* New York: Vintage.

Lukes, S. (1974). *Power: A Radical View.* London: Macmillan.

Lustick, I. (2000). 'Agent-based Modeling of Collective Identity: Testing Constructivist Theory.' *Journal of Artificial Societies and Social Simulation* 3, www. soc.surrey.ac.uk/JASSS/3/1/1.html.

Lustick, I., D. Miodownik, and R. Eidelson (2004). 'Secessionism in Multicultural States: Does Sharing Power Prevent or Encourage It?' *American Political Science Review* 98: 209–29.

MacDonald, P. (2003). 'Useful Fiction or Miracle Maker: The Competing Epistem-ological Foundations of Rational Choice Theory.' *American Political Science Review* 97: 551–65.

MacKinnon, C. (2006). *Are Women Human? And Other International Dialogues.* Cambridge: Belknap Press of Harvard University Press.

Macy, M. and R. Willer (2002). 'From Factors to Actors: Agent-based Modeling and Computational Sociology.' *Annual Review of Sociology* 48: 143–67.

Magnette, P. (2004). 'Coping with Constitutional Incompatibilities: Bargains and Rhetoric in the Convention on the Future of Europe.' Paper presented at the ARENA Research Seminar. Oslo: ARENA Centre for European Studies, University of Oslo.

Mahoney, J. and G. Goertz (2004). 'The Possibility Principle: Choosing Negative Cases in Comparative Research,' *American Political Science Review* 98: 653–99.

Majeski, S. (2004). 'Asymmetric Power Among Agents and the Generation and Maintenance of Cooperation in International Relations.' *International Studies Quarterly* 48: 455–70.

Majeski, S. (2005). 'Do Exploitive Agents Benefit from Asymmetric Power to International Politics?' *British Journal of Political Science* 35: 745–55.

Mallery, J. C. and F. L. Sherman (1993). 'Learning Historical Rules of Major Power Intervention in the Post-War International System.' Paper presented to the International Studies Association.

Marcus, G. (1995). 'Ethnography in/of the World System: The Emergence of Multi-Sited Ethnography.' *Annual Review of Anthropology* 24: 95–117.

Marcus, G. and M. Fischer (1986). *Anthropology as Cultural Critique* . Chicago: University of Chicago Press.

Mayntz, R. (2003). 'Mechanisms in the Analysis of Macro-Social Phenomena.' MPIfG Working Paper, 03/3. Cologne: Max Planck Institute for the Study of Societies (April).

McClelland, D. (1975). *Power: The Inner Experience*. New York: Irvington.

McFate, M. (2005). 'The Military Utility of Understanding Adversary Culture.' *Joint Force Quarterly* 38: 42–8.

Mey, J. (2001). *Pragmatics: An Introduction*, 2nd edn. London: Blackwell.

Milliken, J. (1999). 'The Study of Discourse in International Relations: A Critique of Research and Methods.' *European Journal of International Relations* 5: 225–54.

Monroe, K. R., ed. (2005). *Perestroika: The Raucous Rebellion in Political Science*. New Haven: Yale University Press.

Moos, F. (2005a). 'Anthropologists as Spies.' *Anthropology Today* 21 (3): 25–6.

Moos, F. (2005b). 'Some Thoughts on Anthropological Ethics and Today's Conflicts.' *Anthropology Newsletter* 46 (6): 40–2.

Moravcsik, A. (1999). 'Is Something Rotten in the State of Denmark? Constructivism and European Integration.' *Journal of European Public Policy* 5: 669–81.

Moyser, G. and M. Wagstaffe (1987). *Research Methods for Elite Studies*. London: Allen and Unwin.

Myerhoff, B. (1976). *Peyote Hunt: The Sacred Journey of the Huichol Indians*. Ithaca: Cornell University Press.

Nader, L. (1974). 'Up the Anthropologist: Perspectives Gained from Studying Up.' In *Reinventing Anthropology*, ed. D. Hymes. New York: Vintage.

Nahavandi, A. (2003). *The Art and Science of Leadership*, 3rd edn. Upper Saddle River, NJ: Prentice-Hall.

Narayan, U. (1997). *Dislocating Cultures: Identities, Traditions, and Third-World Feminism*. New York: Routledge.

National Science Foundation, Political Science Program, Directorate for Social, Behavioral, and Economic Sciences (2002). *Empirical Implications of Theoretical Models Report*. Washington, DC: National Science Foundation.

Neumann, I. (1996). *Russia and the Idea of Europe. A Study in Identity and International Relations*. London: Routledge.

Neumann, I. (1997). 'Book Review Essay: Ringmar on Identity and War.' *Cooperation and Conflict* 32: 309–30.

Neumann, I. (1999). *Uses of the Other: 'The East' in European Identity Formation.* Minneapolis: University of Minnesota Press.

Neumann, I. (2001). *Norge – en kritikk. Begrepsmakt i Europa-debatten.* Oslo: Pax.

Neumann, I. (2002). 'This Little Piggy Stayed at Home: Why Norway is Not a Member of the EU.' In *European Integration and National Identity: The Challenge of the Nordic States*, eds L. Hansen and O. Wæver. London: Routledge.

Neumann, I. (2004). 'Deep Structure, Free-Floating Signifier, or Something in Between? Europe's Alterity in Putin's Russia.' In *Identity and Global Politics: Empirical and Theoretical Elaborations*, eds P. M. Goff and K. C. Dunn. London: Palgrave.

Neumann, I. (2007). 'A Speech that the Entire Ministry May Stand For.' *International Political Sociology* 1: 183–200.

Neumann, I. and D. Nexon (2006). 'Harry Potter and the Study of World Politics.' In *Harry Potter and Global Politics*, eds D. Nexon and I. B. Neumann. Lanham, MD: Rowman and Littlefield.

Newbury, D. (1998). 'Understanding Genocide.' *African Studies Review* 41: 73–97.

Nordstrom, C. (2004). *Shadows of War: Violence, Power, and International Profiteering in the Twenty-First Century.* Berkeley: University of California Press.

Nussbaum, M. (2001). *Upheavals of Thought: The Intelligence of Emotions.* Cambridge: Cambridge University Press.

Odell, J. (2006). 'A Major Milestone with One Major Limitation.' *Qualitative Methods: Newsletter of the American Political Science Association Organized Section on Qualitative Methods* 4 (Spring): 37–40.

Orbell, J., R. Dawes, and A. Van de Kragt (1988). 'Explaining Discussion-Induced Cooperation.' *Journal of Personality and Social Psychology* 34: 811–19.

Oreskes, N., K. Shrader-Frechette, and K. Belitz (1994). 'Verification, Validation, and Confirmation of Numerical Models in the Earth Sciences.' *Science* 263: 641–46.

Page, S. (1999). 'Computational Models from A to Z.' *Complexity* 5: 35–41.

Parker, D. (2005). 'Integration of Geographic Information Systems and Agent-Based Models of Land Use: Challenges and Prospects.' In *GIS, Spatial Analysis and Modeling*, eds D. Maguire, M. Goodchild, and M. Batty. Redlands, CA: ESRI Press.

Parker, D., S. Manson, M. Janssen, M. J. Hoffmann, and P. Deadman (2003). 'Multi-Agent Systems for the Simulation of Land-Use and Land-Cover Change: A Review.' *Annals of the Association of American Geographers* 93: 314–37.

Pateman, C. (1988). *The Sexual Contract.* Stanford: Stanford University Press.

Pepinsky, T. (2005). 'From Agents to Outcomes: Simulation in International Relations.' *European Journal of International Relations* 11: 367–94.

Perloff, R. (1993). *The Dynamics of Persuasion.* Hillsdale, NJ: Erlbaum Associates.

Peterson, S. and M. J. Tierney with D. Maliniak (2005). 'Teaching and Research Practices, Views on the Discipline, and Policy Attitudes of International Relations Faculty at US Colleges and Universities.' College of William and Mary, http://www.wm.edu/irtheoryandpractice/trip/papers.php.

Peterson, V. (1990). 'Whose Rights? A Critique of the "Givens" in Human Rights Discourse.' *Alternatives* 15: 303–44.

Pettman, J. (1992). *Living in the Margins: Racism, Sexism, and Feminism in Australia.* North Sydney, Australia: Allen and Unwin.

Post, J. (1980). 'The Seasons of a Leader's Life: Influences on the Life cycle in Political Behaviour.' *Political Psychology* 2: 35–49.

Post, J. (1993). 'Current Concepts of Narcissism: Implications for Political Psychology.' *Political Psychology* 14: 99–121.

Post, J. (2005). *The Psychological Assessment of Political Leaders.* Ann Arbor: University of Michigan Press.

Pouliot, V. (2003). 'La Russie et la communauté atlantique. Vers une culture commune de sécurité?' *Études Internationales* 34: 25–51.

Pouliot, V. (2007). 'Sobjectivism: Toward a Constructivist Methodology.' *International Studies Quarterly* 51: 359–84.

Preston, T. (2001). *The President and His Inner Circle: Leadership Style and the Advisory Process in Foreign Policy.* New York: Columbia University Press.

Preston, T. and M. Hermann (2003). 'Presidential Leadership Style and the Foreign Policy Advisory Process.' In *The Domestic Sources of American Foreign Policy*, eds E. Wittkopf and J. McCormick. New York: Rowman and Littlefield.

Price, D. (2000). 'Anthropologists as Spies.' *The Nation*, 2 November.

Price, D. (2004). *Threatening Anthropology: McCarthyism and the FBI's Surveillance of Activist Anthropologists.* Durham: Duke University Press.

Price, D. and H. Gusterson (2005). 'Spies in Our Midst.' *Anthropology Newsletter* 46 (6): 39–40.

Price, R. (1997). *The Chemical Weapons Taboo.* Ithaca: Cornell University Press.

Ragin, C. (2000). *Fuzzy-set Social Science.* Chicago: University of Chicago Press.

Reich, W. (1933). *Character Analysis.* New York: Orgone Institute Press.

Rescher, N. (1977). *Dialectics.* Albany: SUNY Press.

Ringmar, E. (1996). *Identity, Interest and Action: A Cultural Explanation of Sweden's Intervention in the Thirty Years War.* Cambridge: Cambridge University Press.

Risman, B. (2004). 'Gender as a Social Structure: Theory Wrestling with Activism.' *Gender & Society* 18: 429–50.

Rosaldo, R. (1989). *Culture and Truth: The Remaking of Social Analysis.* Boston: Beacon Press.

Rosato, S. (2003). 'The Flawed Logic of Democratic Peace Theory.' *American Political Science Review* 97: 585–602.

Rotter, J. (1966). 'Generalized Expectancies for Internal Versus External Control of Reinforcement.' *Psychological Monographs* 80 (Whole No. 609).

Rousseau, D. and M. van der Veen (2005). 'The Emergence of a Shared Identity: An Agent-Based Computer Simulation of Idea Diffusion.' *Journal of Conflict Resolution* 49: 686–712.

Ruggie, J. (1998). *Constructing the World Polity: Essays on International Institutionalization.* London: Routledge.

Sahlins, M. (2000). 'Review of James Tierney's Darkness in El Dorado.' *Washington Post Book World*, December 10 (1).

Said, E. (1978). *Orientalism.* Harmondsworth: Penguin.

Sandoval, C. (2000). *Methodology of the Oppressed.* Minneapolis: University of Minnesota Press.

Sanjek, R. (1990). *Fieldnotes: The Makings of Anthropology.* Ithaca: Cornell University Press.

Sartori, G. (1970). 'Concept Misinformation in Comparative Politics.' *American Political Science Review* 64: 1033–53.

Schafer, M. (2000). 'Issues in Assessing Psychological Characteristics at a Distance: An Introduction to the Symposium.' *Political Psychology* 21: 511–27.

Schimmelfennig, F. (2003). *The EU, NATO and the Integration of Europe: Rules and Rhetoric*. Cambridge: Cambridge University Press.

Schimmelfennig, F. (2005). 'Strategic Calculation and International Socialization: Membership Incentives, Party Constellations, and Sustained Compliance in Central and Eastern Europe.' *International Organization* 59: 827–60.

Schwartz-Shea, P. (2005). 'The Graduate Student Experience: "Hegemony" or Balance in Methodological Training?' In *Perestroika: The Raucous Rebellion in Political Science*, ed. K. Monroe. New Haven: Yale University Press.

Searle, J. (1969). *Speech Acts*. Cambridge: Cambridge University Press.

Sherman, F. L. (1994). 'SherFACS: A Cross-Paradigm, Hierarchical and Contextually Sensitive Conflict Data Set.' *International Interactions* 20: 79–100.

Sherman, F. L., J. C. Mallery, S. C. Unseld, and G. Duffy (1992). 'Grammars of Conflict and Cooperation in the Post-War International System.' Paper presented to the International Studies Association.

Shusterman, R., ed. (1999). *Bourdieu: A Critical Reader*. Oxford: Blackwell.

Simon, M. and H. Starr (2000). 'Two-Level Security Management and the Prospects for New Democracies: A Simulation Analysis.' *International Studies Quarterly* 44: 391–422.

Smith, L. (1999). *Decolonizing Methodologies: Research and Indigenous Peoples*. London: Zed.

Sprinz, D. and Y. Wolinsky-Nahmias (2004). "Introduction: Methodology in International Relations Research." In *Models, Numbers and Cases: Methods for Studying International Relations*, eds D. Sprinz and Y. Wolinsky-Nahmias. Ann Arbor: University of Michigan Press.

Stacey, J. (1999). 'Ethnography Confronts the Global Village.' *Journal of Contemporary Ethnography* 28: 687–97.

Stack, C. (1997). *All Our Kin* , 2nd edn. New York: Basic Books.

Staeheli, L. and R. Nagar (2002). 'Feminists Talking across Worlds.' *Gender, Place and Culture* 9: 167–72.

Steinmetz, G., ed. (2005). *The Politics of Method in the Human Sciences: Positivism and Its Epistemological Others*. Durham: Duke University Press.

Stern, M. (2006). 'Racism, Sexism, Classism and Much More: Reading Security-Identity in Marginalized Sites.' In *Feminist Methodologies for International Relations*, eds B. Ackerly, M. Stern, and J. True. Cambridge: Cambridge University Press.

Stolberg, S. (1999). 'The Biotech Death of Jesse Gelsinger.' *New York Times Magazine*, November 28.

Stoller, P. (1989). *The Taste of Ethnographic Things: The Senses in Anthropology*. Philadelphia: University of Pennsylvania Press.

Suedfeld, P. (1992). 'Cognitive Misers and Their Critics.' *Political Psychology* 13: 435–53.

Suedfeld, P. and M. Wallace (1995). 'President Clinton as a Cognitive Manager.' In *The Clinton Presidency: Campaigning, Governing and the Psychology of Leadership*, ed. S. Renshon. Boulder: Westview Press.

Sun, M. (1983). 'The Mysterious Expulsion of Steven Mosher.' *Science* 220 (May 13): 692.

Suu Kyi, A. (1991). *Freedom from Fear: And Other Writings*. New York: Penguin.

Sylvester, C. (1994). *Feminist Theory and International Relations in a Postmodern Era*. Cambridge: Cambridge University Press.

Tannenwald, N. (2007). *The Nuclear Taboo: The United States and the Non-Use of Nuclear Weapons since 1945*. Cambridge: Cambridge University Press.

Tetlock, P. (1991). *An Integratively Complex Look at Integrative Complexity*. Paper presented at the annual meeting of the American Psychological Association, San Francisco, August.

Tetlock, P. and A. Belkin (1996). *Counterfactual Thought Experiments in World Politics*. Princeton: Princeton University Press.

Tierney, P. (2000). *Darkness in El Dorado: How Scientists and Journalists Devastated the Amazon*. New York: Norton.

Tilly, C. (1984). *Big Structures, Large Processes, Huge Comparisons*. New York: Russell Sage Foundation.

Tilly, C. (2001). 'Mechanisms in Political Processes.' *Annual Review of Political Science* 4: 21–41.

Torfing, J. (1999). *New Theories of Discourse: Laclau, Mouffe and Zizek*. Oxford: Blackwell.

Trachtenberg, M. (2006). *The Craft of International History: A Guide to Method*. Princeton: Princeton University Press.

Turner, W. (1983). 'Stanford Ousts a PhD. Candidate over his use of data on China.' *New York Times*, February 26 (A7).

Unseld, S. and J. Mallery (1991). 'Inductive Interaction Detection for Complex Datamodels.' *MIT Artificial Intelligence Laboratory Memo* 1298.

Vaillant, G. (1992). *Ego Mechanisms of Defense: A Guide for Clinicians and Researchers*. Washington, DC. American Psychiatric Press.

Vélez-Ibáñez, C. (1983). *Rituals of Marginality: Politics, Process, and Culture Change in Urban Central Mexico, 1969-1974*. Berkeley: University of California Press.

Wacquant, L. (2003). *Body and Soul: Notebooks of an Apprentice Boxer*. New York: Oxford University Press.

Wacquant, L., ed. (2005). *Pierre Bourdieu and Democratic Politics: The Mystery of Ministry*. Cambridge: Polity.

Wæver, O. (1999). 'Identity, Community and Foreign Policy: Discourse Analysis as Foreign Policy Theory.' In *Between Nations and Europe: Regionalism, Nationalism and the Politics of Union*, eds L. Hansen and O. Wæver. London: Routledge.

Wakin, E. (1992). *Anthropology Goes to War: Professional Ethics and Counterinsurgency in Thailand* . Madison: University of Wisconsin Center for Southeast Asian Studies Monograph.

Walker, S. (1983). 'The Motivational Foundations of Political Belief Systems: A Re-Analysis of the Operational Code Construct.' *International Studies Quarterly* 27: 179–201.

Wax, M. (2003). 'Wartime Dilemmas of an Ethical Anthropology.' *Anthropology Today* 19 (3): 23–4.

Weber, C. (1995). *Simulating Sovereignty: Intervention, the State, and Symbolic Exchange* . Cambridge: Cambridge University Press.

Weber, C. (1999). *Faking It: U.S. Hegemony in a 'Post-Phallic' Era*. Minneapolis: University of Minnesota Press.

Weber, R. (1990). *Basic Content Analysis*. Newbury Park: Sage.

Weber, S. (1994). 'Origins of the European Bank for Reconstruction and Development.' *International Organization* 48: 1–38.

Weldes, J. (1999). *Constructing National Interests: The United States and the Cuban Missile Crisis*. Minneapolis: University of Minnesota Press.

Weldes, J., M. Laffey, H. Gusterson, and R. Duvall (1999). 'Introduction: Constructing Insecurity.' In *Cultures of Insecurity. States, Communities, and the Production of Danger*, eds J. Weldes, M. Laffey, H. Gusterson, and R. Duvall. Minneapolis: University of Minnesota Press.

Wendt, A. (1999). *Social Theory of International Politics*. Cambridge: Cambridge University Press.

Wessels, W. (1998). 'Comitology: Fusion in Action – Politico-Administrative Trends in the EU System.' *Journal of European Public Policy* 5: 209–34.

White, H. (1978). *Tropics of Discourse: Essays in Cultural Criticism*. Baltimore: John Hopkins University Press.

Wight, C. (2002). 'Philosophy of Social Science and International Relations.' In *Handbook of International Relations*, eds W. Carlsnaes, T. Risse, and B. Simmons. London: Sage.

Wilson, J. (1990). *Politically Speaking: The Pragmatic Analysis of Political Language*. Oxford: Basil Blackwell.

Winter, D. (1973). *The Power Motive*. New York: Free Press.

Winter, D. (1992). 'Personality and Foreign Policy: Historical Overview.' In *Political Psychology and Foreign Policy*, eds E. Singer and V. Hudson. Boulder: Westview.

Winter, D. (1995). 'Presidential Psychology and Governing Styles: A Comparative Psychological Analysis of the 1992 Presidential Candidates.' In *The Clinton Presidency: Campaigning, Governing and the Psychology of Leadership*, ed. S. Renshon. Boulder: Westview.

Winter, D. (2005). 'Measuring the Motives of Political Actors at a Distance.' In *The Psychological Assessment of Political Leaders*, ed. J. Post. Ann Arbor: University of Michigan Press.

Winter, D. and A. Stewart (1977). 'Content Analysis as a Technique for Assessing Political Leaders.' In *A Psychological Examination of Political Leaders*, ed. M. Hermann. New York: Free Press.

Winter, D., M. Hermann, W. Weintraub, and S. G. Walker (1991). 'The personalities of Bush and Gorbachev Measured at a Distance: Procedures, Portraits, and Policy.' *Political Psychology* 12: 215–43.

Wolf, D., ed. (1996). *Feminist Dilemmas in Fieldwork*. Boulder: Westview.

Wolf, M. (1992). *A Thrice-Told Tale: Feminism, Postmodernism, and Ethnographic Responsibility*. Stanford: Stanford University Press.

World Social Forum Panel (2004a). 'A Debate on International Issues among Social Movements.' In *World Social Forum, Centre for Equity Studies, January 18*. Mumbai, India.

World Social Forum Panel (2004b). 'A Dialogue between Movements: Breaking Barriers and Building Bridges.' In *World Social Forum, National Network of Autonomous Women's Groups (DAWN, AFM, and WICEJ), January 19*. Mumbai, India.

World Social Forum Panel (2004c). 'A Dialogue between Various Movements on Sexuality Issues.' In *World Social Forum, Rainbow Planet, January 17*. Mumbai, India.

Yanow, D. and P. Schwartz-Shea, eds (2006). *Interpretation and Method: Empirical Research Methods and the Interpretive Turn*. Armonk, NY: M. E. Sharpe.

Young, I. (1990). *Justice and the Politics of Difference*. Princeton: Princeton University Press.

Young, I. (2001). 'Activist Challenges to Deliberative Democracy.' *Political Theory* 29: 670–90.

Young, M. (2000). 'Automating Assessment at a Distance.' *The Political Psychologist* 5: 17–23.

Young, M. and M. Schafer (1998). 'Is There Method in Our Madness? Ways of Assessing Cognition in International Relations.' *Mershon International Studies Review* 42: 63–96.

Zehfuss, M. (2002). *Constructivism in International Relations: The Politics of Reality.* Cambridge: Cambridge University Press.

Zimbardo, P. and M. Leippe (1991). *The Psychology of Attitude Change and Social Influence.* NewYork: McGraw Hill.

Zürn, M. and J. Checkel (2005). 'Getting Socialized to Build Bridges: Constructivism *and* Rational Choice, Europe *and* the Nation State.' *International Organization* 59: 1045–79.

Index